All About
FOREX
TRADING

Other Titles in the "All About" Finance Series

All About
FOREX
TRADING

JOHN JAGERSON
S. WADE HANSEN

New York   Chicago   San Francisco   Lisbon   London   Madrid
Mexico City   Milan   New Delhi   San Juan   Seoul
Singapore   Sydney   Toronto

5 6 7 8 9 10   DOC/DOC   1 6 5 4

ISBN   978-0-07-176822-1
MHID   0-07-176822-X

e-ISBN   978-0-07-176823-8
e-MHID   0-07-176823-8

This publication is designed to provide accurate and authoritative information in regard to the subject matter covered. It is sold with the understanding that neither the author nor the publisher is engaged in rendering legal, accounting, securities trading, or other professional services. If legal advice or other expert assistance is required, the services of a competent professional person should be sought.

—From a Declaration of Principles Jointly Adopted by
a Committee of the American Bar Association and
a Committee of Publishers and Associations

McGraw-Hill books are available at special quantity discounts to use as premiums and sales promotions or for use in corporate training programs. To contact a representative, please e-mail us at bulksales@mcgraw-hill.com.

This book is printed on acid-free paper.

CONTENTS

Chapter 10

Chapter 11

Chapter 12

Chapter 13

Chapter 14

$4 TRILLION A DAY

That's $4 trillion; $4,000,000,000,000; or four million million. No matter how you write it or say it, $4 trillion is a massive number.

To put it into perspective, if you were to spend $1,000 per second every single second of the day, it would take you nearly 127 years to spend $4 trillion. That's a whopping $86,400,000 per day! Try to wrap your head around that one for a minute.

Hopefully, you are starting to grasp the magnitude of that number, because you are going to need to if you truly want to appreciate the Forex market. After all, according to the "2010 Triennial Central Bank Survey" conducted by the Bank for International Settlements (BIS), $4 trillion is the average daily turnover in the Forex market. That's right, $4 trillion *per day*.

The Forex market is so massive that it touches each one of us every day of our lives, even if we're not aware of it. Whether you are reading this book while you are sipping a cup of coffee brewed from imported coffee beans or while you are on vacation in Amsterdam (and if you are, you should really put it down and go see some van Gogh and Vermeer, take a canal cruise, and eat some Indonesian food), the Forex market is affecting your life right now.

Now, if you are like so many people who have been drawn in by the siren song of the Forex market, you are hoping that the Forex market can affect you right in the wallet. Let's be honest; the astronomical sums of money we have been discussing are precisely the reason that you are interested in this market and why you are reading this book. After all, $4 trillion a day is quite a seductive number, don't you think? It's a number that entices you in with thoughts of a never-ending pool of money that provides access to quick and easy riches. After all, if there is $4 trillion changing hands every day, there has to be plenty to go around, and some of it might as well find its way into your trading account, right?

Well, to be perfectly honest, there is plenty to go around. The tricky part is that this pool of money is incredibly slippery, especially if you don't know how to handle it. And that's exactly why we wrote this book.

Too many people dive head first into currency trading because they have seen an advertisement online or read a report promising huge profits in the Forex market with little or no risk. All you need is the latest black-box trading system or magical piece of proprietary trading software. Unfortunately, it's not that easy.

In this book, we are going to try to answer the questions that you have about the Forex market. We're also going to introduce you to a lot of little-known and often misunderstood intermarket relationships and institutions—like the Bank for International Settlements—because the better you understand the nuances of the Forex market, the easier it is going to be for you to take some of that $4 trillion and put it in your pocket.

BEING PART OF THE 33 PERCENT

The retail Forex market has a dirty little secret. Are you ready for it? Here it comes. The majority of retail Forex traders—and just to clarify, when we say "retail traders," we mean you—lose money when they trade currencies. It's true. Just looking at the percentage of traders who lose money when they trade, you would have to conclude that the odds of making money trading currencies are not in your favor.

This is something that those of us who have been in the business for a while have always known, but we had never been able to put a real value on it until recently. We knew that more than half of all traders were losing money, but was the losing percentage closer to 50 percent or closer to 95 percent? No one knew.

Before Monday, October 18, 2010, unless you were one of the privileged few in upper management who were "in the know" at one of the major Forex dealers, there was no way to know just how many people were making money in their accounts and how many people were losing money. That all changed thanks to the passage of the Dodd-Frank Wall Street Reform and Consumer Protection Act of 2009, H.R. 4173 2010 ("Dodd-Frank"), which became law on July 15, 2010, and its implementation by the Commodity Futures Trading Commission (CFTC). Now Forex dealers [those who are registered as retail foreign exchange dealers (RFEDs) with the CFTC] are required to disclose the percentage of their accounts that have been profitable each quarter.

This news has been quite enlightening. First of all, based on how excruciatingly difficult it is to find this "publicly accessible" information (you basically have to set up an account with each dealer to get the information in the disclosure), we get the feeling that Forex dealers don't really want this information to be too widely disseminated. Second, the numbers don't look promising for the average Joe.

It turns out, based on a weighted average of the self-reported numbers of the largest RFEDs in the United States, that approximately 67 percent of retail Forex traders lose money during any given quarter. That's a sobering number. Just think about it—two out of every three retail Forex traders are losing money.

TABLE I-1

Retail Account Profitability at Various U.S. Forex Dealers (Q4 2010 Results)

Dealer	% Profitable	% Unprofitable	Total Open Nondiscretionary Accounts
OANDA Corporation[a]	43.5%	56.5%	48,866
Global Futures & Forex Ltd. (GFT)[b]	32%	68%	9,878
FX Direct Dealer LLC[c]	32%	68%	7,893
Alpari (US) LLC[d]	30%	70%	1,547
Interbank FX LLC[e]	28%	72%	13,699
GAIN Capital Group LLC[f]	28%	72%	14,628
FX Solutions LLC[g]	27%	73%	5,481
MB Trading Futures, Inc.[h]	26%	74%	4,478
IG Markets[i]	26%	74%	378
Forex Capital Markets LLC[j]	23%	77%	18,362
Advanced Markets LLC[k]	46%	54%	108
Principal Financial Group, Inc.[l]	21.3%	78.7%	1,791
Forex Club Financial Company, Inc.[m]	19%	81%	2,465

[a] http://fxtrade.oanda.com/shared/documents/pdf/account/risk_disclosure.pdf.
[b] http://www.gftForex.com/documents/risk_disclosure_document_us.pdf?ts=.
[c] http://www.fxdd.com/fileadmin/template/main/downloads/pdfs/en_US-customer_agreement-fxdd.pdf.
[d] http://static.alpari-us.com/docs_updated/RiskProfitability_Disclosure_V1.2.pdf.
[e] https://www2.interbankfx.com/Agreements/CftcRiskDisclosure/index.php?format=html&locale=en_US.
[f] http://www.Forex.com/pdf/individual_application.pdf.
[g] http://www.fxsolutions.com/documents/account_application.pdf.
[h] http://tonihansen.mbtrading.com/f/SolePropApp.pdf.
[i] http://www.igmarkets.com/content/files/ForexRiskDisclosureStatement_usm_en_US.pdf.
[j] www.fxcm.co.uk/docs_pdfs/risk-disclosure-statement.pdf.
[k] http://www.advancedmarketsfx.com/tr_CFTC_disclosure.htm.
[l] http://www.pfgbest.com/accounts/pdfs/riskDisclosures/Forex_Risk_Disclosure.pdf.
[m] https://secure.fxclub.com/fx?plugin=nfa_warning.

Looking at Table I-1, you can see the profitability breakdown by dealer. Of course, one important thing to mention here before we dive into the data is that these are self-reported numbers from the dealers. It is our understanding that the CFTC asked[1] each dealer to use the following formula (or something similar to it) in its calculations:

Profitability = Ending Balance – Beginning Balance + All Withdrawals – All Deposits + Fees and Commissions

However, we haven't seen an audited report from the CFTC, so we don't know whether each dealer used exactly the same criteria and calculations or whether there were any discrepancies in the methodologies used. That means that we're conducting this analysis in slightly murky waters at best. However, since we're not trying to use these numbers to plot coordinates to the moon, having a general sense of what these numbers are trying to tell us is good enough for what we are trying to accomplish—and that is making sure that you are approaching currency trading with realistic expectations.

Also, some of you may be wondering what an "open" account is. If so, you're not alone. The National Futures Association (NFA) actually clarified this in a notice issued on January 25, 2011.[2] An open account is an account that executed any trades during the quarter and/or had an open position at any time during the quarter. You may also be wondering what a nondiscretionary account is. A nondiscretionary account is a trading account that is controlled solely by the account holder. Many Forex trading accounts allow the account holder to assign trading rights to a third party, such as a money manager or an automated trading system administrator, but the profitability, or lack thereof, of these accounts is not included in these figures. We could speculate on the profitability of discretionary accounts, but we figure that you are most likely reading this book because you are planning to place your

---

[1] http://www.cftc.gov/LawRegulation/FederalRegister/FinalRules/2010-21729.html.

[2] http://www.nfa.futures.org/news/newsNotice.asp?ArticleID=3746.

own Forex trades, so the information we have from the nondiscretionary accounts should be enough for now.

As you can see, there is quite a range of profitability among dealers. We're not exactly sure why there is such a large gap between the performance of account holders at OANDA at the top and Forex Club at the bottom, but we do know that the discrepancy had an impact on the weighted average. OANDA's massive account base definitely skewed the profitable numbers a little higher.

We're also limited in what we can infer from the profitability data. We don't know whether the traders who lost money lost 1 percent of their account value, lost 5 percent of their account value, or completely blew up their accounts and left them in ruins.

So what's the message you should take away from all of this? Hopefully, these numbers will disabuse you of any notion that Forex trading is easy. Is it possible to be a profitable Forex trader? You bet it is. Is it easy? Not in the least.

EASY? NO. POSSIBLE? YES

So enough of the "we hope you know what you're getting into" lecture. Let's take a look at the flip side of the coin and talk about how exciting the Forex market can be. If 67 percent of retail Forex traders lose money, that means that 33 percent (and we're proud to include ourselves in that group) of traders make money. The big question is, how do you become part of the 33 percent and not part of the 67 percent? Is it even possible for a retail trader like you?

Yes, it is.

You can be part of the 33 percent by doing the following three things:

- Learning how the Forex market really works
- Practicing
- Staying disciplined in your trading

This book can help you learn how the Forex market really works, but you are on your own for the other two.

So what are we waiting for? Let's dive in and see if we can't claim some of that $4 trillion for ourselves.

CHAPTER 1

Forex Basics

TWO QUESTIONS YOU NEED TO ASK AND ANSWER

The Forex market is an exciting, fast-paced, 24-hour bonanza of billion-dollar trades, macroeconomic forces, and global geopolitical tensions. Incredible profits can materialize and then vanish again in the space of a few seconds. It is an unforgiving, zero-sum game kind of market, and yet it stands with its arms wide open, waiting for you to build up enough courage to jump in.

Isn't that exciting? We think it is.

However, you shouldn't just jump into the Forex market willy-nilly. As we pointed out in the Introduction, diving into the Forex market without a plan and without taking the time to figure out what makes this global market tick is a recipe for disaster. It will land you squarely among the 66 percent of traders who lose money in this market, and that is not a place you want to be.

So how do you go about getting ready to embark on a successful adventure as a Forex trader? You should be asking yourself and discovering the answers to the following two questions:

- Why do currencies move the way they do?
- How can I profit from that movement?

In fact, we organized this book around those two basic questions.

Why Do Currencies Move the Way They Do?

Understanding why currencies move the way they do is fundamental to your success as a Forex trader because once you understand why they move, you can start to predict where they will move under certain circumstances. And once you can start to predict where currencies are going to move, you have arrived as a currency trader.

The first part of this book answers the question of why currencies move the way they do.

> **What drives currency prices:** We start off with a discussion of the fundamental forces of supply and demand that drive currency prices and the global factors that influence those basic forces. This will lay the foundation for all of your analysis.
>
> **Who drives currency prices:** Once you understand what drives currency prices, it's time to turn your attention to who is driving those prices. After all, even though the market itself may seem like a cold, unfeeling place, it is driven by hot-blooded, emotional traders who aren't always rational. The more you understand these individuals and their motivations, the easier it will be for you to place intelligent trades.
>
> **The individual personality of each currency:** While the same general forces tend to have an impact on all currencies, the severity of the impact will vary depending on the currency. Just like snowflakes, no two currencies are alike, so it is important for you to understand their individual personalities.
>
> **How currencies react to economic announcements and other news:** Economic announcements and other news events are the wild cards in the Forex market. There is no way to predict when news is going to explode, but understanding how different currencies tend to react to various news events will enable you to make quick and nimble adjustments to your portfolio.
>
> **Which indicators you should be watching:** Finally, Forex traders are lucky because there are a number of indicators

they can watch that will give them early warning signs of where a currency may be headed. Some of these indicators are based on market forces that actually move the Forex market, and some of them are merely correlated with those movements. Either way, it's always nice to have something to watch on the horizon.

How Can I Profit from That Movement?

Once you have a handle on what makes currencies move the way they do, you can start to place trades and make investments that will make you money.

Where you can invest your money: It used to be that if you wanted to invest in the Forex market, you literally had to exchange one currency for another at the bank. Nowadays, you have a stellar selection of asset classes and investment vehicles to choose from if you want to trade currencies. You can trade spot Forex, buy an exchange-traded fund (ETF), sell a futures contract, and more. The choice is yours, but it is important that you understand the pros and cons of each investment before you sink any money into it.

How to execute short-term trading strategies: Because of the fast pace and high leverage that are available in the Forex market, many traders are drawn to short-term trading strategies. The rapid-fire nature of getting into and out of a trade quickly can be intoxicating. If you're not careful, though, it can also be deadly. We'll cover what you need to know to give yourself a fighting chance as a short-term trader.

How to invest for the longer term: For those who are drawn to the Forex market by the promise of quick riches, investing for the longer term may seem counterintuitive. However, the nature of the fundamental moves that take place in the Forex market make it an ideal environment for longer-term trades. We'll show you what to look for and how to stay the course.

How the currency market functions and how you can protect yourself: Understanding how the Forex market works and who is regulating the market can help you avoid some of the pitfalls that have tripped up many traders who have gone before you. In fact, regulatory and technological changes in the Forex market have done a lot to level the playing field for individual investors, like you. It's a great time to be a Forex trader.

Getting Started

That's all there is to it. If you can answer those two basic questions, you are set to go. Of course, that is easier said than done, but you've come to the right place to get started.

Before we conduct a more thorough examination of these two questions, however, we need to take a moment to familiarize you with a few of the idiosyncrasies of the Forex market—namely, the concepts of currency pairs and pips.

CURRENCIES DON'T FLY SOLO

When you are a currency trader, you never buy or sell only one currency. That's just not how it works. When you are a currency trader, you always sell one currency and then use the proceeds to buy another currency. Currencies don't fly solo.

Think about it. How much is one U.S. dollar worth? Well . . . it's worth one dollar. How much is one British pound worth? It's worth one pound. All by themselves, currencies are pretty boring. The excitement happens when you couple two currencies into a pair. When you are looking at a currency pair, not just a single currency, you have a point of comparison. Now you can ask the question, how much is one U.S. dollar worth compared to one British pound? Or, to phrase it slightly differently, how many U.S. dollars can you buy with one British pound?

This concept of trading in pairs is one of the hardest concepts for first-time Forex traders to wrap their heads around. It seems so foreign to traders who are used to buying or selling a share of stock or buying or selling a mutual fund to think in terms of a currency pair instead of a single currency. So if you are struggling with this idea, don't worry. You're not alone. We promise that you will get used to it.

Currency Pairs

When you look at a currency pair, the first currency that is listed is called the *base currency*, and the second currency is called the *quote currency*. Here's an easy way to remember which is which: the movement of the currency pair is based on how strong or weak the base currency is, and the price of the currency pair is quoted in terms of the quote currency.

For example, the most widely traded currency pair is the EUR/USD (euro vs. the U.S. dollar). In this case, the euro (EUR) is the base currency and the U.S. dollar (USD) is the quote currency. Whether the currency pair moves up or down in value depends on how strong or weak the euro is compared to the U.S. dollar. If the euro is strong compared to the U.S. dollar, the currency pair will move higher based on this relationship. If the euro is weak compared to the U.S. dollar, the currency pair will move lower. Here's a little something to help you gauge where a currency pair will be moving:

- Base stronger than quote = rising currency pair
- Base weaker than quote = falling currency pair
- Quote stronger than base = falling currency pair
- Quote weaker than base = rising currency pair

Remember, it takes two to tango. And when you are trading a currency pair, movement can be generated by either the base or the quote currency getting stronger or weaker.

The price of the EUR/USD is quoted in terms of how many U.S. dollars it takes to buy one euro. So if the price is 1.3055, you know that it takes 1.3055 U.S. dollars to buy 1 euro. Similarly, if the price moves up to 1.4277, you know that it now takes 1.4277 U.S. dollars to buy 1 euro.

So who decided which currency should be listed first in the pair and which currency should be listed second? Interestingly enough, this important task was given to the International Organization for Standardization (ISO), a nongovernmental group that seeks to bring a little more order to this crazy, crazy world.

Currency pairs are typically divided into the following three major groups:

- Major currency pairs
- Emerging market currency pairs
- Currency crosses

Major Currency Pairs

The major currency pairs are those pairs that include the most important currency in the global markets, the U.S. dollar (USD), combined with one of six other globally significant currencies, the euro (EUR), the Japanese yen (JPY), the British pound (GBP), the Australian dollar (AUD), the Swiss franc (CHF), and the Canadian dollar (CAD).

Take some time to learn the following major currency pairs, because you will probably be using them extensively:

- EUR/USD   (euro/U.S. dollar)
- USD/JPY   (U.S. dollar/Japanese yen)
- GBP/USD   (British pound/U.S. dollar)
- AUD/USD   (Australian dollar/U.S. dollar)
- USD/CHF   (U.S. dollar/Swiss franc)
- USD/CAD   (U.S. dollar/Canadian dollar)

Emerging Market Currency Pairs

The emerging market currency pairs are those pairs that, once again, include the most important currency in the global markets, the U.S. dollar (USD), but this time combined with any currency that is not considered a major currency. Emerging market currencies, like the Swedish krona (SEK), the New Zealand dollar (NZD), or the South African rand (ZAR), are called emerging market currencies because they are less liquid currencies. However, these emerging market currencies are becoming more popular, which is improving their liquidity.

Take a look at the following list of emerging market currency pairs because you may be interested in diversifying your Forex portfolio with a few uncorrelated currency pairs:

- USD/HKD   (U.S. dollar/Hong Kong dollar)
- USD/SEK   (U.S. dollar/Swedish krona)
- NZD/USD   (New Zealand dollar/U.S. dollar)
- USD/SGD   (U.S. dollar/Singapore dollar)
- USD/NOK   (U.S. dollar/Norwegian krone)
- USD/MXN   (U.S. dollar/Mexican peso)
- USD/ZAR   (U.S. dollar/South African rand)
- USD/DKK   (U.S. dollar/Danish krone)
- USD/THB   (U.S. dollar/Thai baht)

Currency Crosses

Currency crosses are currency pairs in which neither currency is the U.S. dollar (USD). The euro (EUR) paired with the British pound (GBP) and the Australian dollar (AUD) paired with the Japanese yen (JPY) would be considered currency crosses.

The following is a list of some of the more popular currency crosses:

- GBP/JPY   (British pound/Japanese yen)
- EUR/GBP   (euro/British pound)
- AUD/JPY   (Australian dollar/Japanese yen)
- EUR/CHF   (euro/Swiss franc)
- CAD/JPY   (Canadian dollar/Japanese yen)

CURRENCY PAIRS MOVE IN PIPS

If you are used to trading stocks, bonds, or commodity futures, you are accustomed to prices being quoted in dollars and cents. That's not how it works in the Forex market. Currency pair prices are quoted in pips.

So what's a pip? Pip is short for "price interest point." You will also hear pips referred to as "basis points."

In most cases, a single pip represents one ten-thousandth of a single unit of a currency. However, there are some exceptions, such as the Japanese yen, where a pip is one one-hundredth of a yen. Historically, a pip has been the smallest tradable price point in the Forex market, but currency dealers have recently made a move toward trading even smaller increments. This started with "half-pip" pricing on pairs such as the EUR/GBP and the EUR/CHF, but it has since expanded, so that some dealers are now quoting prices to one-tenth of a pip—that's going out five decimal places on most prices.

The Value of a Pip

So how much is a pip worth? That's a great question, and coming up with the right answer depends on a few variables. It isn't like trading a stock, where you know that each penny that the stock moves up or down translates directly into a penny gained or a penny lost. To calculate the value of each pip—or each tenth of a pip, as the case may be—you have to know which currency is the base currency and how large the contract you are trading is, or the notional amount. We'll talk more about contract sizes when we discuss various investment vehicles in the Forex market in Chapter 12, but for the time being, just know that full-size contracts cover 100,000 units of currency and mini contracts cover 10,000 units. That being said, here is the formula you use to calculate the value of a pip:

$$(1 \text{ Pip/Exchange Rate}) \times \text{Notional Amount} = \text{Pip Value}$$

Let's plug some actual numbers into that formula to illustrate. Suppose you want to know the value of a 1-pip move on a full-size contract on the USD/JPY (U.S. dollar vs. Japanese yen) currency pair at a time when they exchange rate is 82.65. To figure it out, you would use the following formula:

$$(0.01/82.65) \times 100,000 = \$12.10$$

Now suppose you want to know the value of a 1-pip move on a mini contract on the EUR/USD (euro vs. U.S. dollar) currency pair at a time when the exchange rate is 1.3387. To figure it out, you would use the following formula:

$$(0.0001/1.3387) \times 10,000 = €0.74699$$

Of course, if you want to know how much a pip is worth in U.S. dollars and the USD is not the base currency, you are going to have to go through one more step to calculate the value of the pip. To convert a pip value from a currency other than the U.S. dollar back into a dollar-based value, you simply look at the exchange rate of that currency pair using the following formula:

$$\text{Pip Value} \times \text{Exchange Rate} = \text{USD-based Pip Value}$$

In the case of the EUR/USD example given earlier, the equation would look like this:

$$€0.74699 \times 1.3387 = \$1$$

You can do this conversion for any currency you want.

Okay, okay—that's enough math for now. It's time to expand our horizons and talk about the global forces that drive these currency pairs, sometimes pushing them thousands of pips in no time at all.

CHAPTER 2

What Drives Currency Prices

UNDERSTANDING THE PAST TO MAKE SENSE OF THE FUTURE

It really is a shame, but if you talk to most traders, you will find that they have no clue as to what forces converged in history to shape the Forex market. They don't know why the U.S. dollar is the world's reserve currency. They don't know that if it hadn't been for Richard Nixon, they wouldn't be able to make money trading currencies today. They just don't know. But don't you worry, we're going to rectify that right now.

Why do we care about the history of the Forex market? No, knowing the date when the Jamaica Agreement was signed is not going to affect your trading returns. We care because if we understand the forces that led to the creation of a free-floating currency market, we will better understand the forces that continue to drive currencies today. We care because the more we learn from the past, the better prepared we are going to be for the future.

So here's what we're going to do. We're going to walk through the following key events that led to the Forex market as we know it today:

- Bretton Woods Accord
- Beginning of the end of the Bretton Woods Accord

- End of U.S. dollar convertibility into gold (Nixon Shock)
- Smithsonian Agreement
- European Joint Float
- End of the Smithsonian Agreement and the European Joint Float
- Jamaica Agreement
- European Monetary System

As we do so, we're going to cover only the important information—the details that illustrate how and why the Forex market developed the way it did. We recommend that you learn more about each of these events on your own, but this book is not the place for a deep dive into each event in history.

Bretton Woods Accord

The first thing you are going to notice as we talk about the history of the Forex market as we know it today is that the names for many of the key turning points in our financial history refer to the specific place where an agreement was made. So it only seems fitting that we start our journey back into Forex history in Bretton Woods, New Hampshire.

That's right. Leaders from around the globe came together after World War II—July 1 through July 22, 1944—in a small town in New Hampshire (at the Mount Washington Hotel, to be exact) to determine the fate of the world's monetary system. And to honor this small town, we have referred to the agreement that was reached there as the Bretton Woods Accord ever since. The official name of the event was actually the United Nations Monetary and Financial Conference, but you will never hear it referred to by its full name. Bretton Woods is just a lot easier.

So what happened all those years ago?

The world was reeling as it tried to recover from the devastation brought about by World War II, and one thing that the delegates to this United Nations conference realized was the fact that they needed a stable monetary system if they were to have any chance of pulling themselves out of the chaos. They debated the pros and cons of various monetary methods and approaches, and by the end of the conference, they had come up with what we now refer to as the Bretton Woods monetary system.

Here are the details of that system:

- All participating countries had to peg their currencies to the value of the U.S. dollar, making the greenback the world's reserve currency, a position it still holds. The peg allowed for some leeway: as long as a currency didn't drift higher or lower by more than 1 percent, it was considered to be successfully pegged.
- If a currency moved more than 1 percent above or below the price of the U.S. dollar, the country was required to step in and intervene in the markets to bring prices back into balance.
- In turn, as a sign of good faith and to imbue some confidence in the market, the United States agreed to peg the value of the U.S. dollar to gold at a rate of $35 per ounce.
- If they wanted to, other countries could exchange their U.S. dollars for gold. This provision would later prove to be the undoing of the entire system.

The Bretton Woods Accord also established the International Monetary Fund (IMF) and the International Bank for Reconstruction and Development (IBRD), which is now part of the World Bank Group. Both of these institutions have had an impact on the Forex market in the years since their creation.

Okay. So far, so good? Remember, the dates aren't important, but the agreement that came out of Bretton Woods literally changed the world.

Beginning of the End of the Bretton Woods Accord

"Guns and butter" signaled the beginning of the end of the Bretton Woods Accord. Guns and butter is the derogatory nickname given to President Lyndon B. Johnson's policy agenda, which tried to both carry on a war in Vietnam and implement his Great Society social welfare programs in the United States at the same time. Unfortunately, instead of trying to pay for both of these massive spending programs by raising taxes or cutting spending somewhere else, the federal government simply began to increase the money supply. This set off a chain reaction that ultimately destroyed the Bretton Woods Accord.

As the money supply grew and inflation picked up steam (reaching close to 9 percent in 1968), consumers in the United States started buying more goods from abroad. After all, U.S. consumers had more and more U.S. dollars in their pockets, and while inflation was making goods and services in the United States more expensive, goods and services overseas were still being priced at a fixed exchange rate.

This increase in imports started to push the United States' trade balance (how much a country exports compared to what it imports) out of whack, which put downward pressure on the value of the U.S. dollar. To compensate for this lopsided trade flow, foreign governments and their central banks, which were obligated to keep their currencies pegged to the U.S. dollar, had to start selling their currencies and buying U.S. dollars to lower the value of their currencies and raise the value of the U.S. dollar (we'll talk about supply and demand in the Forex market in the next chapter).

Finally, in early 1971, the U.S. trade balance moved into negative territory, showing a deficit for the first time since 1945. The United States was officially importing more than it was exporting. This news sent currency speculators—yes, they have been around for a long time—racing to buy the deutsche mark. They figured that the West German government would no longer be able to maintain the deutsche mark's peg to the U.S. dollar, and the value of the mark would skyrocket.

Well, the Bundesbank (Germany's central bank) put up a good fight. It continued to sell the deutsche mark and buy U.S. dollars to maintain the peg for as long as it could. But after being forced to buy $1 billion in one day on May 4, 1971, and another $1 billion during the first hour of trading on May 5, 1971, the German government threw in the towel and let the deutsche mark float.

At this point, instead of trying to revalue their currencies against the U.S. dollar, other countries that had been buying massive amounts of U.S. dollars, just as Germany had been doing, decided to cash in on one of the other aspects of the Bretton Woods monetary system: they started converting their U.S. dollars into gold. England, France, Switzerland, and others gathered up their U.S. dollars and asked the United States to exchange them for gold at a rate of $35 per ounce. This was a great deal for them because they could buy gold from the United States at $35 per ounce and then turn around and sell it on the open market for anywhere from $40 to $58 per ounce, depending on the timing of their sales.

Ultimately, the pressure on the U.S. government became too much to bear, and President Nixon did the unthinkable.

End of U.S. Dollar Convertibility into Gold (Nixon Shock)

On August 15, 1971, the Nixon administration announced from Camp David that it would be suspending the convertibility of the U.S. dollar into gold. You will often hear this referred to as "closing the gold window." As you can imagine, governments around the world were quite upset by this.

While closing the gold window didn't make many friends for the United States, it did give the U.S. government some bargaining power. After all, the U.S. government wanted everyone else to let their currencies appreciate against the U.S. dollar. But while the gold window was open, the U.S. government had no leverage to force a revaluation. Closing it provided all the leverage the government needed.

Smithsonian Agreement

The Smithsonian Agreement—another agreement named after the venue where the meeting took place—moved the world one step closer to a free-floating currency system. On December 18, 1971, at a meeting at the Smithsonian Institution, the Group of Ten (G10)— the United States, the United Kingdom, Germany, France, Italy, Canada, Japan, the Netherlands, Belgium, Sweden, and Switzerland (yes, there are 11 countries in the G10)—agreed to allow the following:

- An 8 percent depreciation in the value of the U.S. dollar
- A widening of the trading band from plus or minus 1 percent to plus or minus 2 percent

- A change in the U.S. dollar's peg to gold from $35 per
  ounce to $38 per ounce

Unfortunately, all the Smithsonian Agreement did was per-
form a hard reset on currency values. It didn't do anything to
address the problems that had led to the end of the Bretton Woods
Accord, and thus it was doomed to a similar fate.

European Joint Float

Even after the Smithsonian Agreement was signed, the Europeans
were still concerned by their exposure to the U.S. dollar. In an
attempt to reduce that exposure, the European Economic Community (West Germany, France, Italy, the Netherlands, Belgium,
and Luxembourg) established the European Joint Float system in
April 1972. The system set up the following guidelines:

- Each country had to stay within the "snake"—a 2.25
  percent price band—in relation to other countries.
- Each country had to stay within the "tunnel"—a 4.5
  percent price band—in relation to the U.S. dollar.

Alas, the European Joint Float made the same mistake that
the Smithsonian Agreement made by not fully addressing the
underlying problems that were plaguing the system. It too was to
be short-lived.

End of the Smithsonian Agreement and the
Joint Float

It didn't take long for the bloom to come off the rose after the establishment of the Smithsonian Agreement and the European Joint
Float. And as soon as it did, the same fundamental factors—namely,
an expansion of the U.S. money supply, a jump in the value of gold
to more than $100 per ounce, and a lack of ability on the part of
foreign governments to continue buying U.S. dollars—forced the
markets to devalue the U.S. dollar.

And so began our free-floating currency system, informal as
it was.

The Jamaica Agreement

Members of the International Monetary Fund (IMF) finally formalized the free-floating currency system on January 7 and 8, 1976, at an IMF meeting in Jamaica. In yet another agreement named after the venue where the meetings took place, members updated the IMF's Articles of Agreement to state the following:

- Floating currency rates were now acceptable.
- IMF members could enter the Forex market as they saw fit to temper "unwarranted" price fluctuations.
- Gold would no longer be used as a reserve asset, and the IMF would return all of its gold to its member nations.

With the Jamaica Agreement, world leaders finally acknowledged that they possessed neither the tools nor the will to control currency rates.

So, What Did We Learn From History?

While it is fun to learn about the geopolitical hubris that blinded world leaders to the fact that they couldn't control currency values forever, that is only one of the lessons that we should draw from this brief look back into Forex history. Here are a few more that you should be paying attention to:

- The basic forces of supply and demand drive the Forex market.
- Trade flows, investment flows, and money supply all play key roles in driving supply and demand.
- Government interventions and currency manipulation can last for only so long.

Pretty exciting stuff, don't you think? By the way, you get an "A" for sticking with us. We promise, you will be glad you did.

SUPPLY AND DEMAND DRIVE THE FOREX MARKET

The forces of supply and demand seem to drive every other market on earth, so why shouldn't they also drive the Forex market? As you just saw in our brief history section, even when the governments of the world's leading economies were trying to control currency prices, the forces of supply and demand won out in the end.

Of course, it is relatively simple to explain the impact that shifts in supply and demand will have on the value of a currency. It is another thing entirely to try to explain what factors cause those shifts, but that is exactly what we are going to do.

Just to make sure that we are all on the same page as we discuss how various fundamental forces affect the Forex market, however, let's take a moment to review the basics of supply and demand.

Figure 2-1 shows a typical supply and demand chart. Demand for a currency is represented by the solid line that is sloping downward from left to right, and supply of a currency is represented by the dashed line that is sloping upward from left to right. The point at which these two lines cross represents the price that the market has set for the currency.

As we look at these charts, we are going to try to keep things as simple as possible. The slope of the lines is not going to change.

FIGURE 2-1

Supply and Demand Chart

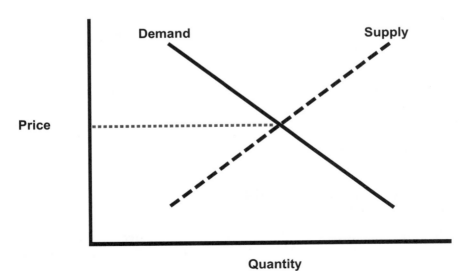

Instead, we are going to focus solely on increases and decreases in the overall level of supply and demand. Here's how it works:

- When supply and demand *increase*, the lines move horizontally from left to right along the *x* axis.
- When supply and demand *decrease*, the lines move horizontally from right to left along the *x* axis.

Now that we've got the basics covered, let's take a look at what happens to the value of a currency when demand for that currency increases. As you can see in Figure 2-2, increasing demand for a currency increases the value of that currency.

So if increasing demand increases the value of a currency, what happens when the supply of that currency increases? As you can see in Figure 2-3, increasing supply of a currency decreases the value of that currency.

We've now seen what happens when we see an increase in either demand or supply. Now let's explore what happens when we see a decrease in either demand or supply. As you can see in

FIGURE 2-2

Price Rises as Demand Increases

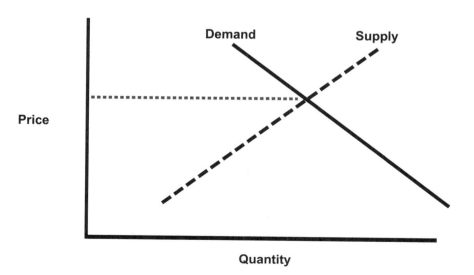

FIGURE 2-3

Price Falls as Supply Increases

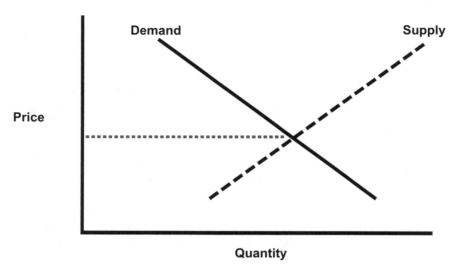

FIGURE 2-4

Price Falls as Demand Decreases

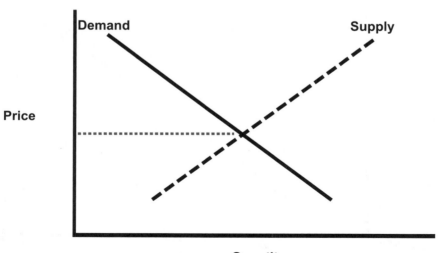

FIGURE 2-5

Price Rises as Supply Decreases

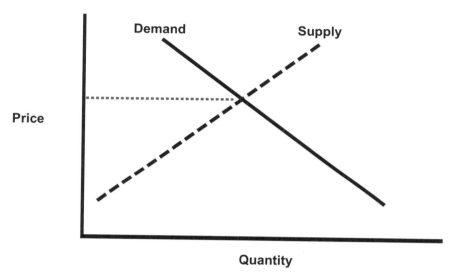

Figure 2-4, decreasing demand for a currency decreases the value of that currency.

And as you have probably guessed by now, and as you can see in Figure 2-5, decreasing supply of a currency increases the value of that currency.

So there you have it—the basics of supply and demand in the Forex market. Now it's time to dig a little deeper and analyze which forces push supply and demand in one direction and which forces push them in the other direction.

Supply and demand in the currency market are driven primarily by the following five factors:

- Trade flows
- Investment flows
- Money supply
- Government interventions and currency manipulation
- Investor fear

Let's take a look at each of these five factors to make sure that we have a handle on why each one is important. Since the U.S.

dollar is the most widely traded currency, we are going to look at each of these factors from a U.S. dollar perspective, but we will be conducting a thorough review of how these five factors relate to each individual currency in Chapter 4, "Getting to Know the Currencies," and we will be discussing the individual currencies in Chapters 5 through 9.

TRADE FLOWS

Trade flows represent the money that flows from one country to another as a result of the trade of goods or services between the two countries. Trade flows are affected by two things:

- Foreign demand for domestic goods
- Domestic demand for foreign goods

Foreign Demand for Domestic Goods

Foreign demand for domestic goods increases the demand for the domestic currency and the supply of the foreign currency. This increase in demand for the domestic currency increases the value of that currency, while the increase in the supply of the foreign currency decreases the value of that currency. Here's how it works.

Suppose a consumer in Spain wants to buy a product that is manufactured in the United States. Naturally, the consumer in Spain would like to pay for the product in euros, but the company that produced the product in the United States would like to be paid in U.S. dollars. To facilitate this process, an exchange must be made. The consumer in Spain must exchange her euros for U.S. dollars to pay the producer.

This exchange increases the supply of euros in the market and increases demand for U.S. dollars, which means that the value of the euro should decline and the value of the U.S. dollar should increase.

Domestic Demand for Foreign Goods

Domestic demand for foreign goods increases the demand for the foreign currency and the supply of the domestic currency. This increase in demand for the foreign currency increases the value of that currency, while the increase in the supply of the domestic currency decreases the value of that currency.

We could provide another illustration here, but it would be exactly like the one between Spain and the United States that we just outlined, except that the roles would be reversed, so we won't bore you with another one.

All you need to remember right now is that when buyers and sellers engage in international trade, the flow of money from the buyers to the sellers increases the value of the sellers' currency and decreases the value of the buyers' currency.

Monitoring Trade Flows

Monitoring trade flows is a relatively straightforward process, thanks to the various government agencies around the world that report monthly *trade balance* numbers. For instance, every month, the U.S. Census Bureau and the Bureau of Economic Analysis (BEA), part of the U.S. Department of Commerce, release the U.S. International Trade in Goods and Services numbers. We'll cover the trade balance announcement in more depth in Chapter 10, "Navigating the Economic Calendar," but here are the basics.

If a country has a trade surplus with another country, it means that there was greater foreign demand for domestic goods than there was domestic demand for foreign goods. This should lead to a strengthening of the domestic currency compared to the foreign currency, all other things being equal.

If a country has a trade deficit with another country, it means that there was greater domestic demand for foreign goods than there was foreign demand for domestic goods. This should lead to a strengthening of the foreign currency compared to the domestic currency, all other things being equal.

Balance of Payments Theory

This concept of a currency getting stronger when the country has a trade surplus and getting weaker when it has a trade deficit is the basic premise of a currency-pricing model called the *balance of payments theory*.

The balance of payments theory suggests that currency markets are self-regulating and will always bring the import and export levels of individual countries back into balance. The thinking goes something like this:

1. If a country has a *trade deficit*, the value of its currency will start to decline because the supply of the currency is so high.
2. As the value of the currency starts to decline, the goods and services offered by that country will become less expensive for (and thus more attractive to) foreign consumers.
3. The less expensive the goods and services become, the more foreign consumers will buy.
4. The more foreign consumers buy, the smaller the trade deficit becomes until trade ultimately comes back into balance . . . in theory, anyway.

Conversely:

1. If a country has a *trade surplus*, the value of its currency will start to increase because demand for the currency is so high.
2. As the value of the currency starts to increase, the goods and services offered by that country will become more expensive for (and thus less attractive to) foreign consumers.
3. The more expensive the goods and services become, the less foreign consumers will buy.
4. The less foreign consumers buy, the smaller and smaller the trade surplus becomes until trade ultimately comes back into balance . . . in theory, anyway.

While this theory offers some basic guidance on the relationship between trade flows and currency values, and how either one can eventually drive the other, it does have some flaws. Most glaringly, it accounts only for trade-based demand when looking at what drives currency prices. But as you will see as we continue to move through this chapter, currency prices are driven by many other factors, such as investment flows, money supply, interventions, and investor fear. These other factors can wreak havoc on the balance of payments theory by keeping the value of a currency from a country with a trade deficit high or by keeping the value of a currency from a country with a trade surplus low, effectively preventing a move back toward balanced trade.

Why is any of this important? The balance of payments theory illustrates how international trade can drive currency prices, which it is important for you to understand if you want to make money in this market. The flaws in the theory also illustrate how dangerous it is to try to oversimplify your analysis as you look at what is driving currency prices. This is also crucial for you to understand if you want to make money in this market. You have to look for nuances.

INVESTMENT FLOWS

Investment flows represent the money that flows from one country to another as a result of the purchase or sale of assets in one country by an investor from another country. Investment flows are affected by three things:

- Foreign demand for domestic assets
- Domestic demand for foreign assets
- Repatriation of assets

Foreign Demand for Domestic Assets

Foreign demand for domestic assets increases the demand for the domestic currency and the supply of the foreign currency. This increase in demand for the domestic currency increases the value of that currency, while the increase in the supply of the foreign currency decreases the value of that currency. Here's how it works.

Suppose an investor in Japan wants to buy a government bond in New Zealand. Naturally, the investor in Japan would like to pay for the product in Japanese yen, but the New Zealand government would like to be paid in New Zealand dollars. To facilitate this process, an exchange must be made. The investor in Japan must exchange his Japanese yen for New Zealand dollars to pay the bond issuer.

This exchange increases the supply of Japanese yen in the market and increases demand for New Zealand dollars, which means that the value of the Japanese yen should decline and the value of the New Zealand dollar should increase.

Domestic Demand for Foreign Assets

Domestic demand for foreign assets increases the demand for the foreign currency and the supply of the domestic currency. This increase in demand for the foreign currency increases the value of that currency, while the increase in the supply of the domestic currency decreases the value of that currency.

We could provide another illustration here, but once again, it would be exactly like the one between Japan and New Zealand that we just outlined, except that the roles would be reversed, so we won't bore you with another one.

All you need to remember right now is that when buyers and sellers engage in international asset purchasing, the flow of money from the buyers to the sellers increases the value of the sellers' currency and decreases the value of the buyers' currency.

Repatriation of Assets

Repatriation of assets increases the demand for the domestic currency and the supply of the foreign currency. This increase in demand for the domestic currency increases the value of that currency, while the increase in the supply of the foreign currency decreases the value of that currency. Here's how it works.

When a corporation makes money overseas, it has two choices as to what to do with that money: it can leave the money overseas, or it can repatriate the money by bringing it back home. There are advantages to both, but in most cases, you would imagine that the corporation would want to bring the money back home so that it can efficiently reallocate it throughout the rest of the corporation or distribute it to shareholders.

The process of repatriation requires the corporation to convert the profits from whatever currency they are denominated in to the local currency where the corporation is headquartered. For instance, if General Electric makes money in Japan but wants to bring those profits back home, it will have to sell Japanese yen and buy U.S. dollars.

One thing you can watch to gauge just how much money may be being repatriated is the earnings announcements of large multinational corporations. If a company like General Electric is making a lot of money overseas, the chances are good that some of that money is going to be brought home. Seeing an increase in overseas earnings can be an effective signal that repatriation activity is going to increase.

Changes in tax policy can also affect the level of repatriation. One shining example of this was the Homeland Investment Act of 2003 (H.R. 767).[1] The Homeland Investment Act allowed corporations that earned foreign profits to repatriate those earnings at a tax rate of only 5.25 percent, instead of being taxed at their standard corporate rates, which could be as high as 35 percent. This decrease in tax rates prompted corporations that had left a large portion of their foreign earnings overseas to repatriate those funds. Some estimate that as much as $600 billion was repatriated thanks to this change in tax policy. As you can imagine, this had a bullish effect on the value of the U.S. dollar as all of that money flowed in, increasing demand for the U.S. dollar.

Monitoring Investment Flows

Unfortunately, monitoring investment flows isn't as straightforward as monitoring trade flows. The information just isn't as readily available from every country in a timely manner as the monthly trade balance numbers are. However, the United States, via the U.S. Department of the Treasury, does do a pretty good job of summarizing investment flow data in its monthly Treasury International Capital (TIC) Data reports. We'll cover the TIC announcement in more depth in Chapter 10, "Navigating the Economic Calendar," but here are the basics.

If foreign investors are buying an increasing amount of U.S. securities, demand for the U.S. dollar will also be increasing. This

---

[1] http://thomas.loc.gov/cgi-bin/query/z?c108:H.R.767.

should lead to a strengthening of the U.S. dollar compared to the foreign currency, all other things being equal.

If foreign investors are buying a decreasing amount of U.S. securities, demand for the U.S. dollar will also be decreasing. This should lead to a weakening of the U.S. dollar compared to the foreign currency, all other things being equal.

While it may not be easy to track the exact amount of investment flows between one country and another, you can get a general idea of whether investment demand is going to be increasing or decreasing by watching the performance of the asset markets—bond markets, stock markets, real estate markets, and so on—that foreign investors may be looking to put their money into.

For example, if the interest rates offered on government bonds in one country are much higher than the interest rates offered on government bonds in another country, you could reasonably conclude that investors from around the world are going to be interested in investing their money in the bonds with the higher interest rates. This would most likely lead to an increase in investment flows into that country, which should increase the value of that currency.

We'll cover this concept in more depth in Chapter 11, "Indicators That Forex Traders Watch," but this should give you a general understanding of the concept.

Interest-Rate Parity Theory

This concept of a currency getting stronger when the country it represents offers higher interest rates than other countries is the basic premise of another currency-pricing model called the *interest-rate parity theory.*

The interest-rate parity theory suggests that investors are always looking for the highest return on their money for the least amount of risk, and that countries that offer higher interest rates on their bonds without being extreme credit risks are going to attract more foreign investment than other countries. The thinking goes something like this:

1. If a country offers high interest rates, demand for that country's bonds will increase.

2. Because you have to pay for bonds and other assets in the currency of the issuing country, this increase in demand for local bonds will increase demand for the local currency.
3. This increase in demand for the local currency will push the value of the currency higher.

While this theory offers some basic guidance on the relationship between investment flows and currency values, it does have some flaws. Like the balance of payments theory, the interest-rate parity theory takes only one source of demand for a currency into account, and we know that this is a little too simplistic.

Why do we care about any of this? The interest-rate parity theory illustrates how international investing trends can drive currency prices. And as a current, or aspiring, Forex trader, you need to understand the impact that traders like you, when looked at as one cohesive group, can have on the markets.

MONEY SUPPLY

The money supply represents the total amount of a currency that is circulating through the economy. That may seem like a strange concept, but in this day and age of fiat currencies (currencies that are not backed by any physical asset, such as gold) and computers, the supply of any given currency can change in literally less than a second. No longer do government treasuries have to fire up the printing presses to increase the supply of money, although they can still do that if they want to. Nowadays, the same thing can be accomplished with a few keystrokes on a computer.

The supply of money in the economy is important to us as currency traders because it has a direct impact on the value of a currency. More money in circulation tends to lead to lower currency values, while less money in circulation tends to lead to higher currency values.

The money supply in a given country is typically dictated by

- The government's Treasury
- The country's central bank

Role of the Treasury in Determining the Money Supply

As we mentioned previously, the Treasury typically controls the printing presses at the mint. And since fiat currencies aren't backed by any physical asset, all the Treasury has to do to increase the money supply is place an order for paper (or cotton, as is the case in the United States) and ink and turn on the presses. As these new bills are distributed into the economy, the supply of money increases.

Of course, if these new bills are being created to replace old, tattered bills that are going to be collected and destroyed once the new bills are distributed, the supply of physical money in the marketplace will remain unchanged. However, the important thing to remember here is just how easy it is to flip a switch and start printing.

Role of the Central Bank in Determining Money Supply

As easy as it may be to flip a switch and start printing, it is even easier for a central bank to increase or decrease the money supply. All a central bank has to do to increase or decrease the money supply is type a few numbers into a computer and hit "Enter." In fact, central banks engage in the creation and destruction of money every day as they implement their monetary policies. We'll cover how central banks affect the Forex market in more depth in Chapter 3, "Who Drives Currency Prices," but here are the basics of how central banks affect the money supply. We'll use the U.S. central bank—the Federal Reserve, or the Fed—as an example.

- When the Fed wants to lower interest rates in the economy, it will start to increase the money supply by making short-term collateralized loans (called *repurchase agreements*, or "repos" for short) to its primary dealers (large banks). In a repo, the Fed borrows U.S. Treasuries from a primary dealer in exchange for crediting the dealer's reserve account with the Fed. At the end of the term of the repo, the Fed gives the U.S. Treasuries back to the primary dealer and debits the dealer's reserve account with the Fed.

- When the Fed wants to raise interest rates in the economy, it will start to decrease the money supply by taking short-term collateralized loans (called *reverse repurchase agreements*, or "reverse repos" for short) from its primary dealers (large banks). In a reverse repo, the Fed lends U.S. Treasuries to the primary dealer in exchange for debiting the dealer's reserve account with the Fed. At the end of the term of the reverse repo, the Fed takes the U.S. Treasuries back from the primary dealer and credits the dealer's reserve account with the Fed.[2]

The amazing thing about all of this is that there is no physical creation or destruction of money. It all takes place via a simple computer entry. The Fed doesn't have stacks of 100-dollar bills and stacks of U.S. Treasuries sitting around that it distributes back and forth to big banks. All it has are computers and a team of people that make credit and debit entries into accounts.

Of course, as we have seen in the wake of the financial crisis of 2008, the Fed and other central banks aren't limited to short-term repos or reverse repos when they want to increase the money supply. They can engage in quantitative easing.

Quantitative Easing

Quantitative easing is a method of increasing the money supply and driving down interest rates that requires the central bank to actually purchase assets—such as U.S. Treasuries, mortgage-backed securities (MBSs), and other collateralized debt obligations (CDOs)— instead of just borrowing them in short-term transactions. Because the transaction is a purchase and not a loan, the central bank is under no obligation to return the assets, and the banks and other institutions from which the central bank purchased the assets are under no obligation to return the money.

This begs the question: where did the central bank get the money to buy the assets? The answer: it didn't get it from anywhere. It created it when it made the credit entry in the seller's account.

---

[2] http://www.newyorkfed.org/aboutthefed/fedpoint/fed04.html.

Inflation

Whenever you hear talk of money creation or "printing" money, the word that inevitably follows next in the discussion is *inflation*. Inflation is a phenomenon that occurs when there is an increase in the money supply that leads to a general and persistent rise in prices as too many dollars chase too few goods.

Inflation is a concern for everyone because it robs us of our purchasing power. Put another way, inflation makes every dollar that we own worth less tomorrow than it is worth today because, as prices rise, we won't be able to buy the same amount of goods tomorrow as we can today for that same dollar.

As you can imagine, inflation is also a major concern for Forex investors. Nobody wants to buy a currency that is going to be losing value because of an increase in the money supply. It's like owning an autographed Babe Ruth baseball card. It is valuable not only because Babe Ruth was an incredible baseball player, but also because the cards are so rare. If everyone had an autographed Babe Ruth baseball card, they wouldn't be worth that much.

So as you analyze the various driving forces in the Forex market, make sure to pay close attention to inflation rates, as rising inflation often leads to a weaker currency. We'll be discussing inflation in more detail in Chapter 10, "Navigating the Economic Calendar," because there are some caveats concerning the effect that rising inflation may have on a currency, but overall, inflation is typically bad news for the value of a currency.

Purchasing Power Parity Theory

This concept of a currency getting weaker when the country that issues it starts experiencing a rise in inflation is the basic premise of another currency-pricing model called the *purchasing power parity theory*.

The purchasing power parity theory suggests that you should be able to buy the same basket of goods for the same amount of money, regardless of which country you are in. Here's how it works. The theory suggests that if you can buy a basket of goods in the United States for $100 and the exchange rate between the U.S.

dollar and the Swiss franc (USD/CHF) is 1.1500, then you should be able to buy the same basket of goods in Switzerland for Fr115. Unfortunately, that is not often the case.

Here's where the theory comes in. The theory holds that an imbalance in purchasing power parity will ultimately be rectified by a change in the value of the currencies. The thinking goes something like this: if a basket of goods in one country is more expensive than the same basket of goods in another country, the value of the currency with the more expensive goods should decrease to bring prices back into balance.

While this theory offers some basic guidance on the relationship between inflation rates and currency values, it does have some flaws. Like the balance of payments theory and the interest-rate parity theory, the purchasing power parity theory looks at only one source of the decrease in demand for a currency with rising inflation, and as we have clearly seen, it is impossible to get an accurate reading on the fundamental forces that are driving the value of a currency by looking at any one of them in a vacuum.

However, if you want to explore the purchasing power you currently have in any one country, you can look at the purchasing power parities (PPPs) data kept by the Organisation for Economic Co-operation and Development (OECD).[3] You can also check out the "Big Mac Index" that is maintained by the folks at *The Economist*.[4] This takes the purchasing power parity idea down from what it would cost to buy a basket of goods to a simpler question of what it would cost to buy a Big Mac—because you can buy a Big Mac pretty much anywhere in the world.

GOVERNMENT INTERVENTIONS AND CURRENCY MANIPULATION

Government interventions and currency manipulation are situations in which a government, typically through its central bank, takes specific action in the Forex market to increase or decrease the

---

[3] http://www.oecd.org/document/47/0,3746,en_2825_495691_36202863_1_1_1_1,00.html.

[4] http://www.economist.com/markets/bigmac/about.cfm.

value of its currency. That specific action can come in one of two forms: outright intervention or verbal intervention.

Outright intervention occurs when a government actually goes out and manipulates the value of its currency by either buying or selling that currency on the open market. *Verbal intervention* occurs when a government threatens to manipulate the value of its currency via open-market transactions, but doesn't actually pull the trigger.

Naturally, a government has a much greater likelihood of manipulating the value of its currency if it is actually engaged in buying or selling that currency, but sometimes the mere threat of intervention is enough to achieve the government's desired results without its having to put to put a lot of money on the line.

Here's another wrinkle. Both outright and verbal intervention can come in two forms: coordinated intervention and unilateral intervention.

Coordinated intervention occurs when more than one government body gets together and decides to intervene in the markets, either through outright intervention or through verbal intervention. *Unilateral intervention* occurs when a government decides to act on its own and takes matters into its own hands when trying to manipulate the value of its currency.

As you will see, coordinated intervention is much more effective in the long run than unilateral intervention. Sure, unilateral intervention can have a huge impact on the market in the short run, but its effects tend not to last as long.

So why would a government want to intervene in the currency market? Governments intervene because they are

- Worried that the currency is getting too strong
- Worried that the currency is getting too weak
- Pegging the currency to another currency

Worried That the Currency Is Getting Too Strong

Why would a government worry that its currency was getting too strong? Having a strong currency is usually a sign that your economy is doing well and that your currency is in high demand, right?

Well, it seems that governments don't mind having a strong currency until it starts to interfere with the country's exports. If a country can't export its goods and services, jobs start drying up, the public starts to blame the government, and the government decides to take action so that all of the politicians who are in office can stay there.

Let us illustrate the concept by walking you through the basics of the Plaza Accord, another Forex agreement that was named after the venue where the agreement was signed.

Plaza Accord

In the mid-1980s, the U.S. dollar was flying high. Foreign investors were flooding the U.S. markets with capital to take advantage of the ridiculously high interest rates that were available thanks to the actions that Paul Volcker (then chairman of the Federal Reserve) had taken to combat the rampant inflation that had crippled the U.S. economy in the late 1970s and early 1980s. Imagine being able to buy U.S. Treasuries that were yielding more than 20 percent. You would be snapping those up as fast as you could.

Unfortunately, this influx of investment demand was driving the value of the U.S. dollar higher, even though the country had a trade deficit and a weak economy. This caused a negative feedback loop in the United States. The U.S. dollar continued to get stronger, which meant that it was more expensive for foreign consumers to buy U.S. goods and services, which in turn made it harder and harder for the United States to climb out of its recent recession.

Luckily for the U.S. government, it was able to bring the finance ministers and others from the United Kingdom, West Germany, France, and Japan together at the Plaza Hotel in New York City and convince them that they all needed to take coordinated action to devalue the U.S. dollar. On September 22, 1985, these men signed the Plaza Accord and instructed their respective trading desks to start selling U.S. dollars. This sudden influx of U.S. dollars into the market immediately started to drive the value of the U.S. dollar lower, enabling the United States to reduce its trade deficit.

Recent Intervention

If you're interested in a more recent example of a country that intervened in the currency market because it felt that its currency was becoming overvalued, you don't have to look any further than

Japan on September 15, 2010. On this date in history, the Japanese Ministry of Finance (MOF), via the Bank of Japan (BOJ), injected ¥2.12 trillion into the market[5] in an attempt to stop the rise in value of the Japanese yen.

You see, Japan's economy is heavily dependent on exports, and as the Japanese yen got stronger and stronger, it was becoming harder and harder for companies like Toyota and Sony to export their products and compete in the United States and other major global markets. By intervening, the Japanese government hoped that it could keep prices low enough to allow its exporters to remain competitive.

The value of the Japanese yen did stabilize during the months following the intervention, but that can't all be attributed to the actions taken by the Japanese government. The rebounding global economy and the resurgence of the U.S. dollar have a lot to do with the Japanese yen getting a little weaker. Also, the Japanese government intervened unilaterally. And as we'll see in just a moment, unilateral moves seem to be far less effective than coordinated interventions.

Worried That the Currency Is Getting Too Weak

Why would a government worry that its currency was getting too weak? Doesn't a weak currency make it easier for the country to export its goods and services?

Yes, it does. However, governments start to worry about price instability if their currencies lose too much value. Also, other governments whose currencies are stronger start to worry when a country's currency starts getting too weak and putting added pressure on the global economy.

Let us illustrate this concept by explaining the antithesis of the Plaza Accord—the Louvre Accord. (Hey, another agreement named after the place where it was signed.)

Louvre Accord

On February 22, 1987, only a year and a half after the Plaza Accord had been signed, officials from the same countries, plus Canada,

---

[5] http://search.japantimes.co.jp/cgi-bin/nb20101109a1.html.

gathered at the Louvre in Paris, France, to reverse course. In a testament to the effectiveness of the coordinated intervention put into motion by the Plaza Accord, the U.S. dollar had continued to move lower and lower until instead of being uncomfortably overvalued, it was now uncomfortably undervalued.

The Plaza Accord had helped the United States pull its trade deficit with Western Europe back into a respectable range, but it hadn't done much to address the U.S. trade deficit with Japan, and the countries of Western Europe were sick of supporting a weaker U.S. dollar. After all, a weaker U.S. dollar meant that U.S. consumers couldn't import as many goods from Western Europe as they used to, and that was hurting the Western European economies.

So after 17 short months, the Louvre Accord canceled out the Plaza Accord, and each country went on its merry way.

Recent Intervention

More recently, if you can call a decade ago more recent, we saw the Eurozone (via the European Central Bank [ECB]) and the United States (via the Federal Reserve) intervene in the currency market to stabilize a declining euro.

The euro had just been launched at the beginning of 2000, and, much to the dismay of the members of the Eurozone and the rest of the global community, it had been dropping ever since. Finally, on September 22, 2000,[6] the European Central Bank decided to step in and intervene in the market to try to buoy the value of the euro by buying euros. A few weeks later, on November 3, 2000,[7] the European Central Bank stepped in again and intervened in the same way.

Just in case you were wondering whether this action was a unilateral action, five days later, on November 8, 2000,[8] the Federal Reserve jumped in and started buying euros in a coordinated effort with the European Central Bank.

These actions eventually stabilized the value of the euro, and it has been a dominant player on the Forex world stage ever since.

---

[6] http://www.ecb.int/press/pr/date/2000/html/pr000922.en.html.
[7] http://www.ecb.int/press/pr/date/2000/html/pr001103.en.html.
[8] http://www.ny.frb.org/newsevents/news/markets/2000/fx001108.html.

Pegging the Currency to Another Currency

Some governments—like China, Hong Kong, Saudi Arabia, Denmark, and others—peg their currencies to another currency—like the U.S. dollar or the euro—in an attempt to maintain a level of stability as they operate in the global financial markets.

Pegging a currency to another currency requires constant intervention in and manipulation of the Forex market. Any time the demand for a pegged currency picks up, that government has to respond by increasing the supply of its currency by selling and/or creating more of the currency if it wants to ensure that prices remain stable. Conversely, any time the demand for a pegged currency drops off, that government has to respond by decreasing the supply of its currency by buying and/or destroying more of the currency if it wants to ensure that prices remain stable.

China has perhaps the most notorious currency peg in the world. The Chinese government decided a long time ago to peg the value of the Chinese renminbi (yuan) to the value of the U.S. dollar, and while it has updated its peg from following only the U.S. dollar to following a basket of currencies (including the U.S. dollar, the euro, the Japanese yen, and so on), it has continued to maintain its peg even in the midst of mounting international pressure to revalue the renminbi. This isn't to say that the Chinese government hasn't let the value of the renminbi appreciate slowly over time, but it is still far from becoming a free-floating currency.

So how does China do it? How does the country peg the Chinese renminbi to the U.S. dollar? We'll discuss that in Chapter 3, "Who Drives Currency Prices," when we address central banks. For now, all you need to focus on is the fact that intervention can come in many forms. Some are more effective than others, but whenever you hear about intervention, or possible intervention, in the Forex market, you had better sit up and take notice.

INVESTOR FEAR

One of the most important things to remember when you are trading in the Forex market is that the market is populated by people just like you. Ultimately, it is people who drive this market, and that means that human emotions (especially fear) are ever present.

Investor fear is one of the most potent forces in today's currency market. In fact, it is so important that it tends to trump many other fundamental factors when it starts to rear its ugly head. Investor fear can send some currencies crashing down when times turn sour. The opposite is also true: investor fear can send some currencies soaring when times are rough.

To take advantage of this market dynamic, you need to know which currencies tend to thrive when times are bad.

Safe-Haven Currencies

Safe-haven currencies thrive when investor fear is running amok. They are called *safe-haven currencies* because of the perceived protection that they offer during times of financial turmoil. At the time of this writing, the U.S. dollar (USD), the Swiss franc (CHF), and the Japanese yen (JPY) seem to be the most popular safe-haven currencies.

Each of these currencies is deemed to be a safe haven for a different reason. The U.S. dollar is a safe-haven currency because investors seem to flock to the safety of U.S. Treasuries when the global financial market enters crisis mode. This increase in demand for U.S. Treasuries leads to an increase in demand for the U.S. dollar, which pushes the value of the U.S. dollar higher. And after all, don't you want your safe-haven currency to appreciate when things look bleak?

The Swiss franc is considered to be a safe-haven currency because a large portion of the Swiss francs in circulation are backed by gold. The percentage of currency that is backed by gold isn't quite as high as it used to be, but compared to many other fiat currencies, the Swiss franc has incredibly stable gold backing. The Swiss economy is also considered to be an incredibly stable economy with low levels of inflation.

The Japanese yen is a safe-haven currency because of the security of the Japanese government debt market. Unlike the U.S. public debt, which is held largely by foreign governments and investors, the Japanese public debt is held almost exclusively by individual Japanese investors. This provides a lot of stability to the Japanese economy and provides less incentive for the government to try to inflate its way out of its debt obligations—something that other countries have been known to do when their debt burdens became too onerous. A currency that faces less risk of inflation is a much safer currency.

Now that you know which currencies like market turmoil, all you have to do is gauge just how fearful or confident the market is in general.

Measuring Investor Fear

Investor fear and confidence are also two of the most nebulous forces to monitor and analyze because there is no quantitative way to measure fear . . . or is there?

One indicator that you can use to gauge investor fear is the CBOE Volatility Index (VIX). We will be discussing this indicator in greater detail in Chapter 11, "Indicators That Forex Traders Watch," but here are the basics:

- The VIX is based on the implied volatility levels of S&P 500 Index options.
- When the VIX is moving higher, it indicates that investor fear is increasing.
- When the VIX is moving lower, it indicates that investor fear is decreasing.

Now, you may be wondering why we are talking about watching an indicator based on stock index options when we are investing in the Forex market, but you would be surprised at how tightly coordinated the financial markets of the world are. We can learn a lot by watching markets other than the Forex market.

CHAPTER 3

Who Drives Currency Prices

HEDGERS, SPECULATORS, MANIPULATORS, AND FACILITATORS

The Forex market is full of all sorts of different people who are trying to accomplish all sorts of different things. Some Forex traders are trying to make money, some are trying not to lose money, and some are trying to affect how much money is worth and how it moves around the world.

It is this diverse cast of characters that makes the Forex market one of the most dynamic markets on earth. On the other hand, it is this same cast of characters that can make it difficult to understand why the market is doing what it is doing. That's why it is important that you take some time to understand what motivates each group. Because the better you understand what is driving the people who are placing the trades, the more successful you will be.

So let's take a look at the four types of players in the Forex market.

Hedgers are market participants who look to the Forex market as a place where they can reduce their exposure to risk. This may seem counterintuitive at first—after all, isn't the Forex market fraught with risk? Yes, it can be. But if you are already exposed to foreign exchange risk through international business transactions or for other reasons, the Forex market can be a great place to offset that exposure and thus reduce your risk.

Speculators are the polar opposite of hedgers. While hedgers look to the Forex market as a place to reduce their risk, speculators look to it as a venue where they can take on risk in the hopes of making a profit. As the name suggests, these traders speculate regarding the direction in which they believe a currency pair is going to move and place their trades accordingly—understanding that if they are wrong, they are going to lose money. Unless you are a corporate treasurer and are reading this book on behalf of your company, you are most likely a speculator.

Manipulators are players whose sole purpose for jumping into the Forex market is to manipulate prices. Now, don't let the negative connotations of the term *manipulators* overwhelm you. Some market manipulation can be viewed as healthy for the market, depending on what your economic philosophy leanings are.

Facilitators are market participants who are not looking to make money by speculating in the Forex on their own. Rather, facilitators look to make money by enabling hedgers, speculators, and manipulators to place their trades in the Forex market.

Now that you understand the four basic categories that Forex market participants typically fall into, let's take a look at some of the most important players in the market and see which category, or categories, they fall into.

CENTRAL BANKS

Central banks are manipulators. Now, don't get us wrong. Central banks are not malicious manipulators. They are not out in the market trying to hurt other traders or to make a lot of money for themselves. They are trying to carry out the mandates they have been given by their governments, and sometimes intervening in the Forex market is the best way—in the eyes of the central bank—to carry out those mandates.

Central banks will typically intervene in the Forex market for one of three reasons:

- To offset the effects of trade imbalances
- To provide liquidity and reduce volatility in the value of the currency during times of financial crisis
- To drive the value of the currency higher or lower

Offsetting the Effects of Trade Imbalances

Central banks that are charged with the responsibility of maintaining a currency peg—whether it is a specific exchange rate or a floating price band—have to constantly combat the effects of trade imbalances. Trade surpluses typically put upward pressure on the value of a currency, and trade deficits typically put downward pressure on the value of a currency.

To offset trade-surplus pressure that pushes the value of the domestic currency higher, the central bank can inject more of the domestic currency into the market by buying the foreign currency. You'll often hear this referred to as the central bank's "printing money." This action will increase the supply of the domestic currency, bringing the value of the domestic currency back down to where the bank wants it. It also builds the foreign exchange reserves of the central bank.

To offset trade-deficit pressure that pushes the value of the domestic currency lower, the central bank can use its foreign exchange reserves to buy the domestic currency. This action will decrease the supply of the domestic currency, bringing the value of the domestic currency back up to where the bank wants it. It also depletes the foreign exchange reserves of the central bank.

It's important to note that these actions taken by the central bank are not without consequences. Injecting too much of the domestic currency into the market to bring the price of the currency down increases the money supply and can lead to inflation. Conversely, taking too much of the domestic currency out of the market to bring the price of the currency back up decreases the money supply and can lead to deflation. Knowing this, the central bank has to decide whether it wants to sterilize the intervention or not.

Unsterilized Currency Intervention

Unsterilized currency intervention is a fancy way of describing what we just outlined—a central bank either injecting more of the domestic currency into the market or pulling more of the domestic currency out of the market, and that's it. With an unsterilized currency intervention, the central bank does not take any further steps to try to combat some of the consequences of the intervention.

Sterilized Currency Intervention

Sterilized currency intervention, on the other hand, does require the central bank to take further steps after it intervenes. Let's look at the two intervention scenarios individually to better understand what a central bank can do to try to sterilize its actions as far as inflation and deflation are concerned.

When a central bank injects more of the domestic currency into the international Forex market to reduce the value of that currency, it risks sparking inflation because the money supply has increased. That's the problem: there is too much of the domestic currency floating around in the market. So if the central bank wants to sterilize its actions, it needs to find a way to reduce the money supply.

Here's the rub. If the central bank were to try to reduce the money supply by using its foreign currency reserves to buy back the domestic currency, it would shrink the money supply, but it would also push the value of the currency right back up, negating its previous actions. So what is a central bank to do if it wants to decrease the value of the currency but not increase the money supply?

To sterilize an injection of the domestic currency into the Forex market, a central bank can use a reverse repo agreement like the ones we talked about in Chapter 2, "What Drives Currency Prices." In a reverse repo, the central bank lends Treasuries or other assets to the primary dealers in exchange for debiting the dealers' reserve accounts with the central bank. At the end of the term of the reverse repo, the central bank takes the Treasuries or other assets back from the primary dealers and credits the dealers' reserve accounts.

By injecting money into the international Forex market and then using a reverse repo in the domestic market to soak that money right back up, the central bank is able to push the value of the currency lower without increasing the money supply.

Now let's take a look at the other side of the sterilized intervention coin. When a central bank uses its foreign currency reserves to buy the domestic currency in the international Forex market to increase the value of that currency, it risks sparking deflation because the money supply has decreased. That's the problem: there is too little of the domestic currency floating around in the market.

So if the central bank wants to sterilize its actions, it needs to find a way to increase the money supply.

Once again, the central bank faces a dilemma. If it were to try to increase the money supply by injecting more of the domestic currency back into the market to buy foreign currencies, it would increase the money supply, but it would also push the value of the currency right back down, negating its previous actions. So what is a central bank to do if it wants to increase the value of the currency but not decrease the money supply?

To sterilize a withdrawal of the domestic currency from the Forex market, a central bank can use a repo agreement. In a repo, the central bank borrows Treasuries or other assets from the primary dealers in exchange for crediting the dealers' reserve accounts with the central bank. At the end of the term of the repo, the central bank gives the Treasuries or other assets back to the primary dealers and debits the dealers' reserve accounts with the central bank.

By pulling money out of the international Forex market and then using a repo in the domestic market, the central bank is able to push the value of the currency higher without decreasing the money supply.

Providing Stability During Financial Crises

Central banks do not like uncertainty or unusual levels of volatility in the Forex market. It is much harder to maintain control of or influence over the market when unusual levels of volatility take control. To that end, central banks may feel compelled to step into the market to provide some stability, especially during times of financial crisis.

One way in which central banks can reduce volatility and help one another at the same time is by issuing temporary reciprocal currency arrangements—central bank liquidity swap lines—with other banks. These liquidity swap lines allow one central bank to borrow foreign currency from another central bank and then disperse that currency in the first bank's domestic economy. Of course, as with any swap transaction, there is a promise to return all of the borrowed funds at some point in the future, but the temporary use of the foreign currency can go a long way toward maintaining order and liquidity in the market. We saw a great example of this during the financial crisis that spawned the Great Recession.

On December 12, 2007, as the global credit markets were seizing up and the financial system was grinding to a halt, the Federal Open Market Committee (FOMC) announced that it had authorized liquidity swap lines with the European Central Bank (ECB) and the Swiss National Bank (SNB) to help provide liquidity in U.S. dollars and stability to overseas markets. Ultimately, many more central banks were given similar deals.[1]

Driving Currency Revaluations

Every now and then, we will see a central bank dive into the Forex market with the simple goal of manipulating currency prices. Sometimes central banks believe that currency prices are too high, and they want to see if they can bring them back down. Other times central banks believe that currency prices are too low, and they want to see if they can bring them back up. We covered these concerns and motivations in great length in the "Government Interventions and Currency Manipulation" section of Chapter 2, "What Drives Currency Prices."

While it may seem as if trying to pull prices back down and trying to push prices back up are two sides of the same coin, there is actually one key difference that central banks have to consider before they move forward with an attempt to manipulate the currency market.

Central banks have a much easier time sustaining a campaign to reduce the value of their currencies because a central bank can always just "print more money" and inject it into the Forex market. Where central banks run into difficulty is when they engage in campaigns to increase the value of their currencies when they don't have sufficient foreign exchange reserves. A central bank can embark on a campaign to increase the value of the currency by taking its foreign exchange reserves and using them to buy the domestic currency on the open market. However, once the central bank

---

[1] http://www.ny.frb.org/aboutthefed/fedpoint/fed27.html.

runs out of foreign exchange reserves, it is out of luck, and the campaign to strengthen the currency will most likely begin to unravel.

BANKS

Banks are facilitators, hedgers, and speculators. We know that is quite a statement, but you have to figure that when a market is often referred to as the interbank Forex market, banks are going to wear many different hats and engage in many different activities.

To get a sense of who some of the banks that make up the interbank market are, let's take a look at the banks that the Federal Reserve Bank of New York surveyed as part of the triennial Forex survey conducted by the Bank for International Settlements (BIS):

- Bank of America
- Bank of Montreal
- Bank of New York Mellon
- Bank of Tokyo-Mitsubishi
- Barclays Capital
- BNP Paribas
- Calyon
- Canadian Imperial Bank of Commerce
- Citigroup
- Credit Suisse Group
- Deutsche Bank
- Goldman Sachs
- HSBC
- JPMorgan Chase
- Mizuho Corporation
- Morgan Stanley
- Royal Bank of Scotland
- Skandinaviska Enskilda Banken
- Société Générale
- Standard Chartered Bank
- State Street Bank & Trust Company
- Sumitomo Mitsui Banking Corp.

- UBS
- Wells Fargo[2]

These are the big names you need to know. Other smaller banks simply don't have as much of an impact. Now that you've met the big players, let's take a look at the three key roles that these banks play.

Banks as Facilitators

Banks facilitate currency transactions for large corporate clients and even individual travelers like you. Some banks also facilitate Forex transactions by serving as a prime broker for some of their clients. We'll discuss prime brokers in the next section, but for right now, let's focus on how banks act as facilitators for their corporate and retail clients. Here's an example.

If a bank has a multinational corporation as a client, and that corporation wants to exchange $100 million for the equivalent number of euros, the bank is going to be more than happy to assist in the transaction. After all, the bank is going to generate some nice commissions from that transaction.

However, by making that currency exchange, the bank is now exposed to currency risk because it now owns an additional $100 million and is short a lot of euros. To offset this risk, the bank must now hedge its position.

Banks as Hedgers

Banks are often hedgers by necessity. They are driven to hedge the currency risks that they assume by acting as counterparty to clients who are looking to exchange currencies. If they have too much of a given currency, they may need to sell some of it or buy a contract that offsets some of that exposure.

Banks also choose to hedge against other investment activities that the bank engages in. Here's how Goldman Sachs put it in a recent 10-Q (quarterly report) filing: "The firm seeks to reduce the impact of fluctuations in foreign exchange rates on its net invest-

---

[2] http://www.newyorkfed.org/markets/triennial/fx_survey.pdf.

ment in certain non-U.S. operations through the use of foreign currency forward contracts and foreign currency-denominated debt. For foreign currency forward contracts designated as hedges, the effectiveness of the hedge is assessed based on the overall changes in the fair value of the forward contracts."[3]

Banks as Speculators

Banks are speculators in a variety of ways. Some banks have their own proprietary trading desks that invest in the Forex market much the way you do, except on a massively larger scale. New financial regulations are forcing some banks to divest themselves of their proprietary trading desks, but many banks still operate robust trading floors.

Banks can also speculate by not fully hedging their currency positions within the bank. In our previous example, if the bank that exchanged the $100 million for euros wanted to speculate that the value of the U.S. dollar was going to go up, it could hold onto that money without hedging it in the market.

PRIME BROKERS

Prime brokers are facilitators. So what is a prime broker, and what does it do? A prime broker is a financial institution (typically a large bank) that provides its clients (typically hedge funds, smaller banks, commodity trading advisors [CTAs], pension funds, endowments, and so on) with the following:

- Access to trade with the banks that make up the interbank Forex market
- Leverage
- The ability to trade in the name of the prime broker
- Trade settlement, clearing, and reporting functionality
- Housing and administration of client accounts

---

[3]http://www.sec.gov/Archives/edgar/data/886982/000095012310046612/y84220e10vq.htm.

As you already know, trading in the Forex market can be a risky proposition. Because of this, the large money-center banks don't want to do business with just anybody. They want to make sure that whomever they do business with is going to be able to make good on their trades. Here's where prime brokers step in.

Here's how the process works. Imagine that a hedge fund manager who is a client of a prime brokerage wants to sell 100 USD/JPY contracts. The first thing the manager will do is look for the best available price at which to sell the contracts. Once he finds the best price, he will place an order with the executing dealer (which could be a bank, another hedge fund, or some other party) that is quoting the price he is interested in.

Now, the hedge fund might not have a direct relationship with this executing dealer, but the hedge fund's prime broker probably does. Therefore, the hedge fund manager will place the trade in the name of the prime broker. At the same time, the hedge fund manager will send the trade information to his prime broker so that it is aware that the trade between the hedge fund and the other bank has been placed.

Once the bank that quoted the price receives the trade order from the hedge fund, it will confirm and place the order with the prime broker. So technically, even though the hedge fund originated the trade, the two counterparties of the trade are the bank and the prime broker. The prime broker then enters into a separate

FIGURE 3-1

FX Prime Brokerage Deal Process

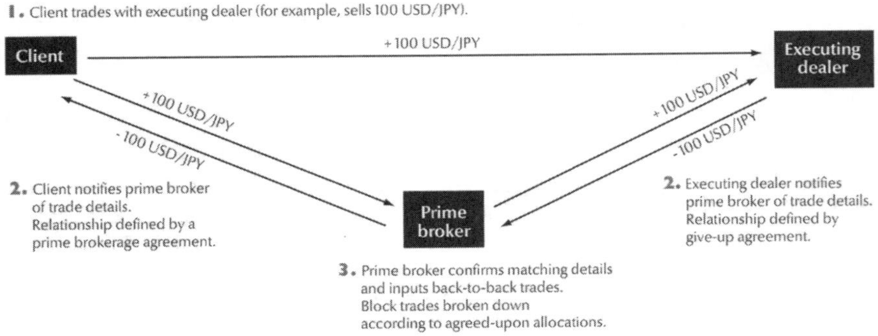

1. Client trades with executing dealer (for example, sells 100 USD/JPY).

+100 USD/JPY

Client   **Executing dealer**

+100 USD/JPY

+100 USD/JPY

−100 USD/JPY

+100 USD/JPY

−100 USD/JPY

2. Client notifies prime broker of trade details. Relationship defined by a prime brokerage agreement.

Prime broker

2. Executing dealer notifies prime broker of trade details. Relationship defined by give-up agreement.

3. Prime broker confirms matching details and inputs back-to-back trades. Block trades broken down according to agreed-upon allocations.

Source: http://www.ny.frb.org/fxc/2005/fxc051219a.pdf.

trade with the hedge fund. Figure 3-1 illustrates the three basic steps of the trade execution and clearing process.

In the end, the hedge fund has a short position on the USD/ JPY, the executing dealer has a long position on the USD/JPY, and the prime broker has no exposure to the Forex market.

At this point, you may be wondering why the prime broker would be willing to do all of this. The answer: fees, fees, fees. Just as your bank charges you to make wire transfers and so on, prime brokerages charge their clients for their services. Every time a client executes anything through the prime brokerage, it has to pay a fee.

The trading facilitation provided by prime brokers has led to huge increases in liquidity in the Forex market by allowing more parties to trade with each other—and everybody benefits when liquidity increases because transaction speeds increase while transaction costs and spreads decrease.

HEDGE FUNDS

Hedge funds are speculators. Hedge funds are pools of money that are raised from wealthy individuals, pension funds, endowments, corporations, and others and are managed by a fund manager. Traditionally, a hedge fund would try to do just what its name suggests: hedge against risks like currency risk. Nowadays, hedge funds are much less concerned with hedging risk. They prefer taking on risk instead—by buying some currencies while selling others— to try to make more money.

Hedge funds typically use massive amounts of leverage when they trade in the Forex market. This means that they borrow money from someone with whom they have a credit agreement (a bank or other large financial institution), then turn around and use that borrowed money to buy and sell currencies.

This system seems to work pretty well when the credit market is functioning well. But when the credit market freezes up and stops functioning, this system of borrowing money to invest in the Forex market can unravel quickly, causing huge price swings in the value of various currencies. We learned this lesson during the financial crisis of 2008.

Heading into 2008, many hedge funds had leveraged up, getting into carry trades with the Japanese yen. A *carry trade* is a currency trade that is established to take advantage of large interest-rate spreads that may exist between two countries. Essentially, you sell the currency with the lower interest rate, and you use the funds to buy the currency with the higher interest rate. By doing so, you will have to pay the lower interest rate for the currency that you sold, but you earn the higher interest rate on the currency that you bought—and you get to keep the difference.

This strategy unraveled for hedge funds in 2008 when the financial crisis caused the credit market to freeze. You see, the money that hedge funds borrow from banks and other financial institutions to leverage their trades is loaned on a short-term basis—often only overnight. So when the credit market froze, hedge funds were cut off from their capital supply and were forced to unwind their carry trades because they could no longer meet their margin requirements—the amount of cash that must be on hand to hold a trade. It didn't matter if the hedge funds thought the trades were still good trades or not. They didn't have the money so they couldn't hold the trades.

MULTINATIONAL CORPORATIONS

Multinational corporations are hedgers. Corporations that operate in multiple countries often run into scenarios in which they have accounts receivable or accounts payable that are denominated in a currency other than that used in the country where the corporation is headquartered.

For example, suppose a U.S.-based corporation has accounts receivable from a customer in Japan, and those accounts receivable are denominated in Japanese yen. The corporation knows that it is most likely not going to collect those accounts receivable for up to 60 days, and it is worried that the value of the Japanese yen compared to the U.S. dollar is going to drop in the meantime. To hedge against this risk of a falling Japanese yen, the corporation could sell the USD/JPY (U.S. dollar vs. Japanese yen) currency pair. That way, if the value of the Japanese yen does decline, the corporation will be able to offset its losses on the accounts receivable with its gains on the currency contract.

Similarly, suppose a British corporation has accounts payable to a vendor in the Netherlands, and those accounts payable are denominated in euros. The corporation knows that it is not going to pay those accounts payable for another 60 days, but it is worried that the value of the euro compared to the British pound is going to increase during that time. To hedge against the risk of a rising euro, the corporation could buy the EUR/GBP (euro vs. British pound) currency pair. That way, if the value of the euro does rise, the corporation will be able to offset its losses on the more expensive accounts payable with its gains on the currency contract.

Corporations have an incentive to hedge these accounts because, according to the Financial Accounting Standards Board (FASB):[4]

> *Transaction gains and losses are a result of the effect of exchange rate changes on transactions denominated in currencies other than the functional currency (for example, a U.S. company may borrow Swiss francs or a French subsidiary may have a receivable denominated in kroner from a Danish customer). Gains and losses on those foreign currency transactions are generally included in determining net income for the period in which exchange rates change unless the transaction hedges a foreign currency commitment or a net investment in a foreign entity.*

Multinational corporations also exchange a lot of money via foreign currency translation. Foreign currency translation is the simple act of transferring profits from one area of the business that operates using one currency to another area of the business that operates using a different currency. A corporation can also hedge these transactions to prevent exchange-rate losses on these profits.

According to the Federal Reserve Bank of New York, corporations continue to represent an important percentage of Forex market activity, even though their significance in comparison with hedge funds and other investors has declined somewhat in recent years.[5]

RETAIL TRADERS

Retail traders are speculators. This one is pretty straightforward. You are a retail trader, and let's face it, you are not getting into the

---

[4] http://www.fasb.org/summary.stsum52.shtml.
[5] http://www.newyorkfed.org/markets/triennial/fx_survey.pdf.

Forex market to hedge your foreign accounts payable exposure, you are not trying to facilitate transactions between institutional traders, and you are definitely not trying to manipulate currency values from within your personal account. You are in the Forex market to make money.

Retail Forex trading activity has grown substantially since 2000. Average daily trading volume on retail Forex platforms (which is somewhere around $118 billion[6]) is relatively small when compared with total daily Forex volume, but it is a segment that continues to grow.

RETAIL FOREIGN EXCHANGE DEALERS (RFEDS)

Retail foreign exchange dealers (RFEDs)—often referred to as "dealers"—are facilitators and speculators. RFEDs play a key role in the life of any retail trader by providing a conduit into the Forex market. However, their dual roles of facilitator on the one hand and speculator on the other hand have led to some controversy in the market.

RFEDs as Facilitators

If you are a retail trader and you want to trade spot Forex, you need to work with an RFED. Without RFEDs, you would be shut out of the spot Forex market. After all, huge megabanks like Deutsche Bank and UBS aren't going to give you, as an individual trader, the time of day when it comes to trading currencies. They have much bigger fish to fry.

By aggregating retail traders' accounts and trade flow, RFEDs are able to establish relationships with big money-center banks and prime brokers, then turn around and share that access with us.

Now, don't misunderstand that statement. RFEDs don't give retail traders access to the interbank market by letting them trade directly with banks and other big players in the market. Instead, RFEDs give retail traders access by acting as counterparty to (taking the other side of) all their trades and then turning around

---

[6]http://Forexmagnates.com/retail-Forex-volumes-survey-september-2010/.

and placing their own trades in the interbank market to offset the currency exposure that they have assumed by acting as counterparty for their clients. Here's how it works.

When a retail trader enters an order to buy 1 EUR/USD contract, she is buying that contract from her RFED. So after this first transaction, the retail trader is long 1 contract on the EUR/USD and the RFED is short 1 contract on the EUR/USD. To eliminate this short exposure to the EUR/USD, the RFED will turn around and buy 1 EUR/USD contract on the interbank market. By holding 1 short EUR/USD contract and 1 long EUR/USD contract, the RFED is able to offset its exposure and risk.

This is a pretty slick system. Retail traders get to place the trades they want, and the RFEDs get to offset their risk. However, this isn't always the way it happens. RFEDs don't always offset their risk—which brings us to the concept of RFEDs as speculators.

RFEDs as Speculators

RFEDs speculate in the Forex market by not offsetting all of their clients' trades.

Going back to the example we just used to illustrate how an RFED can act as a facilitator, recall how the RFED acts as counterparty to the trades that its clients make. This is the service that the RFED provides. However, once a client places a trade, the RFED is under no obligation to offset that trade. So long as the RFED honors the trade with its client, it can choose whether it wants to offset that trade or hold on to it. If the RFED chooses to offset the trade, it puts the trade into its "offset flow," or "A book," and proceeds to place a corresponding trade in the interbank market. Conversely, if the RFED chooses not to offset the trade, it puts the trade into its "managed flow portfolio," or "B book," and maintains its exposure to the trade.

> **Offset flow (A book):** This is the portion of the RFED's portfolio that it chooses to offset by placing corresponding trades in the interbank market.
>
> **Managed flow portfolio (B book):** This is the portion of the RFED's portfolio that it chooses not to offset in the interbank market.

TABLE 3-1

Managed Flow Portfolio—Neutral Position

Client	Action	RFED Action
Client 1	Buys 5 EUR/USD	Sells 5 EUR/USD
Client 2	Buys 3 EUR/USD	Sells 3 EUR/USD
Client 3	Sells 4 EUR/USD	Buys 4 EUR/USD
Client 4	Sells 3 EUR/USD	Buys 3 EUR/USD
Client 5	Sells 1 EUR/USD	Buys 1 EUR/USD

The managed flow portfolio contains trades from many different clients for which the RFED has been the counterparty. In many cases, these trades offset each other naturally, but sometimes they don't. For instance, you could see the trades in Table 3-1 in the managed flow portfolio.

Looking at the sum of the five actions taken by the RFED, you can see that the RFED is in a net neutral position: it sold 8 EUR/USD contracts (5 + 3 = 8), but it also bought 8 EUR/USD contracts (4 + 3 + 1 = 8). In this instance, the actions of the RFED's clients left the RFED in a naturally hedged position.

Now let's take a look at a slightly different scenario. Imagine that you now see the trades in Table 3-2 in the managed flow portfolio.

Looking at the sum of these five actions taken by the RFED, you can see that the RFED is in a net short position: it sold 15 EUR/USD contracts (10 + 5 = 15), and it bought only 10 EUR/USD contracts (6 + 3 + 1 = 10). In this instance, the actions of the RFED's

TABLE 3-2

Managed Flow Portfolio—Bearish Exposure

Client	Action	RFED Action
Client 1	Buys 10 EUR/USD	Sells 10 EUR/USD
Client 2	Buys 5 EUR/USD	Sells 5 EUR/USD
Client 3	Sells 6 EUR/USD	Buys 6 EUR/USD
Client 4	Sells 3 EUR/USD	Buys 3 EUR/USD
Client 5	Sells 1 EUR/USD	Buys 1 EUR/USD

clients left the RFED exposed to price movements in the EUR/ USD. If the EUR/USD goes down, the RFED will make money. If the EUR/USD goes up, the RFED will lose money.

So by determining which client orders it is going to put in the managed flow portfolio, the RFED gets to decide whether it wants to have long or short exposure to any currency pair.

This concept of offsetting some client transactions while not offsetting others was one that was not widely understood among retail traders (and may still not be), but the curtain was pulled back when companies like Gain Capital Holdings (Forex.com) filed their S-1 documents as they prepared for their initial public offerings (IPOs) on the U.S. stock market.[7]

KNOWING WHO IS AWAKE AND TRADING IN THE 24-HOUR CYCLE

Monitoring what is happening throughout the day in the Forex market is much more difficult than monitoring what is happening in the U.S. stock market, for instance, because the Forex market never sleeps. There is no opening or closing bell. Trading activity simply follows the sun as it moves from one financial center to the next around the globe. The trick is knowing which financial center is likely to be most active at different times of the day, because knowing who is awake and trading in the currency market at any given point in time will give you added insight into why a particular currency pair is moving the way it is.

Technically, the trading day starts in New Zealand and Australia. Shortly after that, the Japanese markets come online, followed by Singapore, Hong Kong, and the other Asian markets. Next, Europe starts to join in the fun as Switzerland, Germany, and the United Kingdom wake up and get to work. Lastly, after the Asian markets have wound up their trading day, the United States jumps into action. And then, of course, the entire process starts all over again.

Table 3-3 gives a breakdown of when the major markets open each trading day; all times are in Greenwich mean time (GMT).

---

[7]http://www.sec.gov/Archives/edgar/data/1444363/000095012310108827/ y79727a7sv1za.htm.

TABLE 3-3

24-Hour Forex Cycle

	Open	Close
Sydney	9:00 p.m.	6:00 a.m.
Tokyo	11:00 p.m.	8:00 a.m.
Singapore	12:00 a.m.	9:00 a.m.
Hong Kong	12:30 a.m.	9:30 a.m.
Zurich	7:00 a.m.	3:00 p.m.
London	8:00 a.m.	4:00 p.m.
New York	1:00 p.m.	10:00 p.m.

Of course, when daylight saving rolls around, you will need to make the necessary adjustments by shifting Sydney, Zurich, London, and New York ahead one hour, but this should give you a good idea of which markets are most active during different parts of the trading day.

Although currency trading takes place in financial centers around the world, the bulk of the trading is clustered in a few cities. According to the Bank for International Settlements (BIS),[8] more than half of all Forex transactions take place in either the United Kingdom or the United States. Here's the breakdown:

- London: 36.7 percent
- New York: 18 percent
- Tokyo: 6 percent
- Singapore: 5 percent
- Zurich: 5 percent
- Hong Kong: 5 percent
- Sydney: 4 percent

So what does all this mean? What should we be watching? Here are a few things:

- The London and New York markets are both open between 1:00 p.m. and 4:00 p.m. GMT, which means that there is going to be a lot of liquidity in the market during that period.

---

[8] http://www.bis.org/press/p100901.htm.

- The transition between the close of the trading day in New York and the opening of the trading day in Tokyo is a relatively quiet time in the market.
- Currency pairs involving the Japanese yen are actively traded during the Asian session.
- Liquidity in the euro picks up when the European markets open, and liquidity in the U.S. dollar picks up when the U.S. market opens.

The most important thing for you to take from all of this is the fact that currency pairs trade differently depending on the time of day. So as you get started, try to trade at the same time each day so that you can get used to how the market reacts during those trading hours.

Getting to Know the Currencies: 12 Key Questions to Ask

CURRENCIES HAVE PERSONALITIES

Currencies are just like us . . . they have personalities. Some of them are moody, some of them are volatile, and some of them are pretty boring. That's what makes this market so much fun.

When you trade currencies in the Forex market, you are getting into a relationship with those currencies, so you'd better get to know them. You may actually find that you are more compatible with certain currencies than you are with others.

To help you get to know the currencies a little better, we've set up a speed-dating service of sorts. We know that some of you may be a little shy and that this could feel a little awkward, so we have come up with a list of 12 questions that you need to ask before you trade a currency:

- Does your economy run a trade surplus or a trade deficit?
- What does your economy export?
- To whom does your economy export?
- What does your economy import?

- From whom does your economy import?
- Do you have an attractive government debt market?
- Do you have an attractive equities market?
- Tell me about your central bank. What are its mandates? How much gold and foreign currency reserves does it hold?
- Do you have an overinvolved government that likes to intervene in the Forex market?
- What economic announcements are important to you?
- Are you a safe-haven currency?
- How can I trade you?

So what's so special about these questions? Why should you take the time to learn all this information? First of all, the more you know about a currency, the easier it will be to make good investment choices. That's just common sense. But perhaps even more important, you want to take every precaution you can to avoid being surprised by an unexpected movement in the currency that blows up your account.

Let's go through each of these questions and take a look at why it is pertinent to your investing decisions.

Does Your Economy Run a Trade Surplus or a Trade Deficit?

Why do we care whether a country runs a trade surplus or a trade deficit? We care because trade flows play such an important part in the value of a currency. Countries with a trade surplus tend to have stronger currencies because as demand for the goods and services that the country provides increases, demand for that country's currency tends to increase, since foreign buyers must pay for the goods and services in the local currency. Conversely, countries with a trade deficit tend to have weaker currencies because as consumers exchange their local currency for the currency of the country from which they are buying the goods and services, the supply of the local currency tends to go up, which brings down the value of that currency.

What Does Your Economy Export?

Why do we care what goods or services a country exports? We care because if we know the primary goods and services that a country exports, we know what markets and prices we need to be paying attention to for signs that demand for the local currency may be changing.

For instance, New Zealand is a major exporter of dairy products—everything from butter and cheese to milk and milk powder. Knowing this tunes you into the fact that you should be watching dairy prices. If dairy prices go up, importers will have to exchange more of their local currency and buy more New Zealand dollars in order to buy the same amount of dairy products. This is likely to drive down the value of the local currency by increasing the supply of that currency on the market and drive up the value of the New Zealand dollar by increasing the demand for that currency. The opposite is also true. If dairy prices go down, importers will have to exchange less of their local currency and buy fewer New Zealand dollars in order to buy the same amount of dairy products. This is likely to drive up the value of the local currency by increasing the supply of that currency on the market more slowly and drive down the value of the New Zealand dollar by decreasing the demand for that currency.

You will find that this method of analysis is especially useful when evaluating the currencies of countries with commodity-based economies, such as Australia, New Zealand, and Canada, among others.

As we walk through and classify the goods and services that a country exports, we will be using the classification system used by the World Trade Organization (WTO), which divides goods and services into the following groups:[1]

- Merchandise Trade
  - Agricultural products
  - Fuels and mining products
  - Manufactures
- Commercial Services Trade
  - Transportation

---

[1]http://stat.wto.org/CountryProfile/WSDBCountryPFTechNotes.aspx?Language=E.

- Travel
- Other commercial services

Agricultural products: Food and raw materials. If you see that a majority of a country's merchandise exports come from this group, you know that the currency is going to be sensitive to changes in agricultural commodity prices.

Fuels and mining products: Ores, minerals, fuels, and nonferrous metals. If you see that a majority of a country's merchandise exports come from this group, you know that the currency is going to be sensitive to changes in energy and other commodity prices.

Manufactures: Iron, steel, chemicals, machinery, textiles, clothing, and other consumer goods. If you see that a majority of a country's merchandise exports come from this group, you know that the currency is going to be sensitive to changes in business and consumer sentiment in the destination countries.

Transportation: Airlines, trains, buses, and so on. If you see that a majority of a country's commercial services exports come from this group, you know that the currency is going to be sensitive to changes in business and consumer sentiment in the destination countries.

Travel: Tourism. If you see that a majority of a country's commercial services exports come from this group, you know that the currency is going to be sensitive to changes in employment rates and global threat levels.

Other commercial services: Communication, construction, insurance and financial services, royalties, and license fees. If you see that a majority of a country's commercial services exports come from this group, you know that the currency is going to be sensitive to changes in business growth and expansion.

To Whom Does Your Economy Export?

Why do we care to whom a country exports its goods and services? We care because keeping an eye on the economic health of the countries that are importing goods from the country you are analyzing can tell you a lot about the future demand for those same exports.

For instance, Australia exports more goods to China than to any other country. Another way you could say the same thing is, China imports more of Australia's goods than any other country does. Either way you say it, you know that China is an incredibly important trade partner for Australia.

Knowing this, you can keep an eye on China's GDP, employment rate, manufacturing data, and myriad other economic indicators and get a sense of whether China is going to continue to import as much from Australia in the future. If the economic data coming out of China look strong, Australian exports to China are most likely going to remain robust, and demand for, and therefore the value of, the Australian dollar should remain high. If the economic data coming out of China look weak, Australian exports to China are most likely going to decline, and demand for, and therefore the value of, the Australian dollar should pull back.

What Does Your Economy Import?

Why do we care what goods or services a country imports? We care because if we know the primary goods and services that a country imports, we know what markets and prices we need to be paying attention to for signs that supply of the local currency may be changing.

For instance, Japan is a net importer of oil. In fact, it is the fourth largest importer of oil in the world—behind only the United States, the European Union, and China. Because Japan imports so much oil, and because oil is priced in U.S. dollars, the Japanese yen is sensitive to changes in the price of oil. When oil prices go up, Japanese importers have to sell more Japanese yen and buy more U.S. dollars in order to pay for the same amount of oil. This will probably drive down the value of the Japanese yen by increasing its supply on the market and drive up the value of the U.S. dollar by increasing the demand for that currency. The opposite is also true. When oil prices go down, Japanese importers have to sell fewer Japanese yen and buy fewer U.S. dollars in order to pay for the same amount of oil. This will probably drive up the value of the Japanese yen by increasing its supply on the market more slowly, and drive down the value of the U.S. dollar by decreasing the demand for that currency.

As we walk through and classify the goods and services that a country imports, we will be using the same classification system from the World Trade Organization that we used when we were discussing a country's exports.

From Whom Does Your Economy Import?

Why do we care from whom a country imports its goods and services? We care because the value of the currency of the country from which a country is importing will have a direct effect on the value of the importer's currency.

For instance, more than half of the goods and services that Canada imports come from the United States. This means that the Canadian dollar and the Canadian economy are quite sensitive to changes in the value of the U.S. dollar. If the value of the U.S. dollar goes up, Canadian importers will have to sell more Canadian dollars and buy more U.S. dollars in order to pay for the same amount of goods and services. This is likely to drive down the value of the Canadian dollar by increasing its supply on the market and drive up the value of the U.S. dollar by increasing the demand for that currency. The opposite is also true. If the value of the U.S. dollar goes down, Canadian importers will have to sell fewer Canadian dollars and buy fewer U.S. dollars in order to pay for the same amount of goods and services. This is likely to drive up the value of the Canadian dollar by increasing its supply on the market more slowly and drive down the value of the U.S. dollar by decreasing the demand for that currency.

Do You Have an Attractive Government Debt Market?

Why do we care whether a country has an attractive government debt market? We care because countries with attractive government debt markets tend to draw a lot of foreign investment. As investment flows increase, demand for the currency goes up and the value of the currency typically moves higher.

When investors evaluate a country's government debt market, they are weighing two important questions:

- How risky is this market?
- What yield can I expect on my investment?

Both questions are critically important, but neither should be looked at by itself. For instance, a certain country's debt market may be an incredibly risky place for investors to put their money because there is a chance that the country may not honor all of its debts. However, if that country is offering an appropriately high yield on those debts, it just might make sense for investors to pump their money into that market. On the flip side, a certain country's debt market may be an incredibly safe place for investors to put their money. But if that same country is offering a disappointingly low yield on investments, it will probably not make sense for investors to put their money into that market. Investors have to balance both questions.

Ideally, investors are looking for countries with low default risk and high yields. This probably seems obvious, but you may be asking yourself how a country could have a low default risk and offer high yields at the same time. If you are balancing risk and reward, shouldn't the riskier markets have higher yields and the safer markets have lower yields? Yes and no.

The yields offered by a given country's government debt market are certainly influenced by how risky that market is, but that is not the only influence on yields in the marketplace. Central bank actions to either stimulate the economy or rein in inflation also play a large role in determining the yield in a country's government debt markets. For instance, Australia's government debt market is considered to be quite safe, but because of Australia's booming economy (thanks in large part to the amount of raw materials it exports to China), Australia's central bank, the Reserve Bank of Australia (RBA), has had to keep interest rates quite high to prevent runaway inflation, which has provided investors in the Australian government debt market with a juicy return.

So as we look at the comparative attractiveness of any given country's government debt market, remember to look for stable countries with high interest rates.

To help them evaluate the risk level associated with a country's government debt market, investors can look at two key numbers: the country's *Moody's Long-Term Obligation Rating* and the country's *debt-to-GDP (gross domestic product) ratio*. Of course, institutional investors will dive much deeper as they conduct an exhaustive analysis of a country's debt market, but these two numbers should be enough to give you a general feel for the market from a Forex trader's perspective.

Moody's Long-Term Obligation Ratings

Moody's long-term ratings are opinions of the relative credit risk of financial obligations with an original maturity of one year or more. They address the possibility that a financial obligation will not be honored as promised. These ratings use Moody's Global Scale and reflect both the likelihood of default and any financial loss suffered in the event of default.

- **Aaa:** *Obligations rated Aaa are judged to be of the highest quality, with minimal credit risk.*
- **Aa:** *Obligations rated Aa are judged to be of high quality and are subject to very low credit risk.*
- **A:** *Obligations rated A are considered upper-medium grade and are subject to low credit risk.*
- **Baa:** *Obligations rated Baa are subject to moderate credit risk. They are considered medium grade and as such may possess certain speculative characteristics.*
- **Ba:** *Obligations rated Ba are judged to have speculative elements and are subject to substantial credit risk.*
- **B:** *Obligations rated B are considered speculative and are subject to high credit risk.*
- **Caa:** *Obligations rated Caa are judged to be of poor standing and are subject to very high credit risk.*
- **Ca:** *Obligations rated Ca are highly speculative and are likely in, or very near default, with some prospect of recovery of principal and interest.*
- **C:** *Obligations rated C are the lowest rated class and are typically in default, with little prospect for recovery of principal or interest.*[2]

---

[2]http://www.moodys.com/researchdocumentcontentpage.aspx?docid=
PBC_79004.

In addition, "Moody's appends numerical modifiers 1, 2, and 3 to each generic rating classification from Aa through Caa. The modifier 1 indicates that the obligation ranks in the higher end of its generic rating category; the modifier 2 indicates a mid-range ranking; and the modifier 3 indicates a ranking in the lower end of that generic rating category."

Debt-to-GDP Ratio

The debt-to-GDP ratio measures just how extended a country is. Just as an individual who makes $50,000 a year but owes $60,000 a year in debt payments on a house, two cars, a boat, and five credit cards doesn't look like a great credit risk to most financial institutions, a country with a high debt-to-GDP ratio doesn't look like a great credit risk to most financial institutions.

One thing that having a high debt-to-GDP ratio tends to do is force that country to raise its interest rates to attract more lenders. This goes a long way in helping to bring the risk/reward equation into balance for many investors, but it doesn't meet the ideal scenario of a country with low risk and a high yield.

Do You Have an Attractive Equities Market?

Why do we care if a country has an attractive equities market? We care because countries with attractive equities markets tend to draw a lot of foreign investment. As investment flows increase, demand for the currency goes up and the value of the currency typically moves higher.

When investors evaluate a country's equities market, they are weighing two important questions:

- How risky is the market?
- What yield can I expect on my investments?

Risk in the equities market is driven by many different factors. The size of the market is vitally important. A huge, developed stock market—like the one we enjoy in the United States—is going to provide a safer investment environment than a small, fledgling stock market will. Large equities markets tend to have lots of investors, lots of different stocks for investors to choose from, and a lot of liquidity.

Large equities markets also tend to be more effectively regulated. For instance, the reporting requirements that a company must meet if it is to be listed on the New York Stock Exchange (NYSE) are far more thorough than the reporting requirements for a company that is listed on the Botswana Stock Exchange (BSE). The more accurate the information that investors are able to receive regarding the companies that they are about to invest in, the more confident they will be about investing larger sums of money in those stocks.

Naturally, traders weigh how risky an equities market is against the potential profit that they believe they can receive by investing their money in that market. If an equities market is generating higher returns, it will warrant a higher level of risk. Conversely, if an equities market is generating lower returns, it will not warrant a higher level of risk. Ideally, investors are looking for stable equities markets that are offering high yields on investment.

Tell Me About Your Central Bank. What Are Its Mandates? How Much Gold and Foreign Currency Reserves Does It Hold?

Why do we care about a country's central bank, its mandates, and its gold and foreign currency reserve holdings? We care because, perhaps more than any other institution, a country's central bank can determine whether that country's currency is going to get stronger or weaker.

Thankfully, central banks don't just jump into the market willy-nilly to try to push currency prices higher or lower. The moves they make in the market are typically driven by the mandates they have been given. Some central banks have been charged with keeping economic growth under control by not letting the economy expand too quickly or contract too dramatically. Other central banks have been charged with keeping unemployment levels low. Still other central banks have been charged with both mandates (which can prove to be quite tricky at times). Understanding the mandates that the central bank that watches over the currency you are looking to trade has been given can help you predict the actions that the bank might take in various market circumstances.

Once you understand the mandates that the central bank has been charged with, you need to find out how much gold and foreign currency reserves the bank holds. The amount of reserves the central bank holds is a good indicator of how capable the bank is of intervening in the open market. Central banks with smaller reserves have less ammunition with which to combat volatile currency markets and wild price swings. Conversely, central banks with larger reserves have plenty of latitude to make adjustments in the Forex market if they deem it necessary.

As you keep a watchful eye on these central banks, be on the lookout for any news that might indicate that the banks are making changes to the composition of their foreign exchange reserves. We have seen a trend of central banks trying to diversify away from the U.S. dollar ever so slightly, and if that trend continues into the future, it could affect aggregate demand for the U.S. dollar.

According to the International Monetary Fund (IMF) and its latest Currency Composition of Official Foreign Exchange Reserves (COFER),[3] the U.S. dollar is still the reserve currency of choice by quite a wide margin, but the euro is gaining some ground (see Figure 4-1).

Do You Have an Overinvolved Government That Likes to Intervene in the Forex Market?

Why do we care if the country that issued the currency has an overinvolved government that likes to intervene in the Forex market? We care because knowing just how active a government is in the markets will dictate how we approach trading a currency.

Some governments intervene in the markets every single day because they are actively trying to maintain a peg between their currency and another currency or basket of currencies (as the Chinese government does with the U.S. dollar, the euro, and a few others). Some governments never intervene in the markets, believing that markets should move where they are going to move and that it would be too expensive to try to intervene anyway.

In most cases, however, you can find moments when a government has stepped in and intervened in the market, but the

---

[3] http://www.imf.org/external/np/sta/cofer/eng/index.htm.

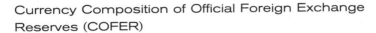

FIGURE 4-1

Currency Composition of Official Foreign Exchange
Reserves (COFER)

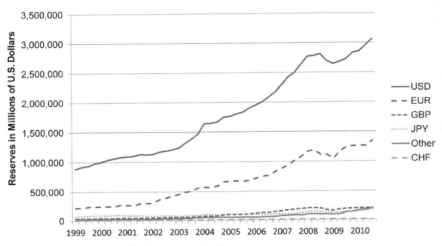

Source: http://www.imf.org/external/np/sta/cofer/eng/index.htm.

incidents are few and far between. For example, the United States
has intervened in the markets, but the last time was on November
8, 2000.

What Economic Announcements Are Important to You?

Why do we care which economic announcements are important
to a country's economy? We care because if we know which economic announcements are most important, we can watch and be
prepared for those announcements when they come up on the economic calendar. The release of most economic announcements is
scheduled months and months ahead of time, so the actual release
should never be a surprise for a currency trader.

For example, knowing that the U.S. dollar tends to have a
strong reaction to the monthly unemployment and nonfarm pay-
roll numbers should put you on high alert whenever we approach
the first Friday of the month (the date when this announcement is

typically released). We'll discuss these announcements more thoroughly in the Chapter 10, "Navigating the Economic Calendar."

Are You a Safe-Haven Currency?

Why do we care whether a country's currency is a safe-haven currency? We care because knowing whether a currency is a safe-haven currency will influence how we will approach trading that currency during times of economic crisis. For instance, knowing that the Swiss franc (CHF) is viewed as a safe-haven currency would lead us to believe that the Swiss franc is going to gain value as investor fear increases. On the other hand, knowing that the New Zealand dollar (NZD) is definitely not considered to be a safe-haven currency would tell us that the New Zealand dollar should be losing value as investor fear increases.

How Can I Trade You?

Why is it important to know which investment vehicles are available for a given currency? We care because we are spending all this time and effort learning about the Forex market and what drives each currency for one specific reason: we want to make some money in this market. Knowing whether you can invest in a currency via a futures contract, an exchange-traded fund, or a spot contract will help you decide where to put your money so that you can make it grow.

We will be addressing the following investment vehicles when we answer this question:

- Spot Forex
- Forex futures
- Exchange-traded funds (ETFs)
- Exchange-traded notes (ETNs)
- Spot Forex options
- Exchange-traded Forex options

Now that you know the important questions that you need to be asking each currency before you put your money on the line, let's dive in and see what makes each currency tick. We'll start with the U.S. dollar and the other currencies from the Americas and move on down the list.

You may be wondering why we have ordered the list of currencies the way we have. There is a method to our madness. First, we decided to group the currencies geographically because so many of the economic and geopolitical forces that shape one currency tend to have a knock-on effect on neighboring currencies. Second, within each geographic designation, we decided to put the currencies in an order based on the percentage of time the currency is used in a Forex transaction. Naturally, the U.S. dollar is used in an extremely high percentage of all Forex transactions, but you might be surprised to see how frequently, or infrequently as the case may be, each currency is used. Here are the numbers according to the Bank for International Settlements:

Currencies of the Americas

- U.S. dollar: 84.9 percent
- Canadian dollar: 5.3 percent
- Mexican peso: 1.3 percent
- Brazilian real: 0.7 percent

Currencies of Western Europe

- Euro: 39.1 percent
- British pound: 12.9 percent
- Swiss franc: 6.4 percent
- Swedish krona: 2.2 percent
- Norwegian krone: 1.3 percent
- Danish krone: 0.6 percent

Currencies of Asia

- Japanese yen: 19 percent
- Hong Kong dollar: 2.4 percent
- South Korean won: 1.5 percent
- Singapore dollar: 1.4 percent
- Indian rupee: 0.9 percent

- New Taiwan dollar: 0.5 percent
- Chinese renminbi: 0.3 percent
- Thai baht: 0.2 percent

Currencies of the Pacific and Africa

- Australian dollar: 7.6 percent
- New Zealand dollar: 1.6 percent
- South African rand: 0.7 percent

Currencies of Eastern Europe

- Russian ruble: 0.9 percent
- Polish zloty: 0.8 percent
- Turkish new lira: 0.7 percent
- Hungarian forint: 0.4 percent
- Czech koruna: 0.2 percent

As you can see, once you start moving away from the U.S. dollar, the percentage of time any other currency is used drops off dramatically. Keep that in mind as you are trading. Currencies that aren't traded as much tend to be more volatile and have wider spreads—something that you will learn more about as we discuss various trading strategies later in the book. In addition, you should note that since most Forex traders focus on the most widely traded currencies, we will be providing more information about those currencies as we get to know them. In the following five chapters, we will answer each of the questions for all of the currencies listed, but we may not go into as much detail on the Czech koruna as we do on the British pound.

CHAPTER 5

Currencies of the Americas

U.S. DOLLAR—THE GREENBACK

As we learned when we were looking at the history of the Forex market at the beginning of Chapter 2, the U.S. dollar (USD) is the reserve currency of the world. This gives the United States a tremendous amount of economic and political clout. The fact that the United States also has the largest economy in the world[1] is another advantage.

With that introduction, let's jump in and get to know the U.S. dollar a little better.

Does Your Economy Run a Trade Surplus or a Trade Deficit?

The United States runs a trade deficit of $561 billion, giving the country a ranking (based on the absolute value of its deficit) of 190 out of the 190 countries tracked by the CIA in *The World Factbook*.[2]

---

[1] https://www.cia.gov/library/publications/the-world-factbook/rankorder/2001rank.html.

[2] https://www.cia.gov/library/publications/the-world-factbook/geos/us.html.

What Does Your Economy Export?

The United States exports agricultural products (soybeans, fruit, and corn), industrial supplies (organic chemicals), capital goods (transistors, aircraft, motor vehicle parts, computers, and telecommunications equipment), and consumer goods (automobiles and medicines).

According to the World Trade Organization (WTO),[3] the United States exports $1,056 billion in goods and merchandise compared to only $474 billion in commercial services. The WTO breaks down those exports as follows (*Note*: The sum may not equal 100 percent.):

- Goods and Merchandise
  - Agricultural products: 11.3 percent
  - Fuels and mining products: 8.4 percent
  - Manufactures: 75.8 percent
- Commercial Services
  - Transportation: 15.2 percent
  - Travel: 25.4 percent
  - Other commercial services: 59.5 percent

To Whom Does Your Economy Export?

The WTO ranks the following countries as the top destinations for exports from the United States:

- European Union: 20.9 percent
- Canada: 19.4 percent
- Mexico: 12.2 percent
- China: 6.6 percent
- Japan: 4.8 percent

What Does Your Economy Import?

The United States imports agricultural products, industrial supplies, crude oil, capital goods (computers, telecommunications equipment, motor vehicle parts, office machines, and electric power

---

[3] http://stat.wto.org/CountryProfile/WSDBCountryPFView.aspx?Language=E&
Country=US.

machinery), and consumer goods (automobiles, clothing, medicines, furniture, and toys).

According to the WTO, the country imports $1,605.3 billion in goods and merchandise compared to only $330.6 billion in commercial services. The WTO breaks down those imports as follows:

- Goods and Merchandise
  - Agricultural products: 6.3 percent
  - Fuels and mining products: 19.4 percent
  - Manufactures: 69.9 percent
- Commercial Services
  - Transportation: 24.4 percent
  - Travel: 23.9 percent
  - Other commercial services: 51.7 percent

From Whom Does Your Economy Import?

The WTO ranks the following countries as the top sources of imports to the United States:

- China: 19.3 percent
- European Union: 17.9 percent
- Canada: 14.2 percent
- Mexico: 11.1 percent
- Japan: 6.1 percent

Do You Have an Attractive Government Debt Market?

The United States currently has a Moody's rating of Aaa. This is the only rating that the country has had in the past 30 years. This is a positive sign for the country's government debt market.[4] However, Moody's has issued a few warnings to the United States recently, stating that the country could be in danger of losing its Aaa status if it is unable to address its long-term debt issues.[5]

---

[4] http://www.moodys.com/credit-ratings/United-States-of-America-credit-rating-600013495.

[5] http://www.nytimes.com/2010/03/16/business/global/16rating.html.

Do You Have an Attractive Equities Market?

The United States has an incredibly attractive equities market. It is the largest equities market in the world, with a total market value of $15.08 trillion.[6]

Tell Me About Your Central Bank. What Are Its Mandates? How Much Gold and Foreign Currency Reserves Does It Hold?

The Federal Reserve has a dual mandate. As stated in Section 2a of the Federal Reserve Act, "The Board of Governors of the Federal Reserve System and the Federal Open Market Committee shall maintain long run growth of the monetary and credit aggregates commensurate with the economy's long run potential to increase production, so as to promote effectively the goals of maximum employment, stable prices, and moderate long-term interest rates."[7]

The U.S. Federal Reserve has foreign currency reserves of $46,358 million and gold deposits of $11,041 million.[8]

Do You Have an Overinvolved Government That Likes to Intervene in the Forex Market?

The U.S. government and the Federal Reserve are not known for their interventionist tendencies. In fact, the last time they intervened in the Forex market was on November 8, 2000.

What Economic Announcements Are Important to You?

When you are watching the economic announcements coming out of the United States, make sure that you keep your eye on the following:

- Federal Open Market Committee (FOMC) federal funds rate
- Nonfarm payrolls

---

[6] https://www.cia.gov/library/publications/the-world-factbook/geos/us.html.

[7] http://www.federalreserve.gov/aboutthefed/section2a.htm.

[8] http://www.imf.org/external/np/sta/ir/IRProcessWeb/data/usa/eng/curusa.htm.

- Unemployment rate
- Consumer price index (CPI)
- Producer price index (PPI)
- Gross domestic product (GDP)
- Trade balance
- Treasury International Capital (TIC) data
- Durable goods orders
- Consumer Confidence Index (Conference Board)
- Consumer Sentiment Index (University of Michigan)
- Retail sales
- Factory orders
- Institute for Supply Management (ISM) Manufacturing Business Survey
- Housing starts and building permits
- Existing home sales
- New home sales
- Standard & Poor's/Case-Shiller Home Price Indices

Are You a Safe-Haven Currency?

Yes, the U.S. dollar is considered to be a safe-haven currency. Increased demand for U.S. Treasuries during times of financial turmoil and crisis drives up demand for the U.S. dollar, which drives up the value of the U.S. dollar.

How Can I Trade You?

You can trade the U.S. dollar using any of the following:

- Spot Forex
- Forex futures
- Exchange-traded funds (ETFs)
- Exchange-traded notes (ETNs)
- Spot Forex options
- Exchange-traded Forex options

CANADIAN DOLLAR—THE LOONIE

The Canadian dollar (CAD) is considered to be a major currency in the Forex market. It is also one of the "commodity" currencies because of the Canadian economy's dependence on commodity exports.

Canada is the world's fourteenth largest economy.[9]

Does Your Economy Run a Trade Surplus or a Trade Deficit?

Canada runs a trade deficit of $40.21 billion, giving the country a ranking of 184 out of the 190 countries tracked by the CIA in *The World Factbook*.[10]

What Does Your Economy Export?

Canada exports motor vehicles and parts, industrial machinery, aircraft, telecommunications equipment, chemicals, plastics, fertilizers, wood pulp, timber, crude petroleum, natural gas, electricity, and aluminum.

According to the World Trade Organization (WTO),[11] Canada exports $316.7 billion in goods and merchandise compared to only $57.5 billion in commercial services. The WTO breaks down up those exports as follows:

- Goods and Merchandise
  - Agricultural products: 13.8 percent
  - Fuels and mining products: 29.4 percent
  - Manufactures: 49.6 percent
- Commercial Services
  - Transportation: 15.5 percent
  - Travel: 23.8 percent
  - Other commercial services: 60.7 percent

---

[9] https://www.cia.gov/library/publications/the-world-factbook/rankorder/2001rank.html.

[10] https://www.cia.gov/library/publications/the-world-factbook/geos/ca.html.

[11] http://stat.wto.org/CountryProfile/WSDBCountryPFView.aspx?Language=E&Country=CA.

To Whom Does Your Economy Export?

The WTO ranks the following countries as the top destinations for exports from Canada:

- United States: 75.0 percent
- European Union: 8.3 percent
- China: 3.1 percent
- Japan: 2.3 percent
- Mexico: 1.3 percent

What Does Your Economy Import?

Canada imports machinery and equipment, motor vehicles and parts, crude oil, chemicals, electricity, and durable consumer goods.

According to the WTO, the country imports $329.9 billion in goods and merchandise compared to only $77.6 billion in commercial services. The WTO breaks down those imports as follows:

- Goods and Merchandise
  - Agricultural products: 8.9 percent
  - Fuels and mining products: 11.9 percent
  - Manufactures: 75.5 percent
- Commercial Services
  - Transportation: 22.3 percent
  - Travel: 31.2 percent
  - Other commercial services: 46.6 percent

From Whom Does Your Economy Import?

The WTO ranks the following countries as the top sources of imports to Canada:

- United States: 51.2 percent
- European Union: 12.4 percent
- China: 10.9 percent
- Mexico: 4.5 percent
- Japan: 3.4 percent

Do You Have an Attractive Government Debt Market?

Canada currently has a Moody's rating of Aaa. It received this latest rating on May 3, 2002. This most recent rating was an upgrade from the Aa1 rating that the country had held previously. This is a positive sign for the country's government debt market.[12]

Do You Have an Attractive Equities Market?

Canada has an attractive equities market. It is the tenth largest equities market in the world, with a total market value of $1.681 trillion.[13]

Tell Me About Your Central Bank. What Are Its Mandates? How Much Gold and Foreign Currency Reserves Does It Hold?

The Bank of Canada (BOC) aims to keep inflation at the 2 percent target, the midpoint of the 1 to 3 percent inflation-control target range. This target is expressed in terms of total CPI inflation, but the bank uses a measure of core inflation as an operational guide. The bank feels that core inflation provides a better measure of the underlying trend of inflation and tends to be a better predictor of future changes in the total CPI.[14]

The BOC has foreign currency reserves of $44,888 million and gold deposits of $153 million.[15]

Do You Have an Overinvolved Government That Likes to Intervene in the Forex Market?

The Canadian government is not known as an aggressive currency manipulator.

---

[12] http://www.moodys.com/credit-ratings/Canada-credit-rating-600013449.
[13] https://www.cia.gov/library/publications/the-world-factbook/geos/ca.html.
[14] http://www.bankofcanada.ca/en/inflation/index.html.
[15] http://www.imf.org/external/np/sta/ir/IRProcessWeb/data/can/eng/curcan.htm.

What Economic Announcements Are Important to You?

When you are watching the economic announcements coming out of Canada, make sure that you keep your eye on the following:

- Bank of Canada (BOC) overnight rate
- Employment change
- Unemployment rate
- Consumer price index (CPI)
- Producer price index (PPI)
- Gross domestic product (GDP)
- Trade balance
- Foreign securities purchases

Are You a Safe-Haven Currency?

No, the Canadian dollar is not considered to be a safe-haven currency.

How Can I Trade You?

You can trade the Canadian dollar using any of the following:

- Spot Forex
- Forex futures
- Exchange-traded funds (ETFs)
- Exchange-traded notes (ETNs)
- Spot Forex options
- Exchange-traded Forex options

MEXICAN PESO

The Mexican peso (MXN) is considered to be an exotic currency in the Forex market. Mexico is the world's eleventh largest economy.[16]

---

[16] https://www.cia.gov/library/publications/the-world-factbook/rankorder/2001rank.html.

Does Your Economy Run a Trade Surplus or a Trade Deficit?

Mexico runs a trade deficit of $7 billion, giving the country a ranking of 173 out of the 190 countries tracked by the CIA in *The World Factbook*.[17]

What Does Your Economy Export?

Mexico exports manufactured goods, oil and oil products, silver, fruits, vegetables, coffee, and cotton.

According to the World Trade Organization (WTO),[18] Mexico exports $229.6 billion in goods and merchandise compared to only $15.4 billion in commercial services. The WTO breaks down those exports as follows:

- Goods and Merchandise
  - Agricultural products: 6.8 percent
  - Fuels and mining products: 15.8 percent
  - Manufactures: 75.1 percent
- Commercial Services
  - Transportation: 10.5 percent
  - Travel: 73.1 percent
  - Other commercial services: 16.4 percent

To Whom Does Your Economy Export?

The WTO ranks the following countries as the top destinations for exports from Mexico:

- United States: 80.7 percent
- European Union: 5.1 percent
- Canada: 3.6 percent
- Colombia: 1.1 percent
- Brazil: 1.1 percent

---

[17] https://www.cia.gov/library/publications/the-world-factbook/geos/mx.html.
[18] http://stat.wto.org/CountryProfile/WSDBCountryPFView.aspx?Language=E&Country=MX.

What Does Your Economy Import?

Mexico imports metalworking machines, steel-mill products, agricultural machinery, electrical equipment, car parts for assembly, repair parts for motor vehicles, aircraft, and aircraft parts.

According to the WTO, the country imports $241.5 billion in goods and merchandise compared to only $21 billion in commercial services. The WTO breaks down those imports as follows:

- Goods and Merchandise
  - Agricultural products: 8.6 percent
  - Fuels and mining products: 9.0 percent
  - Manufactures: 80.4 percent
- Commercial Services
  - Transportation: 13.6 percent
  - Travel: 33.9 percent
  - Other commercial services: 52.5 percent

From Whom Does Your Economy Import?

The WTO ranks the following countries as the top sources of imports to Mexico:

- United States: 48.1 percent
- China: 13.9 percent
- European Union: 11.6 percent
- Japan: 4.9 percent
- South Korea: 4.7 percent

Do You Have an Attractive Government Debt Market?

Mexico currently has a Moody's rating of A1. It received this latest rating on May 24, 2006. This most recent rating was an upgrade from the Baa1 rating that the country had held previously. This is a positive sign for the country's government debt market.[19]

---

[19] http://www.moodys.com/credit-ratings/Mexico-credit-rating-600013480.

Do You Have an Attractive Equities Market?

Mexico has an attractive equities market, but it is not very large. It is the twenty-fifth largest equities market in the world, with a total market value of $340.6 billion.[20]

Tell Me About Your Central Bank. What Are Its Mandates? How Much Gold and Foreign Currency Reserves Does It Hold?

The monetary policy of the Banco de México is to influence interest rates and inflation expectations in order to make price behavior consistent with the objective of ensuring an environment of low and stable inflation. This is how the Banco de México contributes to establishing appropriate conditions for sustained economic growth and the creation of permanent jobs.[21]

The Banco de México has foreign currency reserves of $112,033 million and gold deposits of $326 million.[22]

Do You Have an Overinvolved Government That Likes to Intervene in the Forex Market?

The Mexican government has been known to intervene in the currency market from time to time.

What Economic Announcements Are Important to You?

When you are watching the economic announcements coming out of Mexico, make sure that you keep your eye on the following:

- Interest rates
- Employment
- Inflation

---

[20] https://www.cia.gov/library/publications/the-world-factbook/geos/mx.html.

[21] http://www.banxico.org.mx/politica-monetaria-e-inflacion/monetary-policy-and-inflation.html.

[22] http://www.imf.org/external/np/sta/ir/IRProcessWeb/data/mex/eng/curmex.htm.

- Gross domestic product (GDP)
- Trade balance

Are You a Safe-Haven Currency?

No, the Mexican peso is not considered to be a safe-haven currency.

How Can I Trade You?

You can trade the Mexican peso using any of the following:

- Spot Forex
- Forex futures
- Exchange-traded funds (ETFs)
- Spot Forex options
- Exchange-traded Forex options

BRAZILIAN REAL

The Brazilian real (BRL) is considered to be an exotic currency in the Forex market. Brazil is the world's seventh largest economy.[23]

Does Your Economy Run a Trade Surplus or a Trade Deficit?

Brazil runs a trade deficit of $52.73 billion, giving the country a ranking of 186 out of the 190 countries tracked by the CIA in *The World Factbook*.[24]

What Does Your Economy Export?

Brazil exports transport equipment, iron ore, soybeans, footwear, coffee, and autos.

---

[23] https://www.cia.gov/library/publications/the-world-factbook/rankorder/2001rank.html.

[24] https://www.cia.gov/library/publications/the-world-factbook/geos/br.html.

According to the World Trade Organization (WTO),[25] Brazil exports $153 billion in goods and merchandise compared to only $26.2 billion in commercial services. The WTO breaks down those exports as follows:

- Goods and Merchandise
  - Agricultural products: 37.7 percent
  - Fuels and mining products: 21.3 percent
  - Manufactures: 38.0 percent
- Commercial Services
  - Transportation: 15.4 percent
  - Travel: 20.2 percent
  - Other commercial services: 64.4 percent

To Whom Does Your Economy Export?

The WTO ranks the following countries as the top destinations for exports from Brazil:

- European Union: 22.3 percent
- China: 13.2 percent
- United States: 10.3 percent
- Argentina: 8.4 percent
- Japan: 2.8 percent

What Does Your Economy Import?

Brazil imports machinery, electrical equipment, transport equipment, chemical products, oil, automotive parts, and electronics.

According to the WTO, the country imports $133.7 billion in goods and merchandise compared to only $44.1 billion in commercial services. The WTO breaks down those imports as follows:

---

[25] http://stat.wto.org/CountryProfile/WSDBCountryPFView.aspx?Language=E&Country=BR.

- Goods and Merchandise
  - Agricultural products: 6.4 percent
  - Fuels and mining products: 17.6 percent
  - Manufactures: 75.9 percent
- Commercial Services
  - Transportation: 18.1 percent
  - Travel: 24.7 percent
  - Other commercial services: 57.2 percent

From Whom Does Your Economy Import?

The WTO ranks the following countries as the top sources of imports to Brazil:

- European Union: 22.9 percent
- United States: 15.8 percent
- China: 12.5 percent
- Argentina: 8.8 percent
- Japan: 4.2 percent

Do You Have an Attractive Government Debt Market?

Brazil currently has a Moody's rating of Baa2. It received this latest rating on September 22, 2009. This most recent rating was an upgrade from the Baa3 rating that the country had held previously. This is a positive sign for the country's government debt market.[26]

Do You Have an Attractive Equities Market?

Brazil has an attractive equities market. It is the fifteenth largest equities market in the world, with a total market value of $1.167 trillion.[27]

---

[26] http://www.moodys.com/credit-ratings/Brazil-credit-rating-600013448.

[27] https://www.cia.gov/library/publications/the-world-factbook/geos/br.html.

Tell Me About Your Central Bank. What Are Its Mandates? How Much Gold and Foreign Currency Reserves Does It Hold?

The strategic planning of the Banco Central do Brasil (Central Bank of Brazil) aims to ensure the stability of the currency's purchasing power and a solid and efficient financial system.[28]

The Central Bank of Brazil has foreign currency reserves of $275,968 million and gold deposits of $1,495 million.[29]

Do You Have an Overinvolved Government That Likes to Intervene in the Forex Market?

The Brazilian government has been known to intervene in the currency market from time to time.

What Economic Announcements Are Important to You?

When you are watching the economic announcements coming out of Brazil, make sure that you keep your eye on the following:

- Interest rates
- Employment
- Inflation
- Gross domestic product (GDP)
- Trade balance

Are You a Safe-Haven Currency?

No, the Brazilian real is not considered to be a safe-haven currency.

How Can I Trade You?

You can trade the Brazilian real using any of the following:

---

[28] http://www.bcb.gov.br/?PLAN.

[29] http://www.imf.org/external/np/sta/ir/IRProcessWeb/data/bra/eng/curbra.htm.

- Spot Forex
- Forex futures
- Exchange-traded funds (ETFs)
- Spot Forex options
- Exchange-traded Forex options

CHAPTER 6
Currencies of Western Europe

EURO — THE FIBER

The euro (EUR) is the official currency of the countries that make up the euro area, or Eurozone. This is not to be confused with the European Union, which is a much larger group of countries.

The Eurozone was created on January 1, 1999, and originally included the following 11 member countries:

1. Austria
2. Belgium
3. Finland
4. France
5. Germany
6. Ireland
7. Italy
8. Luxembourg
9. Netherlands
10. Portugal
11. Spain

Additional countries were allowed to join the Eurozone once they could do the following:

1. Keep inflation rates below a ceiling that was set at 1.5 percentage points above the average of the three members with the lowest inflation rates.
2. Keep government deficits below 3 percent of gross domestic product (GDP).
3. Maintain a stable currency within the European exchange-rate mechanism (ERM II) for at least two years.
4. Keep long-term interest rates below a ceiling set at 2 percentage points above the average of the three members with the lowest inflation rates.

Greece joined the euro on January 1, 2001; Slovenia joined on January 1, 2007; Cyprus and Malta joined on January 1, 2008; Slovakia joined on January 1, 2009; and Estonia joined on January 1, 2011.

We're not done yet, though. While the following countries are not officially part of the Eurozone, they do use the euro: Montenegro, Monaco, San Marino, and Vatican City.

What Countries Are Most Important?

As you evaluate the euro, you have to remember that it is important not only to look at the Eurozone as a whole, but also to look at the health and stability of each of the individual countries in the Eurozone.

If you are looking to see which countries drive most of the economic activity in the Eurozone, check out the following:

- Germany, the fifth largest economy in the world
- France, the ninth largest
- Italy, the tenth largest
- Spain, the thirteenth largest[1]

If you are looking to see which countries pose the greatest threat to the monetary union because of their mounting debt burdens and unstable sovereign debt markets, consider the PIIGS, which consist of Portugal, Ireland, Italy, Greece, and Spain. The

---

[1] https://www.cia.gov/library/publications/the-world-factbook/rankorder/2001rank.html.

European sovereign debt crisis of 2010 began in Greece and then spread to Ireland. At the time of the writing of this book, investors are wondering whether the crisis is going to spread to Portugal, then to Spain, and eventually on to Italy and beyond.

You see, one of the fundamental problems facing the Eurozone is it has a unified monetary policy but a fractured fiscal policy. We'll discuss this in more depth shortly, but for now, you need to know that even though the euro has become a successful and dominant currency on the world stage, it still faces some underlying challenges.

Hopefully, this gives you a basic overview of the euro and the Eurozone. As we go through the next few questions, we will be focusing on the top three economies in the Eurozone: Germany, France, and Italy.

Does Your Economy Run a Trade Surplus or a Trade Deficit?

Germany runs a trade surplus of $162.3 billion, giving the country a ranking of 3 out of the 190 countries tracked by the CIA in *The World Factbook*.[2]

France runs a trade deficit of $53.29 billion, giving the country a ranking of 187 out of the 190 countries.[3]

Italy runs a trade surplus of $61.98 billion, giving the country a ranking of 188 out of the 190 countries.[4]

What Does Your Economy Export?

Germany exports machinery, vehicles, chemicals, metals, manufactures, foodstuffs, and textiles.

According to the World Trade Organization (WTO),[5] Germany exports $1,126.4 billion in goods and merchandise compared to

---

[2]https://www.cia.gov/library/publications/the-world-factbook/geos/gm.html.

[3] https://www.cia.gov/library/publications/the-world-factbook/geos/fr.html.

[4] https://www.cia.gov/library/publications/the-world-factbook/geos/it.html.

[5] http://stat.wto.org/CountryProfile/WSDBCountryPFView.aspx?Language=E&Country=DE.

only $226.6 billion in commercial services. The WTO breaks down those exports as follows:

- ■ Goods and Merchandise
  - • Agricultural products: 6.9 percent
  - • Fuels and mining products: 4.7 percent
  - • Manufactures: 86.1 percent
- ■ Commercial Services
  - • Transportation: 22.9 percent
  - • Travel: 15.3 percent
  - • Other commercial services: 61.7 percent

France exports machinery, transportation equipment, aircraft, plastics, chemicals, pharmaceutical products, iron, steel, and beverages.

According to the WTO,[6] France exports $484.7 billion in goods and merchandise compared to only $142.5 billion in commercial services. The WTO breaks down those exports as follows:

- ■ Goods and Merchandise
  - • Agricultural products: 13.2 percent
  - • Fuels and mining products: 5.8 percent
  - • Manufactures: 79.0 percent
- ■ Commercial Services
  - • Transportation: 22.5 percent
  - • Travel: 34.7 percent
  - • Other commercial services: 42.8 percent

Italy exports engineering products, textiles and clothing, production machinery, motor vehicles, transport equipment, chemicals, food, beverages, tobacco, minerals, and nonferrous metals.

According to the WTO,[7] Italy exports $405.8 billion in goods and merchandise compared to only $114.6 billion in commercial services. The WTO breaks down those exports as follows:

---

[6] http://stat.wto.org/CountryProfile/WSDBCountryPFView.aspx?Language=E&Country=FR.

[7] http://stat.wto.org/CountryProfile/WSDBCountryPFView.aspx?Language=E&Country=IT.

- Goods and Merchandise
  - Agricultural products: 8.9 percent
  - Fuels and mining products: 5.5 percent
  - Manufactures: 83.5 percent

- Commercial Services
  - Transportation: 13.4 percent
  - Travel: 39.8 percent
  - Other commercial services: 46.8 percent

To Whom Does Your Economy Export?

The WTO ranks the following countries as the top destinations for exports from Germany:

- European Union: 62.9 percent
- United States: 6.7 percent
- China: 4.5 percent
- Switzerland: 4.4 percent
- Russian Federation: 2.5 percent

The WTO ranks the following countries as the top destinations for exports from France:

- European Union: 62.0 percent
- United States: 5.9 percent
- Switzerland: 3.0 percent
- China: 2.4 percent
- Russian Federation: 1.5 percent

The WTO ranks the following countries as the top destinations for exports from Italy:

- European Union: 56.9 percent
- United States: 5.9 percent
- Switzerland: 4.7 percent
- China: 2.3 percent
- Russian Federation: 2.2 percent

What Does Your Economy Import?

Germany imports machinery, vehicles, chemicals, foodstuffs, textiles, and metals.

According to the WTO, the country imports $938.3 billion in goods and merchandise compared to only $253.1 billion in commercial services. The WTO breaks down those imports as follows:

- Goods and Merchandise
  - Agricultural products: 10.3 percent
  - Fuels and mining products: 14.9 percent
  - Manufactures: 72.7 percent
- Commercial Services
  - Transportation: 20.7 percent
  - Travel: 32.0 percent
  - Other commercial services: 47.3 percent

France imports machinery and equipment, vehicles, crude oil, aircraft, plastics, and chemicals.

According to the WTO, the country imports $559.8 billion in goods and merchandise compared to only $126.4 billion in commercial services. The WTO breaks down those imports as follows:

- Goods and Merchandise
  - Agricultural products: 10.4 percent
  - Fuels and mining products: 15.0 percent
  - Manufactures: 74.0 percent
- Commercial Services
  - Transportation: 26.1 percent
  - Travel: 30.5 percent
  - Other commercial services: 43.3 percent

Italy imports engineering products, chemicals, transport equipment, energy products, minerals and nonferrous metals, textiles and clothing, food, beverages, and tobacco.

According to the WTO, the country imports $412.7 billion in goods and merchandise compared to only $114.6 billion in commercial services. The WTO breaks down those imports as follows:

- Goods and Merchandise
  - Agricultural products: 12.5 percent
  - Fuels and mining products: 21.1 percent
  - Manufactures: 65.2 percent
- Commercial Services
  - Transportation: 20.0 percent
  - Travel: 24.3 percent
  - Other commercial services: 55.7 percent

From Whom Does Your Economy Import?

The WTO ranks the following countries as the top sources of imports to Germany:

- European Union: 58.3 percent
- China: 8.3 percent
- United States: 5.9 percent
- Switzerland: 4.2 percent
- Russian Federation: 3.7 percent

The WTO ranks the following countries as the top sources of imports to France:

- European Union: 60.3 percent
- China: 7.6 percent
- United States: 6.4 percent
- Switzerland: 2.5 percent
- Russian Federation: 2.4 percent

The WTO ranks the following countries as the top sources of imports to Italy:

- European Union: 57.1 percent
- China: 6.5 percent
- Russian Federation: 4.1 percent
- Switzerland: 3.5 percent
- Libyan Arab Jamahiriya: 3.4 percent

Do You Have an Attractive Government Debt Market?

The euro is unique in this area because the Eurozone does not have a single, unified government debt market. Instead, each country within the Eurozone still has its own government debt market. This is part of what led to the sovereign debt crisis of 2010, which started in Greece and then spread to Ireland. So when you are looking at government debt in the Eurozone, you have to look at each country individually. As you do so, try to remember that "a chain is only as strong as its weakest link."

However, Moody's has given the Eurozone a current, cumulative rating of Aaa. This was the first and only rating that the group was given. This is a positive sign for the country's government debt market.[8]

Do You Have an Attractive Equities Market?

Eurozone has many attractive equities markets. France has the sixth largest equities market in the world, with a total market value of $1.972 trillion[9]; Germany has the ninth largest equities market in the world, with a total market value of $1.298 trillion[10]; and Spain has the eleventh largest equities market in the world, with a total market value of $1.297 trillion.[11]

Tell Me About Your Central Bank. What Are Its Mandates? How Much Gold and Foreign Currency Reserves Does It Hold?

The primary objective of the European Central Bank (ECB) is to maintain price stability by keeping inflation rates below but close to 2 percent.[12]

---

[8] http://www.moodys.com/credit-ratings/Eurozone-credit-rating-600049469.

[9] https://www.cia.gov/library/publications/the-world-factbook/geos/fr.html.

[10] https://www.cia.gov/library/publications/the-world-factbook/geos/gm.html.

[11] https://www.cia.gov/library/publications/the-world-factbook/geos/sp.html.

[12] http://www.ecb.europa.eu/mopo/html/index.en.html.

The ECB has foreign currency reserves of $53,699 million and gold deposits of $22,305 million.[13]

Do You Have an Overinvolved Government That Likes to Intervene in the Forex Market?

The European Union and the European Central Bank (ECB) are not known for their interventionist tendencies. In fact, the last time they intervened in the Forex market was on November 3, 2000.[14]

What Economic Announcements Are Important to You?

When you are watching the economic announcements coming out of the Eurozone, make sure that you keep your eye on the following:

- European Central Bank (ECB) minimum bid rate
- Preliminary gross domestic product (GDP)
- Trade balance
- German unemployment
- German industrial production
- German ZEW (Zentrum für Europäische Wirtschaftsforschung) Indicator of Economic Sentiment
- German IFO (Institut für Wirtschaftsforschung) Business Climate Index
- CPI flash estimate
- German consumer price index (CPI)

Are You a Safe-Haven Currency?

No, the euro is not considered to be a safe-haven currency.

---

[13] http://www.imf.org/external/np/sta/ir/IRProcessWeb/data/ECB/eng/CURecb.HTM.

[14] http://www.ecb.int/press/pr/date/2000/html/pr001103.en.html.

How Can I Trade You?

You can trade the euro using any of the following:

- Spot Forex
- Forex futures
- Exchange-traded funds (ETFs)
- Exchange-traded notes (ETNs)
- Spot Forex options
- Exchange-traded Forex options

BRITISH POUND — STERLING, OR THE CABLE

The British pound (GBP) is considered to be a major currency in the Forex market. Because the British and European economies are so closely linked, the British pound and the euro enjoy a strong positive correlation.

The United Kingdom is the eighth largest economy in the world.[15]

Does Your Economy Run a Trade Surplus or a Trade Deficit?

The United Kingdom runs a trade deficit of $40.34 billion, giving the country a ranking of 185 out of the 190 countries tracked by the CIA in *The World Factbook*.[16]

What Does Your Economy Export?

The United Kingdom exports manufactured goods, fuels, chemicals, food, beverages, and tobacco.

According to the World Trade Organization (WTO),[17] the United Kingdom exports $352.5 billion in goods and merchandise

---

[15] https://www.cia.gov/library/publications/the-world-factbook/rankorder/2001rank.html.

[16] https://www.cia.gov/library/publications/the-world-factbook/geos/uk.html.

[17] http://stat.wto.org/CountryProfile/WSDBCountryPFView.aspx?Language=E&Country=GB.

compared to only $233.3 billion in commercial services. The WTO breaks down those exports as follows:

- Goods and Merchandise
  - Agricultural products: 7.4 percent
  - Fuels and mining products: 14.4 percent
  - Manufactures: 73.0 percent
- Commercial Services
  - Transportation: 14.3 percent
  - Travel: 13.0 percent
  - Other commercial services: 72.7 percent

To Whom Does Your Economy Export?

The WTO ranks the following countries as the top destinations for exports from the United Kingdom:

- European Union: 54.8 percent
- United States: 14.9 percent
- China: 2.3 percent
- Switzerland: 1.7 percent
- Canada: 1.6 percent

What Does Your Economy Import?

The United Kingdom imports manufactured goods, machinery, fuels, and foodstuffs.

According to the WTO, the country imports $481.7 billion in goods and merchandise compared to only $160.9 billion in commercial services. The WTO breaks down those imports as follows:

- Goods and Merchandise
  - Agricultural products: 12.1 percent
  - Fuels and mining products: 13.1 percent
  - Manufactures: 69.9 percent
- Commercial Services
  - Transportation: 17.7 percent

- Travel: 30.4 percent
- Other commercial services: 51.9 percent

From Whom Does Your Economy Import?

The WTO ranks the following countries as the top sources of imports to the United Kingdom:

- European Union: 52.7 percent
- United States: 9.7 percent
- China: 9.0 percent
- Norway: 4.8 percent
- Japan: 2.0 percent

Do You Have an Attractive Government Debt Market?

The United Kingdom currently has a Moody's rating of Aaa. This is the only rating that the country has had in the past 30 years. This is a positive sign for the country's government debt market.[18]

Do You Have an Attractive Equities Market?

The United Kingdom has an attractive equities market. It is the fifth largest equities market in the world, with a total market value of $2.796 trillion.[19]

Tell Me About Your Central Bank. What Are Its Mandates? How Much Gold and Foreign Currency Reserves Does It Hold?

The Bank of England (BOE) has two core purposes: monetary stability and financial stability.

---

[18] http://www.moodys.com/credit-ratings/United-Kingdom-credit-rating-600013494.

[19] https://www.cia.gov/library/publications/the-world-factbook/geos/uk.html.

Monetary stability means stable prices (low inflation) and confidence in the currency. Stable prices are defined by the government's inflation target, which the bank seeks to meet through the decisions taken by the Monetary Policy Committee.[20]

A stable financial system is a key ingredient for a healthy and successful economy. People need to have confidence that the system is safe and stable, and that it functions properly to provide critical services to the wider economy. It is important that problems in particular areas do not lead to disruption across the financial system.

The bank has a statutory objective to "contribute to protecting and enhancing the stability of the financial systems of the United Kingdom." It does this through its risk assessment and risk reduction work; market intelligence functions; payments systems oversight; banking and market operations, including, in exceptional circumstances, acting as lender of last resort; and resolution work to deal with distressed banks.[21]

The BOE has foreign currency reserves of $43,489 million and gold deposits of $14,067 million.[22]

Do You Have an Overinvolved Government That Likes to Intervene in the Forex Market?

The British government is not known as an aggressive currency manipulator.

What Economic Announcements Are Important to You?

When you are watching the economic announcements coming out of the United Kingdom, make sure that you keep your eye on the following:

- Bank of England official bank rate
- Claimant count change (unemployment)
- Consumer price index (CPI)

---

[20] http://www.bankofengland.co.uk/monetarypolicy/index.htm.
[21] http://www.bankofengland.co.uk/financialstability/index.htm.
[22] http://www.imf.org/external/np/sta/ir/IRProcessWeb/data/gbr/eng/curgbr.pdf.

- Producer price index (PPI)
- Gross domestic product (GDP)
- Retail sales
- Trade balance
- Manufacturing Purchasing Managers Index (PMI)
- Halifax House Price Index (HPI)

Are You a Safe-Haven Currency?

No, the British pound is not considered to be a safe-haven currency.

How Can I Trade You?

You can trade the British pound using any of the following:

- Spot Forex
- Forex futures
- Exchange-traded funds (ETFs)
- Exchange-traded notes (ETNs)
- Spot Forex options
- Exchange-traded Forex options

SWISS FRANC—THE SWISSY

The Swiss franc (CHF) is considered to be a major currency in the Forex market and the premier safe-haven currency.

Switzerland is the world's thirty-sixth largest economy.[23]

Does Your Economy Run a Trade Surplus or a Trade Deficit?

Switzerland runs a trade surplus of $49.35 billion, giving the country a ranking of 7 out of the 190 countries tracked by the CIA in *The World Factbook*.[24]

---

[23] https://www.cia.gov/library/publications/the-world-factbook/rankorder/2001rank.html.

[24] https://www.cia.gov/library/publications/the-world-factbook/geos/ca.html.

What Does Your Economy Export?

Switzerland exports machinery, chemicals, metals, watches, and agricultural products.

According to the World Trade Organization (WTO),[25] Switzerland exports $172.9 billion in goods and merchandise compared to only $68.8 billion in commercial services. The WTO breaks down those exports as follows:

- Goods and Merchandise
  - Agricultural products: 4.2 percent
  - Fuels and mining products: 5.6 percent
  - Manufactures: 89.4 percent
- Commercial Services
  - Transportation: 8.2 percent
  - Travel: 20.3 percent
  - Other commercial services: 71.5 percent

To Whom Does Your Economy Export?

The WTO ranks the following countries as the top destinations for exports from Switzerland:

- European Union: 59.7 percent
- United States: 10.0 percent
- Japan: 3.8 percent
- China: 2.9 percent
- Hong Kong: 2.9 percent

What Does Your Economy Import?

Switzerland imports machinery, chemicals, vehicles, metals, agricultural products, and textiles.

---

[25] http://stat.wto.org/CountryProfile/WSDBCountryPFView.aspx?Language=E&Country=CA.

According to the WTO, the country imports $155.7 billion in goods and merchandise compared to only $35.5 billion in commercial services. The WTO breaks down those imports as follows:

- Goods and Merchandise
  - Agricultural products: 7.3 percent
  - Fuels and mining products: 11.4 percent
  - Manufactures: 80.6 percent
- Commercial Services
  - Transportation: 20.6 percent
  - Travel: 30.7 percent
  - Other commercial services: 48.7 percent

From Whom Does Your Economy Import?

The WTO ranks the following countries as the top sources of imports to Switzerland:

- European Union: 78.0 percent
- United States: 5.8 percent
- China: 3.0 percent
- Japan: 2.1 percent
- Vietnam: 1.3 percent

Do You Have an Attractive Government Debt Market?

Switzerland currently has a Moody's rating of Aaa. This is the only rating that the country has had in the past 30 years. This is a positive sign for the country's government debt market.[26]

Do You Have an Attractive Equities Market?

Switzerland has an attractive equities market. It is the twelfth largest equities market in the world, with a total market value of $1.071 trillion.[27]

---

[26] http://www.moodys.com/credit-ratings/Switzerland-credit-rating-600013489.
[27] https://www.cia.gov/library/publications/the-world-factbook/geos/sz.html.

Tell Me About Your Central Bank. What Are Its Mandates? How Much Gold and Foreign Currency Reserves Does It Hold?

The Swiss National Bank's (SNB) monetary policy strategy consists of three elements. First, the SNB states how it defines price stability. Second, it bases its monetary policy decisions on a medium-term inflation forecast. Third, it sets an operational target range for its chosen reference interest rate, the three-month LIBOR.[28]

The SNB has foreign currency reserves of $217,227 million and gold deposits of $47,161 million.[29]

Do You Have an Overinvolved Government That Likes to Intervene in the Forex Market?

The Swiss government has been known to intervene in the currency market from time to time.

What Economic Announcements Are Important to You?

When you are watching the economic announcements coming out of Switzerland, make sure that you keep your eye on the following:

- Interest rates
- Retail sales
- KOF Economic Barometer
- Employment
- Inflation
- Gross domestic product (GDP)
- Trade balance

---

[28] http://www.snb.ch/en/iabout/monpol.

[29] http://www.imf.org/external/np/sta/ir/IRProcessWeb/data/che/eng/ curche.htm.

Are You a Safe-Haven Currency?

Yes, the Swiss franc is considered to be a safe-haven currency. An extremely stable economy and the fact that a comparatively large amount of Swiss francs are backed by gold make the Swiss franc an attractive investment during times of market unease and volatility.

How Can I Trade You?

You can trade the Swiss franc using any of the following:

- Spot Forex
- Forex futures
- Exchange-traded funds (ETFs)
- Exchange-traded notes (ETNs)
- Spot Forex options
- Exchange-traded Forex options

SWEDISH KRONA

The Swedish krona (SEK) is considered to be an exotic currency in the Forex market.

Sweden is the world's thirty-second largest economy.[30]

Does Your Economy Run a Trade Surplus or a Trade Deficit?

Sweden runs a trade surplus of $21.68 billion, giving the country a ranking of 16 out of the 190 countries tracked by the CIA in *The World Factbook*.[31]

What Does Your Economy Export?

Sweden exports machinery, motor vehicles, paper products, pulp and wood, iron, steel products, and chemicals.

---

[30] https://www.cia.gov/library/publications/the-world-factbook/rankorder/ 2001rank.html.

[31] https://www.cia.gov/library/publications/the-world-factbook/geos/sw.html.

According to the World Trade Organization (WTO),[32] Sweden exports $131.2 billion in goods and merchandise compared to only $60.8 billion in commercial services. The WTO breaks down those exports as follows:

- Goods and Merchandise
  - Agricultural products: 9.2 percent
  - Fuels and mining products: 10.3 percent
  - Manufactures: 79.5 percent
- Commercial Services
  - Transportation: 15.8 percent
  - Travel: 20.0 percent
  - Other commercial services: 64.3 percent

To Whom Does Your Economy Export?

The WTO ranks the following countries as the top destinations for exports from Sweden:

- European Union: 58.2 percent
- Norway: 10.5 percent
- United States: 6.4 percent
- China: 3.1 percent
- Russian Federation: 1.4 percent

What Does Your Economy Import?

Sweden imports machinery, petroleum and petroleum products, chemicals, motor vehicles, iron, steel, foodstuffs, and clothing.

According to the WTO, the country imports $119.8 billion in goods and merchandise compared to only $45.8 billion in commercial services. The WTO breaks down those imports as follows:

- Goods and Merchandise
  - Agricultural products: 11.7 percent

[32] http://stat.wto.org/CountryProfile/WSDBCountryPFView.aspx?Language=E&Country=SE.

- Fuels and mining products: 14.7 percent
- Manufactures: 73.3 percent
■ Commercial Services
  - Transportation: 16.0 percent
  - Travel: 27.3 percent
  - Other commercial services: 56.7 percent

From Whom Does Your Economy Import?

The WTO ranks the following countries as the top sources of imports to Sweden:

■ European Union: 69.0 percent
■ Norway: 9.0 percent
■ China: 3.8 percent
■ United States: 3.8 percent
■ Russian Federation: 3.4 percent

Do You Have an Attractive Government Debt Market?

Sweden currently has a Moody's rating of Aaa. It received this latest rating on April 4, 2002. This most recent rating was an upgrade from the Aa1 rating that the country had held previously. This is a positive sign for the country's government debt market.[33]

Do You Have an Attractive Equities Market?

Sweden has an attractive equities market, but it is not very large. It is the twenty-second largest equities market in the world, with a total market value of $432.3 billion.[34]

---

[33] http://www.moodys.com/credit-ratings/Sweden-credit-rating-600013488.
[34] https://www.cia.gov/library/publications/the-world-factbook/geos/sw.html.

Tell Me About Your Central Bank. What Are Its Mandates? How Much Gold and Foreign Currency Reserves Does It Hold?

The Sveriges Riksbank is responsible for conducting monetary policy, the objective of which is to maintain a low and stable level of inflation. The bank also has the task of ensuring that payments in the economy can be made safely and efficiently.[35]

The Sveriges Riksbank has foreign currency reserves of $37,918 million and gold deposits of $5,735 million.[36]

Do You Have an Overinvolved Government That Likes to Intervene in the Forex Market?

The Swedish government is not known as an aggressive currency manipulator.

What Economic Announcements Are Important to You?

When you are watching the economic announcements coming out of Sweden, make sure that you keep your eye on the following:

- Interest rates
- Employment
- Inflation
- Gross domestic product (GDP)
- Trade balance

Are You a Safe-Haven Currency?

No, the Swedish krona is not considered to be a safe-haven currency.

---

[35] http://www.riksbank.com/.
[36] http://www.imf.org/external/np/sta/ir/IRProcessWeb/data/can/eng/curcan.htm.

How Can I Trade You?

You can trade the Swedish krona using any of the following:

- Spot Forex
- Forex futures
- Exchange-traded funds (ETFs)
- Spot Forex options
- Exchange-traded Forex options

NORWEGIAN KRONE

The Norwegian krone (NOK) is considered to be an exotic currency in the Forex market. Since Norway is an important exporter of oil, it is also closely tied to oil prices.

Norway is the world's forty-second largest economy.[37]

Does Your Economy Run a Trade Surplus or a Trade Deficit?

Norway runs a trade surplus of $60.23 billion, giving the country a ranking of 5 out of the 190 countries tracked by the CIA in *The World Factbook*.[38]

What Does Your Economy Export?

Norway exports petroleum and petroleum products, machinery, equipment, metals, chemicals, ships, and fish.

According to the World Trade Organization (WTO),[39] Norway exports $120.9 billion in goods and merchandise compared to only $38 billion in commercial services. The WTO breaks down those exports as follows:

---

[37] https://www.cia.gov/library/publications/the-world-factbook/rankorder/2001rank.html.

[38] https://www.cia.gov/library/publications/the-world-factbook/geos/no.html.

[39] http://stat.wto.org/CountryProfile/WSDBCountryPFView.aspx?Language=E&Country=NO.

- Goods and Merchandise
  - Agricultural products: 6.6 percent
  - Fuels and mining products: 68.0 percent
  - Manufactures: 19.6 percent
- Commercial Services
  - Transportation: 41.8 percent
  - Travel: 10.7 percent
  - Other commercial services: 47.6 percent

To Whom Does Your Economy Export?

The WTO ranks the following countries as the top destinations for exports from Norway:

- European Union: 80.4 percent
- United States: 4.8 percent
- Canada: 2.1 percent
- China: 2.0 percent
- South Korea: 1.9 percent

What Does Your Economy Import?

Norway imports machinery and equipment, chemicals, metals, and foodstuffs.

According to the WTO, the country imports $69.3 billion in goods and merchandise compared to only $37.6 billion in commercial services. The WTO breaks down those imports as follows:

- Goods and Merchandise
  - Agricultural products: 9.5 percent
  - Fuels and mining products: 10.3 percent
  - Manufactures: 75.8 percent
- Commercial Services
  - Transportation: 26.3 percent
  - Travel: 32.6 percent
  - Other commercial services: 41.1 percent

From Whom Does Your Economy Import?

The WTO ranks the following countries as the top sources of imports to Norway:

- European Union: 66.3 percent
- China: 7.8 percent
- United States: 6.2 percent
- Japan: 2.5 percent
- Canada: 2.2 percent

Do You Have an Attractive Government Debt Market?

Norway currently has a Moody's rating of Aaa. It received this latest rating on September 30, 1997. This most recent rating was an upgrade from the Aa1 rating that the country had held previously. This is a positive sign for the country's government debt market.[40]

Do You Have an Attractive Equities Market?

Norway has an attractive equities market, but it is not very large. It is the thirty-second largest equities market in the world, with a total market value of $227.2 billion.[41]

Tell Me About Your Central Bank. What Are Its Mandates? How Much Gold and Foreign Currency Reserves Does It Hold?

The Central Bank of Norway's (Norges Bank) activities are regulated by the Norges Bank Act of 1985. The act states that the bank shall be an executive and advisory body for monetary, credit, and foreign exchange policy. The bank shall issue banknotes and coins, promote an efficient payment system domestically as well as vis-à-vis other countries, and monitor developments in the money,

---

[40] http://www.moodys.com/credit-ratings/Norway-credit-rating-600013483.
[41] https://www.cia.gov/library/publications/the-world-factbook/geos/no.html.

credit, and foreign exchange markets. The act authorizes the bank to implement measures customarily or ordinarily taken by a central bank.[42]

The Central Bank of Norway has foreign currency reserves of $39,073 million and no gold deposits.[43]

Do You Have an Overinvolved Government That Likes to Intervene in the Forex Market?

The Norwegian government is not known as an aggressive currency manipulator.

What Economic Announcements Are Important to You?

When you are watching the economic announcements coming out of Norway, make sure that you keep your eye on the following:

- Interest rates
- Employment
- Inflation
- Gross domestic product (GDP)
- Trade balance

Are You a Safe-Haven Currency?

No, the Norwegian krone is not considered to be a safe-haven currency.

How Can I Trade You?

You can trade the Norwegian krone using any of the following:

- Spot Forex
- Forex futures

---

[42] http://www.norges-bank.no/templates/article__12358.aspx.
[43] http://www.imf.org/external/np/sta/ir/IRProcessWeb/data/nor/eng/curnor.htm.

- Spot Forex options
- Exchange-traded Forex options

DANISH KRONE

The Danish krone (DKK) is considered to be an exotic currency in the Forex market.

The most important thing you need to know about the Danish krone is that it is pegged to the euro (EUR) at 7.46 kroner per euro.

Does Your Economy Run a Trade Surplus or a Trade Deficit?

Denmark runs a trade surplus of $14.35 billion, giving the country a ranking of 21 out of the 190 countries tracked by the CIA in *The World Factbook*.[44]

What Does Your Economy Export?

Denmark exports machinery, instruments, meat and meat products, dairy products, fish, pharmaceuticals, furniture, and windmills.

According to the World Trade Organization (WTO),[45] Denmark exports $93.3 billion in goods and merchandise compared to only $55.0 billion in commercial services. The WTO breaks down those exports as follows:

- Goods and Merchandise
  - Agricultural products: 22.2 percent
  - Fuels and mining products: 10.2 percent
  - Manufactures: 64.9 percent
- Commercial Services
  - Transportation: 61.5 percent

---

[44] https://www.cia.gov/library/publications/the-world-factbook/geos/da.html.

[45] http://stat.wto.org/CountryProfile/WSDBCountryPFView.aspx?Language=E&Country=DK.

- Travel: 11.6 percent
- Other commercial services: 27.0 percent

To Whom Does Your Economy Export?

The WTO ranks the following countries as the top destinations for exports from Denmark:

- European Union: 61.5 percent
- Norway: 6.2 percent
- United States: 5.4 percent
- China: 2.1 percent
- Japan: 1.5 percent

What Does Your Economy Import?

Denmark imports machinery, equipment, raw materials, semi-manufactures for industry, chemicals, grain, foodstuffs, and consumer goods.

According to the WTO, the country imports $82.9 billion in goods and merchandise compared to only $51.0 billion in commercial services. The WTO breaks down those imports as follows:

- Goods and Merchandise
  - Agricultural products: 16.2 percent
  - Fuels and mining products: 7.9 percent
  - Manufactures: 74.2 percent
- Commercial Services
  - Transportation: 51.1 percent
  - Travel: 18.1 percent
  - Other commercial services: 30.8 percent

From Whom Does Your Economy Import?

The WTO ranks the following countries as the top sources of imports to Denmark:

- European Union: 69.9 percent
- China: 6.5 percent
- Norway: 5.3 percent
- United States: 3.4 percent
- Singapore: 1.9 percent

Do You Have an Attractive Government Debt Market?

Denmark currently has a Moody's rating of Aaa. It received this latest rating on August 23, 1999. This most recent rating was an upgrade from the Aa1 rating that the country had held previously. This is a positive sign for the country's government debt market.[46]

Do You Have an Attractive Equities Market?

Denmark has an attractive equities market, but it is not very large. It is the thirty-first largest equities market in the world, with a total market value of $186.9 billion.[47]

Tell Me About Your Central Bank. What Are Its Mandates? How Much Gold and Foreign Currency Reserves Does It Hold?

Danmarks Nationalbank is responsible for monetary policy in Denmark. The objective of monetary policy is to keep the krone stable vis-à-vis the euro. Danmarks Nationalbank conducts monetary policy by setting the monetary policy interest rates, that is, the discount rate, the current-account rate, the lending rate, and the rate of interest on certificates of deposit. The interest rates are determined by the Board of Governors of Danmarks Nationalbank, and can be changed as required at any time.[48]

---

[46] http://www.moodys.com/credit-ratings/Denmark-credit-rating-600013457.

[47] https://www.cia.gov/library/publications/the-world-factbook/geos/sw.html.

[48] http://www.nationalbanken.dk/DNUK/MonetaryPolicy.nsf/side/Denmarks_monetary_policy!OpenDocument.

The Danmarks Nationalbank has foreign currency reserves of $64,398 million and gold deposits of $3,017 million.[49]

Do You Have an Overinvolved Government That Likes to Intervene in the Forex Market?

The Danish government is not known as an aggressive currency manipulator.

What Economic Announcements Are Important to You?

When you are watching the economic announcements coming out of Denmark, make sure that you keep your eye on the following:

- Interest rates
- Employment
- Inflation
- Gross domestic product (GDP)
- Trade balance

Are You a Safe-Haven Currency?

No, the Danish krone is not considered to be a safe-haven currency.

How Can I Trade You?

You can trade the Danish krone using any of the following:

- Spot Forex
- Forex futures
- Spot Forex options

---

[49] http://www.imf.org/external/np/sta/ir/IRProcessWeb/data/dnk/eng/curdnk.htm.

CHAPTER 7

Currencies of Asia

JAPANESE YEN—THE YEN

The Japanese yen (JPY) is considered to be a major currency in the Forex market. Japan has had chronically low interest rates for a decade now, and that has made it a popular target for the short side of carry trades. Japan is also quite sensitive to changes in oil prices because the country consumes a lot of oil but produces virtually no oil of its own.

Japan is the third largest economy in the world[1] and has the second largest trade surplus,[2] which is a powerful combination.

Does Your Economy Run a Trade Surplus or a Trade Deficit?

Japan runs a trade surplus of $182.3 billion, giving the country a ranking of 2 out of the 190 countries tracked by the CIA in *The World Factbook*.[3]

---

[1] https://www.cia.gov/library/publications/the-world-factbook/rankorder/2001rank.html.

[2] https://www.cia.gov/library/publications/the-world-factbook/rankorder/2187rank.html.

[3] https://www.cia.gov/library/publications/the-world-factbook/geos/ja.html.

What Does Your Economy Export?

Japan exports transport equipment, motor vehicles, semiconductors, electrical machinery, and chemicals.

According to the World Trade Organization (WTO),[4] Japan exports \$580.7 billion in goods and merchandise compared to only \$125.9 billion in commercial services. The WTO breaks down those exports as follows:

- Goods and Merchandise
  - Agricultural products: 1.4 percent
  - Fuels and mining products: 4.4 percent
  - Manufactures: 87.5 percent
- Commercial Services
  - Transportation: 25.1 percent
  - Travel: 8.2 percent
  - Other commercial services: 66.7 percent

To Whom Does Your Economy Export?

The WTO ranks the following countries as the top destinations for exports from Japan:

- China: 18.9 percent
- United States: 16.4 percent
- European Union: 12.5 percent
- Korea: 8.1 percent
- Taiwan: 6.3 percent

What Does Your Economy Import?

Japan imports machinery and equipment, fuels, foodstuffs, chemicals, textiles, and raw materials.

According to the WTO, the country imports \$552 billion in goods and merchandise compared to only \$147 billion in commercial services. The WTO breaks down those imports as follows:

---

[4]http://stat.wto.org/CountryProfile/WSDBCountryPFView.aspx?Language= E&Country=JP.

- Goods and Merchandise
  - Agricultural products: 12.3 percent
  - Fuels and mining products: 34.0 percent
  - Manufactures: 51.8 percent
- Commercial Services
  - Transportation: 27.6 percent
  - Travel: 17.2 percent
  - Other commercial services: 55.2 percent

From Whom Does Your Economy Import?

The WTO ranks the following countries as the top sources of imports to Japan:

- China: 22.2 percent
- United States: 11.0 percent
- European Union: 10.7 percent
- Australia: 6.3 percent
- Saudi Arabia: 5.3 percent

Do You Have an Attractive Government Debt Market?

Japan currently has a Moody's rating of Aaa. It received this latest rating on October 20, 2002. This most recent rating was an upgrade from the Aa1 rating that the country had held previously. This is a positive sign for the country's government debt market.[5]

Do You Have an Attractive Equities Market?

Japan has an attractive equities market. It is the third largest equities market in the world, with a total market value of $3.378 trillion.[6]

---

[5] http://www.moodys.com/credit-ratings/Japan-credit-rating-600013473.
[6] https://www.cia.gov/library/publications/the-world-factbook/geos/ja.html.

Tell Me About Your Central Bank. What Are Its Mandates? How Much Gold and Foreign Currency Reserves Does It Hold?

The Bank of Japan's (BOJ) objectives are to issue banknotes, carry out currency and monetary control, and ensure the smooth settlement of funds among banks and other financial institutions, thereby contributing to the maintenance of stability of the financial system.[7]

The BOJ has foreign currency reserves of $1,035,817 million and gold deposits of $34,695 million.[8]

Do You Have an Overinvolved Government That Likes to Intervene in the Forex Market?

Japan's Ministry of Finance (MOF) and the Bank of Japan do have an interventionist track record, so you need to be aware of any rumors that may start circulating regarding Japanese intervention.

What Economic Announcements Are Important to You?

When you are watching the economic announcements coming out of Japan, make sure that you keep your eye on the following:

- Bank of Japan overnight call rate
- Tankan Manufacturing Index
- Tokyo core CPI
- Preliminary gross domestic product (GDP)
- Trade balance

Are You a Safe-Haven Currency?

Yes, the yen is seen as a safe-haven currency. Japan's government debt is largely owned by domestic investors, making the country

---

[7] http://www.boj.or.jp/en/type/exp/about/expboj.htm.
[8] http://www.imf.org/external/np/sta/ir/IRProcessWeb/data/jpn/eng/curjpn.htm.

less at risk of the capital flight that can occur when economic or political shocks cause confidence to collapse.

How Can I Trade You?

You can trade the Japanese yen using any of the following:

- Spot Forex
- Forex futures
- Exchange-traded funds (ETFs)
- Exchange-traded notes (ETNs)
- Spot Forex options
- Exchange-traded Forex options

HONG KONG DOLLAR

The Hong Kong dollar (HKD) is considered to be an exotic currency in the Forex market. The most important thing you need to know about the HKD is that it is pegged to the U.S. dollar at an exchange-rate band of 7.75 to 7.85 Hong Kong dollars per 1 U.S. dollar (USD).

Does Your Economy Run a Trade Surplus or a Trade Deficit?

Hong Kong runs a trade surplus of $18.07 billion, giving the country a ranking of 18 out of the 190 countries tracked by the CIA in *The World Factbook*.[9]

What Does Your Economy Export?

Hong Kong exports electrical machinery and appliances, textiles, apparel, footwear, watches and clocks, toys, plastics, precious stones, and printed material.

According to the World Trade Organization (WTO),[10] Hong Kong exports $329.4 billion in goods and merchandise compared

---

[9] https://www.cia.gov/library/publications/the-world-factbook/geos/hk.html.
[10] http://stat.wto.org/CountryProfile/WSDBCountryPFView.aspx?Language=E&Country=HK.

to only $86.3 billion in commercial services. The WTO breaks down those exports as follows:

- Goods and Merchandise
  - Agricultural products: 2.1 percent
  - Fuels and mining products: 1.9 percent
  - Manufactures: 92.6 percent
- Commercial Services
  - Transportation: 29.0 percent
  - Travel: 19.1 percent
  - Other commercial services: 51.9 percent

To Whom Does Your Economy Export?

The WTO ranks the following countries as the top destinations for exports from Hong Kong:

- China: 49.9 percent
- European Union: 13.6 percent
- United States: 11.2 percent
- Japan: 4.3 percent
- Taiwan: 2.3 percent

What Does Your Economy Import?

Hong Kong imports raw materials and semi-manufactures, consumer goods, capital goods, and foodstuffs.

According to the WTO, the country imports $352.2 billion in goods and merchandise compared to only $44.4 billion in commercial services. The WTO breaks down those imports as follows:

- Goods and Merchandise
  - Agricultural products: 4.9 percent
  - Fuels and mining products: 5.4 percent
  - Manufactures: 88.2 percent
- Commercial Services
  - Transportation: 30.7 percent

- Travel: 36.0 percent
- Other commercial services: 33.3 percent

From Whom Does Your Economy Import?

The WTO ranks the following countries as the top sources of imports to Hong Kong:

- China: 45.8 percent
- Japan: 9.2 percent
- European Union: 8.0 percent
- Taiwan: 7.2 percent
- South Korea: 4.9 percent

Do You Have an Attractive Government Debt Market?

Hong Kong currently has a Moody's rating of Aaa. It received this latest rating on November 10, 2010. This most recent rating was an upgrade from the Aa1 rating that the country had held previously. This is a positive sign for the country's government debt market.[11]

Do You Have an Attractive Equities Market?

Hong Kong has an attractive equities market. It is the eighth largest equities market in the world, with a total market value of $2.292 trillion.[12]

Tell Me About Your Central Bank. What Are Its Mandates? How Much Gold and Foreign Currency Reserves Does It Hold?

The primary monetary policy objective of the Hong Kong Monetary Authority (HKMA) is to maintain exchange-rate stability within the framework of the Linked Exchange Rate System through sound

---

[11] http://www.moodys.com/credit-ratings/Hong-Kong-credit-rating-600013464.
[12] https://www.cia.gov/library/publications/the-world-factbook/geos/ hk.html.

management of the Exchange Fund, monetary operations, and other means that are deemed necessary.[13]

Hong Kong has foreign currency reserves of $258,103 million and gold deposits of $94 million.[14]

Do You Have an Overinvolved Government That Likes to Intervene in the Forex Market?

Because the Hong Kong dollar is pegged to the U.S. dollar, the Hong Kong Monetary Authority actively intervenes in the currency market.

What Economic Announcements Are Important to You?

When you are watching the economic announcements coming out of Hong Kong, make sure that you keep your eye on the following:

- Interest rates
- Employment
- Inflation
- Gross domestic product (GDP)
- Trade balance

Are You a Safe-Haven Currency?

No, the Hong Kong dollar is not considered to be a safe-haven currency.

How Can I Trade You?

You can trade the Hong Kong dollar using the following:

- Spot Forex

---

[13] http://www.info.gov.hk/hkma/eng/currency/link_ex/index.htm.

[14] http://www.imf.org/external/np/sta/ir/IRProcessWeb/data/can/eng/curcan.htm.

SOUTH KOREAN WON

The South Korean won (KRW) is considered to be an exotic currency in the Forex market.

South Korea is the world's twelfth largest economy.[15]

Does Your Economy Run a Trade Surplus or a Trade Deficit?

South Korea runs a trade surplus of $36.35 billion, giving the country a ranking of 12 out of the 190 countries tracked by the CIA in *The World Factbook*.[16]

What Does Your Economy Export?

South Korea exports semiconductors, wireless telecommunications equipment, motor vehicles, computers, steel, ships, and petrochemicals.

According to the World Trade Organization (WTO),[17] South Korea exports $363.5 billion in goods and merchandise compared to only $57.3 billion in commercial services. The WTO breaks down those exports as follows:

- Goods and Merchandise
  - Agricultural products: 2.0 percent
  - Fuels and mining products: 8.4 percent
  - Manufactures: 88.7 percent
- Commercial Services
  - Transportation: 50.5 percent
  - Travel: 16.5 percent
  - Other commercial services: 33.0 percent

---

[15] https://www.cia.gov/library/publications/the-world-factbook/rankorder/2001rank.html.

[16] https://www.cia.gov/library/publications/the-world-factbook/geos/ks.html.

[17] http://stat.wto.org/CountryProfile/WSDBCountryPFView.aspx?Language=E&Country=KR.

To Whom Does Your Economy Export?

The WTO ranks the following countries as the top destinations for exports from South Korea:

- China: 23.9 percent
- European Union: 12.8 percent
- United States: 10.4 percent
- Japan: 6.0 percent
- Hong Kong: 5.4 percent

What Does Your Economy Import?

South Korea imports machinery, electronics and electronic equipment, oil, steel, transport equipment, organic chemicals, and plastics.

According to the WTO, the country imports $323.1 billion in goods and merchandise compared to only $75 billion in commercial services. The WTO breaks down those imports as follows:

- Goods and Merchandise
  - Agricultural products: 6.5 percent
  - Fuels and mining products: 35.5 percent
  - Manufactures: 57.6 percent
- Commercial Services
  - Transportation: 31.2 percent
  - Travel: 17.8 percent
  - Other commercial services: 51.1 percent

From Whom Does Your Economy Import?

The WTO ranks the following countries as the top sources of imports to South Korea:

- China: 16.8 percent
- Japan: 15.3 percent
- European Union: 10.0 percent
- United States: 9.0 percent
- Saudi Arabia: 6.1 percent

Do You Have an Attractive Government Debt Market?

South Korea currently has a Moody's rating of Aa2. It received this latest rating on April 14, 2010. This most recent rating was an upgrade from the A1 rating that the country had held previously. This is a positive sign for the country's government debt market.[18]

Do You Have an Attractive Equities Market?

South Korea has an attractive equities market. It is the seventeenth largest equities market in the world, with a total market value of $836.5 billion.[19]

Tell Me About Your Central Bank. What Are Its Mandates? How Much Gold and Foreign Currency Reserves Does It Hold?

The objectives of monetary policy differ over time, depending on the economic situation of a country. The objectives of South Korea's monetary policy have varied over time and in accordance with the state of the economy, but nowadays price stability is regarded as the most important objective of monetary policy. This stems from the conviction that sustainable economic growth, which is the ultimate objective of monetary policy, can be achieved only on the basis of price stability. If inflation accelerates, uncertainties over the future mount, dampening economic activities as a whole. Likewise, economic efficiency declines as a result of the distorted distribution of income and resources.

Like most other central banks, the Bank of Korea takes price stability as the most important objective of its monetary policy. The current Bank of Korea Act clearly sets out price stability as the purpose of the Bank of Korea's establishment and stipulates that it should seek to bring about price stability by setting an inflation

---

[18] http://www.moodys.com/credit-ratings/Korea-credit-rating-600013475.
[19] https://www.cia.gov/library/publications/the-world-factbook/geos/ks.html.

target in consultation with the government and do its utmost to attain this target.[20]

The Bank of Korea has foreign currency reserves of $289,277 million and gold deposits of $80 million.[21]

Do You Have an Overinvolved Government That Likes to Intervene in the Forex Market?

The South Korean government has been known to intervene in the currency market from time to time.

What Economic Announcements Are Important to You?

When you are watching the economic announcements coming out of South Korea, make sure that you keep your eye on the following:

- Interest rates
- Employment
- Inflation
- Gross domestic product (GDP)
- Trade balance

Are You a Safe-Haven Currency?

No, the South Korean won is not considered to be a safe-haven currency.

How Can I Trade You?

You can trade the South Korean won using either of the following:

- Spot Forex
- Forex futures

---

[20] http://eng.bok.or.kr/.

[21] http://www.imf.org/external/np/sta/ir/IRProcessWeb/data/kor/eng/curkor.htm.

SINGAPORE DOLLAR

The Singapore dollar (SGD) is considered to be an exotic currency in the Forex market.

The first thing you need to know about the Singapore dollar is that it is pegged within a tight trading band to an undisclosed basket of currencies. The basket is believed to be made up of currencies from the country's top trading partners, but nobody knows for sure which ones are included and what the weighting of each is.

Singapore is the world's fortieth largest economy.[22]

Does Your Economy Run a Trade Surplus or a Trade Deficit?

Singapore runs a trade surplus of $40.44 billion, giving the country a ranking of 9 out of the 190 countries tracked by the CIA in *The World Factbook*.[23]

What Does Your Economy Export?

Singapore exports machinery and equipment (including electronics), consumer goods, pharmaceuticals, other chemicals, and mineral fuels.

According to the World Trade Organization (WTO),[24] Singapore exports $269.8 billion in goods and merchandise compared to only $87.8 billion in commercial services. The WTO breaks down those exports as follows:

- Goods and Merchandise
  - Agricultural products: 2.3 percent
  - Fuels and mining products: 16.3 percent
  - Manufactures: 73.2 percent
- Commercial Services
  - Transportation: 35.0 percent

---

[22] https://www.cia.gov/library/publications/the-world-factbook/rankorder/2001rank.html.

[23] https://www.cia.gov/library/publications/the-world-factbook/geos/sn.html.

[24] http://stat.wto.org/CountryProfile/WSDBCountryPFView.aspx?Language=E&Country=SG.

- Travel: 10.5 percent
- Other commercial services: 54.6 percent

To Whom Does Your Economy Export?

The WTO ranks the following countries as the top destinations for exports from Singapore:

- Hong Kong: 11.6 percent
- Malaysia: 11.5 percent
- China: 9.7 percent
- Indonesia: 9.7 percent
- European Union: 9.6 percent

What Does Your Economy Import?

Singapore imports machinery and equipment, mineral fuels, chemicals, foodstuffs, and consumer goods.

According to the WTO, the country imports $245.8 billion in goods and merchandise compared to only $81.4 billion in commercial services. The WTO breaks down those imports as follows:

- Goods and Merchandise
  - Agricultural products: 3.6 percent
  - Fuels and mining products: 26.3 percent
  - Manufactures: 66.1 percent
- Commercial Services
  - Transportation: 32.5 percent
  - Travel: 19.4 percent
  - Other commercial services: 48.1 percent

From Whom Does Your Economy Import?

The WTO ranks the following countries as the top sources of imports to Singapore:

- European Union: 13.8 percent
- United States: 11.9 percent

- Malaysia: 11.6 percent
- China: 10.5 percent
- Japan: 7.6 percent

Do You Have an Attractive Government Debt Market?

Singapore currently has a Moody's rating of Aaa. It received this latest rating on June 14, 2002. This most recent rating was an upgrade from the Aa1 rating that the country had held previously. This is a positive sign for the country's government debt market.[25]

Do You Have an Attractive Equities Market?

Singapore has an attractive equities market, but it is not very large. It is the twenty-second largest equities market in the world, with a total market value of $474.8 billion.[26]

Tell Me About Your Central Bank. What Are Its Mandates? How Much Gold and Foreign Currency Reserves Does It Hold?

The Monetary Authority of Singapore is charged with maintaining price stability. The Monetary Authority of Singapore has foreign currency reserves of $222,694 million and gold deposits of $212 million.[27]

Do You Have an Overinvolved Government That Likes to Intervene in the Forex Market?

The Monetary Authority of Singapore (MAS) closely tracks the movement of the Singapore dollar and intervenes whenever the currency moves outside of its prescribed trading band, which is based on an undisclosed basket of currencies.

---

[25] http://www.moodys.com/credit-ratings/Singapore-credit-rating-600013486.
[26] https://www.cia.gov/library/publications/the-world-factbook/geos/sn.html.
[27] http://www.imf.org/external/np/sta/ir/IRProcessWeb/data/sgp/eng/cursgp.htm.

What Economic Announcements Are Important to You?

When you are watching the economic announcements coming out of Singapore, make sure that you keep your eye on the following:

- Interest rates
- Employment
- Inflation
- Gross domestic product (GDP)
- Trade balance

Are You a Safe-Haven Currency?

No, the Singapore dollar is not considered to be a safe-haven currency.

How Can I Trade You?

You can trade the Singapore dollar using the following:

- Spot Forex

INDIAN RUPEE

The Indian rupee (INR) is considered to be an exotic currency in the Forex market.

India is the world's fourth largest economy.[28]

Does Your Economy Run a Trade Surplus or a Trade Deficit?

India runs a trade deficit of $26.91 billion, giving the country a ranking of 181 out of the 190 countries tracked by the CIA in *The World Factbook*.[29]

---

[28] https://www.cia.gov/library/publications/the-world-factbook/rankorder/2001rank.html.

[29] https://www.cia.gov/library/publications/the-world-factbook/geos/in.html.

What Does Your Economy Export?

India exports petroleum products, precious stones, machinery, iron, steel, chemicals, vehicles, and apparel.

According to the World Trade Organization (WTO),[30] India exports $162.6 billion in goods and merchandise compared to only $87.4 billion in commercial services. The WTO breaks down those exports as follows:

- Goods and Merchandise
  - Agricultural products: 10.2 percent
  - Fuels and mining products: 20.6 percent
  - Manufactures: 66.0 percent
- Commercial Services
  - Transportation: 12.3 percent
  - Travel: 12.1 percent
  - Other commercial services: 75.6 percent

To Whom Does Your Economy Export?

The WTO ranks the following countries as the top destinations for exports from India:

- European Union: 20.5 percent
- United Arab Emirates: 14.4 percent
- United States: 10.8 percent
- China: 5.9 percent
- Hong Kong: 4.0 percent

What Does Your Economy Import?

India imports crude oil, precious stones, machinery, fertilizer, iron, steel, and chemicals.

According to the WTO, the country imports $249.6 billion in goods and merchandise compared to only $79.8 billion in commercial services. The WTO breaks down those imports as follows:

---

[30] http://stat.wto.org/CountryProfile/WSDBCountryPFView.aspx?Language=E&Country=IN.

- Goods and Merchandise
  - Agricultural products: 5.6 percent
  - Fuels and mining products: 37.6 percent
  - Manufactures: 46.6 percent

- Commercial Services
  - Transportation: 43.4 percent
  - Travel: 11.6 percent
  - Other commercial services: 45.0 percent

From Whom Does Your Economy Import?

The WTO ranks the following countries as the top sources of imports to India:

- European Union: 14.4 percent
- China: 11.5 percent
- United Arab Emirates: 7.4 percent
- United States: 6.0 percent
- Saudi Arabia: 5.4 percent

Do You Have an Attractive Government Debt Market?

India currently has a Moody's rating of Baa2. It received this latest rating on May 24, 2006. This most recent rating was an upgrade from the Ba1 rating that the country had held previously. This is a positive sign for the country's government debt market.[31]

Do You Have an Attractive Equities Market?

India has an attractive equities market. It is the fourteenth largest equities market in the world, with a total market value of $1.179 trillion.[32]

---

[31] http://www.moodys.com/credit-ratings/India-credit-rating-600013469.

[32] https://www.cia.gov/library/publications/the-world-factbook/geos/in.html.

Tell Me About Your Central Bank. What Are Its Mandates? How Much Gold and Foreign Currency Reserves Does It Hold?

The Reserve Bank of India (RBI) has the following four objectives:

1. Maintain price stability and ensure an adequate flow of credit to productive sectors
2. Maintain public confidence in the system, protect depositors' interests, and provide cost-effective banking services to the public
3. Facilitate external trade and payment and promote orderly development and maintenance of the foreign exchange market in India
4. Give the public an adequate quantity of supplies of currency notes and coins and in good quality[33]

The Reserve Bank of India has foreign currency reserves of $267,814 million and gold deposits of $22,470 million.[34]

Do You Have an Overinvolved Government That Likes to Intervene in the Forex Market?

The Indian government has been known to intervene in the currency market from time to time.

What Economic Announcements Are Important to You?

When you are watching the economic announcements coming out of India, make sure that you keep your eye on the following:

- Interest rates
- Employment
- Inflation

---

[33] http://www.rbi.org.in/scripts/AboutusDisplay.aspx#MF.
[34] http://www.imf.org/external/np/sta/ir/IRProcessWeb/data/ind/eng/curind.htm.

- Gross domestic product (GDP)
- Trade balance

Are You a Safe-Haven Currency?

No, the Indian rupee is not considered to be a safe-haven currency.

How Can I Trade You?

You can trade the Indian rupee using any of the following:

- Spot Forex
- Exchange-traded funds (ETFs)
- Exchange-traded notes (ETNs)

NEW TAIWAN DOLLAR

The New Taiwan dollar (TWD) is considered to be an exotic currency in the Forex market.
    Taiwan is the world's nineteenth largest economy.[35]

Does Your Economy Run a Trade Surplus or a Trade Deficit?

Taiwan runs a trade surplus of $39 billion, giving the country a ranking of 10 out of the 190 countries tracked by the CIA in *The World Factbook*.[36]

What Does Your Economy Export?

Taiwan exports electronics, flat panels, machinery, metals, textiles, plastics, chemicals, and optical, photographic, measuring and medical instruments.

---

[35] https://www.cia.gov/library/publications/the-world-factbook/rankorder/2001rank.html.

[36] https://www.cia.gov/library/publications/the-world-factbook/geos/tw.html.

According to the World Trade Organization (WTO),[37] Taiwan exports $203.7 million in goods and merchandise compared to only $30.6 million in commercial services. The WTO breaks down those exports as follows:

- Goods and Merchandise
  - Agricultural products: 2.1 percent
  - Fuels and mining products: 7.7 percent
  - Manufactures: 88.5 percent
- Commercial Services
  - Transportation: 17.9 percent
  - Travel: 22.7 percent
  - Other commercial services: 59.4 percent

To Whom Does Your Economy Export?

The WTO ranks the following countries as the top destinations for exports from Taiwan:

- China: 26.6 percent
- Hong Kong: 14.5 percent
- United States: 11.6 percent
- European Union: 10.5 percent
- Japan: 7.1 percent

What Does Your Economy Import?

Taiwan imports electronics, machinery, crude petroleum, precision instruments, organic chemicals, and metals.

According to the WTO, Taiwan imports $174.4 million in goods and merchandise compared to only $29.1 million in commercial services. The WTO breaks down those imports as follows:

- Goods and Merchandise
  - Agricultural products: 5.9 percent

---

[37] http://stat.wto.org/CountryProfile/WSDBCountryPFView.aspx?Language=E&Country=TW.

- • Fuels and mining products: 27.9 percent
- • Manufactures: 64.5 percent
- ▪ Commercial Services
  - • Transportation: 27.1 percent
  - • Travel: 26.8 percent
  - • Other commercial services: 46.1 percent

From Whom Does Your Economy Import?

The WTO ranks the following countries as the top sources of imports to Taiwan:

- ▪ Japan: 20.8 percent
- ▪ China: 14.0 percent
- ▪ United States: 10.5 percent
- ▪ European Union: 9.0 percent
- ▪ Korea: 6.0 percent

Do You Have an Attractive Government Debt Market?

Taiwan currently has a Moody's rating of Aa3. It received this rating on March 24, 1994. This is the only rating that Taiwan has ever had.[38]

Do You Have an Attractive Equities Market?

Taiwan has an attractive equities market, but it is not very large. It is the twenty-first largest equities market in the world, with a total market value of $354.7 billion.[39]

---

[38] http://www.moodys.com/credit-ratings/Taiwan-credit-rating-600013490.
[39] https://www.cia.gov/library/publications/the-world-factbook/geos/sw.html.

Tell Me About Your Central Bank. What Are Its Mandates? How Much Gold and Foreign Currency Reserves Does It Hold?

The Central Bank of the Republic of China (Taiwan) states that according to the Central Bank of China Act, the bank's operational objectives include promoting financial stability, ensuring sound banking operations, maintaining the stable internal and external value of the currency, and, within the scope of the previous three objectives, fostering economic development.[40]

The foreign currency reserves and gold deposit information for Taiwan is not available.

Do You Have an Overinvolved Government That Likes to Intervene in the Forex Market?

The Taiwanese government has been known to intervene in the currency market from time to time.

What Economic Announcements Are Important to You?

When you are watching the economic announcements coming out of Taiwan, make sure that you keep your eye on the following:

- Interest rates
- Employment
- Inflation
- Gross domestic product (GDP)
- Trade balance

Are You a Safe-Haven Currency?

No, the New Taiwan dollar is not considered to be a safe-haven currency.

---

[40] http://www.cbc.gov.tw/lp.asp?ctNode=453&CtUnit=271&BaseDSD=7& mp=2.

How Can I Trade You?

You cannot currently trade the New Taiwan dollar, but spot Forex dealers do have plans to offer pairs including the New Taiwan dollar in the future.

CHINESE YUAN

The Chinese yuan (CNY) is considered to be an exotic currency in the Forex market.

The most important thing you need to know about the Chinese yuan is that it is pegged to a basket of currencies, the most important of which are the U.S. dollar (USD), the euro (EUR), and the Japanese yen (JPY). Before July 21, 2005, the yuan was pegged at 8.11 yuan per U.S. dollar. However, at the time of this writing, the value of the yuan has climbed to 6.60 yuan per U.S. dollar.

China is the world's second largest economy.[41]

Does Your Economy Run a Trade Surplus or a Trade Deficit?

China runs a trade surplus of $272.5 billion, giving the country a ranking of 1 out of the 190 countries tracked by the CIA in *The World Factbook*.[42]

What Does Your Economy Export?

China exports electrical and other machinery, data-processing equipment, apparel, textiles, iron, steel, and optical and medical equipment.

According to the World Trade Organization (WTO),[43] China exports $1,201.5 billion in goods and merchandise compared to only $128.6 billion in commercial services. The WTO breaks down those exports as follows:

---

[41] https://www.cia.gov/library/publications/the-world-factbook/geos/ch.html.

[42] https://www.cia.gov/library/publications/the-world-factbook/geos/ch.html.

[43] http://stat.wto.org/CountryProfile/WSDBCountryPFView.aspx?Language= E&Country=CN.

- Goods and Merchandise
  - Agricultural products: 3.4 percent
  - Fuels and mining products: 2.9 percent
  - Manufactures: 93.6 percent
- Commercial Services
  - Transportation: 18.4 percent
  - Travel: 30.9 percent
  - Other commercial services: 50.8 percent

To Whom Does Your Economy Export?

The WTO ranks the following countries as the top destinations for exports from China:

- European Union: 19.7 percent
- United States: 18.4 percent
- Hong Kong: 13.8 percent
- Japan: 8.1 percent
- Korea: 4.5 percent

What Does Your Economy Import?

China imports electrical and other machinery, oil, mineral fuels, optical equipment, medical equipment, metal ores, plastics, and organic chemicals.

According to the WTO, the country imports $133.8 billion in goods and merchandise compared to only $37.8 billion in commercial services. The WTO breaks down those imports as follows:

- Goods and Merchandise
  - Agricultural products: 7.6 percent
  - Fuels and mining products: 24.9 percent
  - Manufactures: 67.1 percent
- Commercial Services
  - Transportation: 29.5 percent
  - Travel: 27.6 percent
  - Other commercial services: 42.9 percent

From Whom Does Your Economy Import?

The WTO ranks the following countries as the top sources of imports to China:

- Japan: 13.0 percent
- European Union: 12.7 percent
- Korea: 10.2 percent
- China: 8.6 percent
- Taipei: 8.5 percent

Do You Have an Attractive Government Debt Market?

China currently has a Moody's rating of Aa3. It received this latest rating on November 11, 2010. This most recent rating was an upgrade from the A1 rating that the country had held previously. This is a positive sign for the country's government debt market.[44]

Do You Have an Attractive Equities Market?

China has an attractive equities market. It is the fourth largest equities market in the world, with a total market value of $5.008 trillion.[45]

Tell Me About Your Central Bank. What Are Its Mandates? How Much Gold and Foreign Currency Reserves Does It Hold?

The objective of the monetary policy of the People's Bank of China (PBC) is to maintain the stability of the value of the currency and thereby promote economic growth.[46]

The People's Bank of China has foreign currency reserves of $2,850,000 million[47] and gold deposits of $371,000,000 million.[48]

---

[44] http://www.moodys.com/credit-ratings/China-credit-rating-600013451.

[45] https://www.cia.gov/library/publications/the-world-factbook/geos/ch.html.

[46] http://www.pbc.gov.cn/publish/english/970/index.html.

[47] http://www.nytimes.com/2011/01/12/business/global/12yuan.html.

[48] http://www.safe.gov.cn/model_safe_en/news_en/new_detail_en.jsp?ID=30100000000000000,240.

Do You Have an Overinvolved Government That Likes to Intervene in the Forex Market?

Since the Chinese yuan is pegged to a basket of currencies, the Chinese government frequently intervenes in the Forex market.

What Economic Announcements Are Important to You?

When you are watching the economic announcements coming out of China, make sure that you keep your eye on the following:

- Interest rates and reserve requirements
- Inflation
- Gross domestic product (GDP)
- Trade balance

Are You a Safe-Haven Currency?

No, the Chinese yuan is not considered to be a safe-haven currency.

How Can I Trade You?

You can trade the Chinese yuan using either of the following:

- Exchange-traded funds (ETFs)
- Exchange-traded notes (ETNs)

THAI BAHT

The Thai baht (THB) is considered to be an exotic currency in the Forex market.

Thailand is the world's twenty-fourth largest economy.[49]

---

[49] https://www.cia.gov/library/publications/the-world-factbook/rankorder/2001rank.html.

Does Your Economy Run a Trade Surplus or a Trade Deficit?

Thailand runs a trade surplus of $12.29 billion, giving the country a ranking of 22 out of the 190 countries tracked by the CIA in *The World Factbook*.[50]

What Does Your Economy Export?

Thailand exports textiles, footwear, fishery products, rice, rubber, jewelry, automobiles, computers, and electrical appliances.

According to the World Trade Organization (WTO),[51] Thailand exports $152.5 billion in goods and merchandise compared to only $29.9 billion in commercial services. The WTO breaks down those exports as follows:

- Goods and Merchandise
  - Agricultural products: 18.4 percent
  - Fuels and mining products: 6.2 percent
  - Manufactures: 71.7 percent
- Commercial Services
  - Transportation: 19.4 percent
  - Travel: 53.1 percent
  - Other commercial services: 27.5 percent

To Whom Does Your Economy Export?

The WTO ranks the following countries as the top destinations for exports from Thailand:

- European Union: 11.9 percent
- United States: 10.9 percent
- China: 10.6 percent
- Japan: 10.3 percent
- Hong Kong: 6.2 percent

---

[50] https://www.cia.gov/library/publications/the-world-factbook/geos/th.html.
[51] http://stat.wto.org/CountryProfile/WSDBCountryPFView.aspx?Language=E&Country=TH.

What Does Your Economy Import?

Thailand imports capital goods, intermediate goods, raw materials, consumer goods, and fuels.

According to the WTO, the country imports $133.8 billion in goods and merchandise compared to only $37.8 billion in commercial services. The WTO breaks down those imports as follows:

- Goods and Merchandise
  - Agricultural products: 7.0 percent
  - Fuels and mining products: 22.6 percent
  - Manufactures: 67.3 percent
- Commercial Services
  - Transportation: 45.6 percent
  - Travel: 11.0 percent
  - Other commercial services: 43.4 percent

From Whom Does Your Economy Import?

The WTO ranks the following countries as the top sources of imports to Thailand:

- Japan: 18.7 percent
- China: 12.7 percent
- European Union: 9.1 percent
- Malaysia: 6.4 percent
- United States: 6.3 percent

Do You Have an Attractive Government Debt Market?

Thailand currently has a Moody's rating of A2. It received this latest rating on October 28, 2010. This most recent rating was an upgrade from the A3 rating that the country had held previously. This is a positive sign for the country's government debt market.[52]

---

[52] http://www.moodys.com/credit-ratings/Thailand-credit-rating-600013491.

Do You Have an Attractive Equities Market?

Thailand has an attractive equities market, but it is not very large. It is the thirty-fifth largest equities market in the world, with a total market value of $138.2 billion.[53]

Tell Me About Your Central Bank. What Are Its Mandates? How Much Gold and Foreign Currency Reserves Does It Hold?

The main objective of the Bank of Thailand (BoT) is to ensure price stability in the economy, which is defined as low and stable inflation. Price stability helps facilitate decision making and planning of consumption, production, saving, and investment by the private sector, which in turn supports sustainable economic growth and employment in the long run. This is because low and stable inflation helps to

- Preserve the purchasing power of consumers and savers.
- Maintain the price competitiveness of businesses in both domestic and international markets.
- Reduce the volatility of the real interest rate.
- Promote a good overall economic environment through reduced uncertainty, which would otherwise negatively affect private-sector consumption and investment planning and decision making.[54]

The Bank of Thailand has foreign currency reserves of $161,152 million and gold deposits of $4,480 million.[55]

Do You Have an Overinvolved Government That Likes to Intervene in the Forex Market?

The Thai government has been known to intervene in the currency market from time to time.

---

[53] https://www.cia.gov/library/publications/the-world-factbook/geos/th.html.
[54] http://www.bot.or.th/English/MonetaryPolicy/Target/Pages/PriceStability.aspx.
[55] http://www.imf.org/external/np/sta/ir/IRProcessWeb/data/tha/eng/curtha.htm.

What Economic Announcements Are Important to You?

When you are watching the economic announcements coming out of Thailand, make sure that you keep your eye on the following:

- Interest rates
- Employment
- Inflation
- Gross domestic product (GDP)
- Trade balance

Are You a Safe-Haven Currency?

No, the Thai baht is not considered to be a safe-haven currency.

How Can I Trade You?

You can trade the Thai baht using the following:

- Spot Forex

Currencies of Oceania and Africa

AUSTRALIAN DOLLAR—THE AUSSIE

The Australian dollar (AUD) is considered to be a major currency in the Forex market. It is also one of the "commodity" currencies because of the Australian economy's dependence on commodity exports.

Australia is the world's seventeenth largest economy.[1]

Does Your Economy Run a Trade Surplus or a Trade Deficit?

Australia runs a trade deficit of $35.23 billion, giving the country a ranking of 182 out of the 190 countries tracked by the CIA in *The World Factbook*.[2]

What Does Your Economy Export?

Australia exports coal, iron ore, gold, meat, wool, alumina, wheat, machinery, and transport equipment.

---

[1] https://www.cia.gov/library/publications/the-world-factbook/rankorder/2001rank.html.

[2] https://www.cia.gov/library/publications/the-world-factbook/geos/as.html.

According to the World Trade Organization (WTO),[3] Australia exports $154.2 billion in goods and merchandise compared to only $41.2 billion in commercial services. The WTO breaks down those exports as follows:

- Goods and Merchandise
  - Agricultural products: 15.2 percent
  - Fuels and mining products: 56.8 percent
  - Manufactures: 14.9 percent
- Commercial Services
  - Transportation: 12.5 percent
  - Travel: 62.8 percent
  - Other commercial services: 24.6 percent

To Whom Does Your Economy Export?

The WTO ranks the following countries as the top destinations for exports from Australia:

- China: 21.6 percent
- Japan: 19.5 percent
- European Union: 8.7 percent
- South Korea: 8.0 percent
- India: 7.4 percent

What Does Your Economy Import?

Australia imports machinery and transport equipment, computers and office machines, telecommunication equipment and parts, crude oil, and petroleum products.

According to the WTO, the country imports $165.5 billion in goods and merchandise compared to only $41.4 billion in commercial services. The WTO breaks down those imports as follows:

- Goods and Merchandise
  - Agricultural products: 6.2 percent

---

[3] http://stat.wto.org/CountryProfile/WSDBCountryPFView.aspx?Language=E&Country=AU.

- Fuels and mining products: 13.9 percent
- Manufactures: 72.2 percent
- Commercial Services
  - Transportation: 25.3 percent
  - Travel: 44.1 percent
  - Other commercial services: 30.6 percent

From Whom Does Your Economy Import?

The WTO ranks the following countries as the top sources of imports to Australia:

- European Union: 19.7 percent
- China: 17.8 percent
- United States: 11.3 percent
- Japan: 8.3 percent
- Thailand: 5.8 percent

Do You Have an Attractive Government Debt Market?

Australia currently has a Moody's rating of Aaa. It received this latest rating on October 20, 2002. This most recent rating was an upgrade from the Aa2 rating that the country had held previously. This is a positive sign for the country's government debt market.[4]

Do You Have an Attractive Equities Market?

Australia has an attractive equities market. It is the thirteenth largest equities market in the world, with a total market value of $1.258 trillion.[5]

---

[4] http://www.moodys.com/credit-ratings/Australia-credit-rating-600013445.
[5] https://www.cia.gov/library/publications/the-world-factbook/geos/as.html.

Tell Me About Your Central Bank. What Are Its Mandates? How Much Gold and Foreign Currency Reserves Does It Hold?

The Reserve Bank of Australia's (RBA) obligations with respect to monetary policy are laid out in Sections 10(2) and 11(1) of the Reserve Bank Act of 1959. Section 10(2) of the act, which is often referred to as the bank's "charter," says: "It is the duty of the Reserve Bank Board, within the limits of its powers, to ensure that the monetary and banking policy of the Bank is directed to the greatest advantage of the people of Australia and that the powers of the Bank . . . are exercised in such a manner as, in the opinion of the Reserve Bank Board, will best contribute to:

1. The stability of the currency of Australia;
2. The maintenance of full employment in Australia; and
3. The economic prosperity and welfare of the people of Australia."[6]

The RBA has foreign currency reserves of $32,397 million and gold deposits of $3,608 million.[7]

Do You Have an Overinvolved Government That Likes to Intervene in the Forex Market?

The Australian government is not known as an aggressive currency manipulator.

What Economic Announcements Are Important to You?

When you are watching the economic announcements coming out of Australia, make sure that you keep your eye on the following basics:

- Reserve Bank of Australia (RBA) cash rate
- Employment change
- Unemployment rate

[6]http://www.rba.gov.au/about-rba/our-role.html.
[7]http://www.imf.org/external/np/sta/ir/IRProcessWeb/data/aus/eng/curaus.htm.

- Consumer price index (CPI)
- Producer price index (PPI)
- Gross domestic product (GDP)
- Trade balance
- Commodity prices
- Retail sales

Are You a Safe-Haven Currency?

No, the Australian dollar is not considered to be a safe-haven currency.

How Can I Trade You?

You can trade the Australian dollar using any of the following:

- Spot Forex
- Forex futures
- Exchange-traded funds (ETFs)
- Exchange-traded notes (ETNs)
- Spot Forex options
- Exchange-traded Forex options

NEW ZEALAND DOLLAR—THE KIWI

The New Zealand dollar (NZD) is considered to be a major currency in the Forex market. It is also one of the "commodity" currencies because of the economy's dependence on commodity exports.

New Zealand is the world's sixty-second largest economy.[8]

---

[8] https://www.cia.gov/library/publications/the-world-factbook/rankorder/2001rank.html.

Does Your Economy Run a Trade Surplus or a Trade Deficit?

New Zealand runs a trade deficit of $4.5 billion, giving the country a ranking of 168 out of the 190 countries tracked by the CIA in *The World Factbook.*[9]

What Does Your Economy Export?

New Zealand exports dairy products, meat, wood and wood products, fish, and machinery.

According to the World Trade Organization (WTO),[10] New Zealand exports $24.9 billion in goods and merchandise compared to only $7.5 billion in commercial services. The WTO breaks down those exports as follows:

- Goods and Merchandise
  - Agricultural products: 61.8 percent
  - Fuels and mining products: 8.0 percent
  - Manufactures: 25.3 percent
- Commercial Services
  - Transportation: 19.7 percent
  - Travel: 58.9 percent
  - Other commercial services: 21.4 percent

To Whom Does Your Economy Export?

The WTO ranks the following countries as the top destinations for exports from New Zealand:

- Australia: 23.0 percent
- European Union: 13.0 percent
- United States: 10.0 percent
- China: 9.1 percent
- Japan: 7.1 percent

---

[9] https://www.cia.gov/library/publications/the-world-factbook/geos/nz.html.
[10] http://stat.wto.org/CountryProfile/WSDBCountryPFView.aspx?Language=
    E&Country=NZ.

What Does Your Economy Import?

New Zealand imports machinery and equipment, vehicles and aircraft, petroleum, electronics, textiles, and plastics.

According to the WTO, the country imports $25.5 billion in goods and merchandise compared to only $7.7 billion in commercial services. The WTO breaks down those imports as follows:

- Goods and Merchandise
  - Agricultural products: 11.3 percent
  - Fuels and mining products: 16.3 percent
  - Manufactures: 71.4 percent
- Commercial Services
  - Transportation: 28.9 percent
  - Travel: 33.2 percent
  - Other commercial services: 37.9 percent

From Whom Does Your Economy Import?

The WTO ranks the following countries as the top sources of imports to New Zealand:

- Australia: 18.4 percent
- European Union: 17.3 percent
- China: 15.1 percent
- United States: 10.8 percent
- Japan: 7.4 percent

Do You Have an Attractive Government Debt Market?

New Zealand currently has a Moody's rating of Aaa. It received this latest rating on October 20, 2002. This most recent rating was an upgrade from the Aa2 rating that the country had held previously. This is a positive sign for the country's government debt market.[11]

---

[11] http://www.moodys.com/credit-ratings/New-Zealand-credit-rating-600013482.

Do You Have an Attractive Equities Market?

New Zealand has an attractive equities market, but it is not very large. It is the fifty-eighth largest equities market in the world, with a total market value of $67.06 billion.[12]

Tell Me About Your Central Bank. What Are Its Mandates? How Much Gold and Foreign Currency Reserves Does It Hold?

The Reserve Bank of New Zealand (RBNZ) uses monetary policy to maintain price stability as defined in the Policy Targets Agreement (PTA). The current PTA requires the bank to keep inflation between 1 and 3 percent on average over the medium term. The bank implements monetary policy by setting the Official Cash Rate (OCR), which is reviewed eight times a year.[13]

The RBNZ has foreign currency reserves of $13,835 million and no gold deposits.[14]

Do You Have an Overinvolved Government That Likes to Intervene in the Forex Market?

The New Zealand government is not known as an aggressive currency manipulator.

What Economic Announcements Are Important to You?

When you are watching the economic announcements coming out of New Zealand, make sure that you keep your eye on the following:

- Reserve Bank of New Zealand Official Cash Rate
- Employment

---

[12] https://www.cia.gov/library/publications/the-world-factbook/geos/nz.html.

[13] http://www.rbnz.govt.nz/monpol/index.html.

[14] http://www.imf.org/external/np/sta/ir/IRProcessWeb/data/nzl/eng/curnzl.htm.

- Consumer price index (CPI)
- Gross domestic product (GDP)
- Trade balance
- Retail sales
- NZIER (New Zealand Institute of Economic Research) Business Confidence
- NBNZ (National Bank of New Zealand) Business Confidence

Are You a Safe-Haven Currency?

No, the New Zealand dollar is not considered to be a safe-haven currency.

How Can I Trade You?

You can trade the New Zealand dollar using any of the following:

- Spot Forex
- Forex futures
- Exchange-traded funds (ETFs)
- Spot Forex options
- Exchange-traded Forex options

SOUTH AFRICAN RAND

The South African rand (ZAR) is considered to be an exotic currency in the Forex market. It is also one of the "commodity" currencies because of the economy's dependence on commodity exports.

South Africa is the world's twenty-fifth largest economy.[15]

---

[15]https://www.cia.gov/library/publications/the-world-factbook/rankorder/ 2001rank.html.

Does Your Economy Run a Trade Surplus or a Trade Deficit?

South Africa runs a trade deficit of $16.51 billion, giving the country a ranking of 178 out of the 190 countries tracked by the CIA in *The World Factbook*.[16]

What Does Your Economy Export?

South Africa exports gold, diamonds, platinum, other metals and minerals, machinery, and equipment.

According to the World Trade Organization (WTO),[17] South Africa exports $62.6 billion in goods and merchandise compared to only $14.3 billion in commercial services. The WTO breaks down those exports as follows:

- Goods and Merchandise
  - Agricultural products: 10.7 percent
  - Fuels and mining products: 34.8 percent
  - Manufactures: 51.8 percent
- Commercial Services
  - Transportation: 11.8 percent
  - Travel: 65.5 percent
  - Other commercial services: 22.7 percent

To Whom Does Your Economy Export?

The WTO ranks the following countries as the top destinations for exports from South Africa:

- European Union: 26.5 percent
- China: 10.5 percent
- United States: 9.0 percent
- Japan: 7.6 percent
- Switzerland: 4.2 percent

---

[16] https://www.cia.gov/library/publications/the-world-factbook/geos/sf.html.
[17] http://stat.wto.org/CountryProfile/WSDBCountryPFView.aspx?Language=E&Country=ZA.

What Does Your Economy Import?

South Africa imports machinery, equipment, chemicals, petroleum products, scientific instruments, and foodstuffs.

According to the WTO, the country imports $73.2 billion in goods and merchandise compared to only $14.3 billion in commercial services. The WTO breaks down those imports as follows:

- Goods and Merchandise
  - Agricultural products: 7.4 percent
  - Fuels and mining products: 23.3 percent
  - Manufactures: 68.3 percent
- Commercial Services
  - Transportation: 41.2 percent
  - Travel: 28.9 percent
  - Other commercial services: 29.9 percent

From Whom Does Your Economy Import?

The WTO ranks the following countries as the top sources of imports to South Africa:

- European Union: 32.2 percent
- China: 13.1 percent
- United States: 7.8 percent
- Saudi Arabia: 5.0 percent
- Japan: 4.9 percent

Do You Have an Attractive Government Debt Market?

South Africa currently has a Moody's rating of A1. It received this latest rating on July 16, 2009. This most recent rating was an upgrade from the A3 rating that the country had held previously. This is a positive sign for the country's government debt market.[18]

---

[18]http://www.moodys.com/credit-ratings/South-Africa-credit-rating-600014299.

Do You Have an Attractive Equities Market?

South Africa has an attractive equities market. It is the eighteenth largest equities market in the world, with a total market value of $704.8 billion.[19]

Tell Me About Your Central Bank. What Are Its Mandates? How Much Gold and Foreign Currency Reserves Does It Hold?

The South African Reserve Bank (the SARB) is the central bank of the Republic of South Africa. It regards its primary goal in the South African economic system as "the achievement and maintenance of price stability."[20]

The South African Reserve Bank has foreign currency reserves of $35,427 million and gold deposits of $5,654 million.[21]

Do You Have an Overinvolved Government That Likes to Intervene in the Forex Market?

The South African government is not known as an aggressive currency manipulator.

What Economic Announcements Are Important to You?

When you are watching the economic announcements coming out of South Africa, make sure that you keep your eye on the following:

- Interest rates
- Employment
- Inflation
- Gross domestic product (GDP)
- Trade balance

---

[19] https://www.cia.gov/library/publications/the-world-factbook/geos/sf.html.
[20] http://www.reservebank.co.za/.
[21] http://www.imf.org/external/np/sta/ir/IRProcessWeb/data/zaf/eng/curzaf.htm.

Are You a Safe-Haven Currency?

No, the South African rand is not considered to be a safe-haven currency.

How Can I Trade You?

You can trade the South African rand using any of the following:

- Spot Forex
- Forex futures
- Exchange-traded funds (ETFs)
- Spot Forex options
- Exchange-traded Forex options

CHAPTER 9

Currencies of Eastern Europe

RUSSIAN RUBLE

The Russian ruble (RUB) is considered to be an exotic currency in the Forex market.

The Russian Federation is the world's sixth largest economy.[1]

Does Your Economy Run a Trade Surplus or a Trade Deficit?

The Russian Federation runs a trade surplus of $68.85 billion, giving the country a ranking of 4 out of the 190 countries tracked by the CIA in *The World Factbook*.[2]

What Does Your Economy Export?

The Russian Federation exports petroleum and petroleum products, natural gas, metals, wood and wood products, chemicals, and a wide variety of civilian and military manufactures.

---

[1] https://www.cia.gov/library/publications/the-world-factbook/rankorder/2001rank.html.

[2] https://www.cia.gov/library/publications/the-world-factbook/geos/rs.html.

According to the World Trade Organization (WTO),[3] the Russian Federation exports $303.4 billion in goods and merchandise compared to only $41.2 billion in commercial services. The WTO breaks down those exports as follows:

- Goods and Merchandise
  - Agricultural products: 6.9 percent
  - Fuels and mining products: 69.0 percent
  - Manufactures: 21.1 percent
- Commercial Services
  - Transportation: 30.0 percent
  - Travel: 22.8 percent
  - Other commercial services: 47.2 percent

To Whom Does Your Economy Export?

The WTO ranks the following countries as the top destinations for exports from the Russian Federation:

- European Union: 45.9 percent
- China: 5.6 percent
- Turkey: 3.6 percent
- Ukraine: 3.4 percent
- Kazakhstan: 3.1 percent

What Does Your Economy Import?

The Russian Federation imports machinery, vehicles, pharmaceutical products, plastic, semifinished metal products, meat, fruits and nuts, optical instruments, medical instruments, iron, and steel.

According to the WTO, the country imports $191.8 billion in goods and merchandise compared to only $59.4 billion in commercial services. The WTO breaks down those imports as follows:

---

[3] http://stat.wto.org/CountryProfile/WSDBCountryPFView.aspx?Language=E&Country=RU.

- Goods and Merchandise
  - Agricultural products: 15.2 percent
  - Fuels and mining products: 3.8 percent
  - Manufactures: 79.8 percent
- Commercial Services
  - Transportation: 15.9 percent
  - Travel: 35.0 percent
  - Other commercial services: 49.1 percent

From Whom Does Your Economy Import?

The WTO ranks the following countries as the top sources of imports to the Russian Federation:

- European Union: 45.2 percent
- China: 14.2 percent
- Ukraine: 5.6 percent
- United States: 5.4 percent
- Japan: 4.5 percent

Do You Have an Attractive Government Debt Market?

The Russian Federation currently has a Moody's rating of A2. It received this latest rating on May 24, 2006. This most recent rating was an upgrade from the Baa1 rating that the country had held previously. This is a positive sign for the country's government debt market.[4]

Do You Have an Attractive Equities Market?

The Russian Federation has an attractive, yet volatile, equities market. It is the seventh largest equities market in the world, with a total market value of $861.4 billion.[5]

---

[4] http://www.moodys.com/credit-ratings/Russia-credit-rating-600018920.
[5] https://www.cia.gov/library/publications/the-world-factbook/geos/rs.html.

Tell Me About Your Central Bank. What Are Its Mandates? How Much Gold and Foreign Currency Reserves Does It Hold?

Under Article 75 of the Russian Constitution, the principal function of the Bank of Russia is to protect the ruble and guarantee its stability.[6]

The Central Bank of Russia has foreign currency reserves of $426,029 million and gold deposits of $35,788 million.[7]

Do You Have an Overinvolved Government That Likes to Intervene in the Forex Market?

The Russian Federation government has been known to intervene in the currency market from time to time.

What Economic Announcements Are Important to You?

When you are watching the economic announcements coming out of the Russian Federation, make sure that you keep your eye on the following:

- Interest rates
- Employment
- Inflation
- Gross domestic product (GDP)
- Trade balance

Are You a Safe-Haven Currency?

No, the Russian ruble is not considered to be a safe-haven currency.

---

[6] http://www.cbr.ru/eng/today/status_functions/.
[7] http://www.imf.org/external/np/sta/ir/IRProcessWeb/data/ind/eng/curind.htm.

How Can I Trade You?

You can trade the Russian ruble using any of the following:

- Spot Forex
- Forex futures
- Exchange-traded funds (ETFs)

POLISH ZLOTY

The Polish zloty (PLN) is considered to be an exotic currency in the Forex market.

Poland is the world's twentieth largest economy.[8]

Does Your Economy Run a Trade Surplus or a Trade Deficit?

Poland runs a trade deficit of $12.33 billion, giving the country a ranking of 177 out of the 190 countries tracked by the CIA in *The World Factbook*.[9]

What Does Your Economy Export?

Poland exports machinery, transport equipment, intermediate manufactured goods, miscellaneous manufactured goods, food, and live animals.

According to the World Trade Organization (WTO),[10] Poland exports $134.5 billion in goods and merchandise compared to only $28.8 billion in commercial services. The WTO breaks down those exports as follows:

- Goods and Merchandise
  - Agricultural products: 12.3 percent
  - Fuels and mining products: 6.7 percent
  - Manufactures: 80.8 percent

---

[8] https://www.cia.gov/library/publications/the-world-factbook/rankorder/2001rank.html.

[9] https://www.cia.gov/library/publications/the-world-factbook/geos/pl.html.

[10] http://stat.wto.org/CountryProfile/WSDBCountryPFView.aspx?Language=E&Country=PL.

- Commercial Services
  - Transportation: 30.1 percent
  - Travel: 31.3 percent
  - Other commercial services: 38.7 percent

To Whom Does Your Economy Export?

The WTO ranks the following countries as the top destinations for exports from Poland:

- European Union: 77.9 percent
- Russian Federation: 5.2 percent
- Ukraine: 3.7 percent
- Norway: 1.7 percent
- United States: 1.4 percent

What Does Your Economy Import?

Poland imports machinery, chemicals, semifinished goods, fuels, and transport equipment.

According to the WTO, the country imports $146.6 billion in goods and merchandise compared to only $23.7 billion in commercial services. The WTO breaks down those imports as follows:

- Goods and Merchandise
  - Agricultural products: 9.7 percent
  - Fuels and mining products: 12.4 percent
  - Manufactures: 75.3 percent
- Commercial Services
  - Transportation: 21.8 percent
  - Travel: 30.9 percent
  - Other commercial services: 47.3 percent

From Whom Does Your Economy Import?

The WTO ranks the following countries as the top sources of imports to Poland:

- European Union: 62.0 percent
- Russian Federation: 9.8 percent
- China: 8.0 percent
- South Korea: 2.5 percent
- United States: 2.2 percent

Do You Have an Attractive Government Debt Market?

Poland currently has a Moody's rating of Aa1. It received this latest rating on May 24, 2006. This most recent rating was an upgrade from the A2 rating that the country had held previously. This is a positive sign for the country's government debt market.[11]

Do You Have an Attractive Equities Market?

Poland has an attractive equities market, but it is not very large. It is the thirty-ninth largest equities market in the world, with a total market value of $135.3 billion.[12]

Tell Me About Your Central Bank. What Are Its Mandates? How Much Gold and Foreign Currency Reserves Does It Hold?

The basic objective of the monetary policy of the National Bank of Poland is maintaining price stability.[13]

The National Bank of Poland has foreign currency reserves of $81,431 million and gold deposits of $4,666 million.[14]

---

[11] http://www.moodys.com/credit-ratings/Poland-credit-rating-600016274.

[12] https://www.cia.gov/library/publications/the-world-factbook/geos/pl.html.

[13] http://www.nbp.pl/homen.aspx?f=/en/onbp/informacje/polityka_pieniezna.html.

[14] http://www.imf.org/external/np/sta/ir/IRProcessWeb/data/pol/eng/curpol.htm.

Do You Have an Overinvolved Government That Likes to Intervene in the Forex Market?

The Polish government has been known to intervene in the currency market from time to time.

What Economic Announcements Are Important to You?

When you are watching the economic announcements coming out of Poland, make sure that you keep your eye on the following:

- Interest rates
- Employment
- Inflation
- Gross domestic product (GDP)
- Trade balance

Are You a Safe-Haven Currency?

No, the Polish zloty is not considered to be a safe-haven currency.

How Can I Trade You?

You can trade the Polish zloty using either of the following:

- Spot Forex
- Forex futures

TURKISH NEW LIRA

The Turkish new lira (TRY) is considered to be an exotic currency in the Forex market.

Turkey is the world's sixteenth largest economy.[15]

---

[15] https://www.cia.gov/library/publications/the-world-factbook/rankorder/2001rank.html.

Does Your Economy Run a Trade Surplus or a Trade Deficit?

Turkey runs a trade deficit of $38.82 billion, giving the country a ranking of 183 out of the 190 countries tracked by the CIA in *The World Factbook*.[16]

What Does Your Economy Export?

Turkey exports apparel, foodstuffs, textiles, metal manufactures, and transport equipment.

According to the World Trade Organization (WTO),[17] Turkey exports $102.1 billion in goods and merchandise compared to only $32.8 billion in commercial services. The WTO breaks down those exports as follows:

- Goods and Merchandise
  - Agricultural products: 10.7 percent
  - Fuels and mining products: 6.9 percent
  - Manufactures: 76.5 percent
- Commercial Services
  - Transportation: 23.1 percent
  - Travel: 64.9 percent
  - Other commercial services: 12.0 percent

To Whom Does Your Economy Export?

The WTO ranks the following countries as the top destinations for exports from Turkey:

- European Union: 46.8 percent
- Iraq: 5.0 percent
- Switzerland: 3.9 percent
- United States: 3.2 percent
- Russian Federation: 3.1 percent

---

[16] https://www.cia.gov/library/publications/the-world-factbook/geos/tu.html.
[17] http://stat.wto.org/CountryProfile/WSDBCountryPFView.aspx?Language=E&Country=TR.

What Does Your Economy Import?

Turkey imports machinery, chemicals, semifinished goods, fuels, and transport equipment.

According to the WTO, the country imports $141 billion in goods and merchandise compared to only $15.6 billion in commercial services. The WTO breaks down those imports as follows:

- Goods and Merchandise
  - Agricultural products: 6.8 percent
  - Fuels and mining products: 26.7 percent
  - Manufactures: 63.5 percent
- Commercial Services
  - Transportation: 41.9 percent
  - Travel: 26.6 percent
  - Other commercial services: 31.5 percent

From Whom Does Your Economy Import?

The WTO ranks the following countries as the top sources of imports to Turkey:

- European Union: 40.2 percent
- Russian Federation: 14.0 percent
- China: 9.0 percent
- United States: 6.1 percent
- Iran: 2.4 percent

Do You Have an Attractive Government Debt Market?

Turkey currently has a Moody's rating of Ba1. It received this latest rating on May 24, 2006. This most recent rating was an upgrade from the Ba3 rating that the country had held previously. This is a positive sign for the country's government debt market.[18]

---

[18] http://www.moodys.com/credit-ratings/Turkey-credit-rating-600013493.

Do You Have an Attractive Equities Market?

Turkey has an attractive equities market, but it is not very large. It is the thirty-third largest equities market in the world, with a total market value of $225.7 billion.[19]

Tell Me About Your Central Bank. What Are Its Mandates? How Much Gold and Foreign Currency Reserves Does It Hold?

The primary objective of the Central Bank of the Republic of Turkey is to achieve and maintain price stability.[20]

The Central Bank of the Republic of Turkey has foreign currency reserves of $79,042 million and gold deposits of $5,258 million.[21]

Do You Have an Overinvolved Government That Likes to Intervene in the Forex Market?

The Turkish government is not known as an aggressive currency manipulator.

What Economic Announcements Are Important to You?

When you are watching the economic announcements coming out of Turkey, make sure that you keep your eye on the following:

- Interest rates
- Employment
- Inflation
- Gross domestic product (GDP)
- Trade balance

---

[19] https://www.cia.gov/library/publications/the-world-factbook/geos/tu.html.
[20] http://www.tcmb.gov.tr/yeni/eng/.
[21] http://www.imf.org/external/np/sta/ir/IRProcessWeb/data/tur/eng/curtur.htm.

Are You a Safe-Haven Currency?

No, the Turkish new lira is not considered to be a safe-haven currency.

How Can I Trade You?

You can trade the Turkish new lira using either of the following:

- Spot Forex
- Forex futures

HUNGARIAN FORINT

The Hungarian forint (HUF) is considered to be an exotic currency in the Forex market.

Hungary is the world's fifty-fourth largest economy.[22]

Does Your Economy Run a Trade Surplus or a Trade Deficit?

Hungary runs a trade deficit of $631 million, giving the country a ranking of 124 out of the 190 countries tracked by the CIA in *The World Factbook*.[23]

What Does Your Economy Export?

Hungary exports machinery, equipment, food products, raw materials, fuels, and electricity.

According to the World Trade Organization (WTO),[24] Hungary exports $83.8 million in goods and merchandise compared to only $18.1 million in commercial services. The WTO breaks down those exports as follows:

---

[22] https://www.cia.gov/library/publications/the-world-factbook/rankorder/2001rank.html.

[23] https://www.cia.gov/library/publications/the-world-factbook/geos/hu.html.

[24] http://stat.wto.org/CountryProfile/WSDBCountryPFView.aspx?Language=E&Country=HU.

- Goods and Merchandise
  - Agricultural products: 8.4 percent
  - Fuels and mining products: 3.9 percent
  - Manufactures: 85.6 percent
- Commercial Services
  - Transportation: 18.9 percent
  - Travel: 31.6 percent
  - Other commercial services: 49.5 percent

To Whom Does Your Economy Export?

The WTO ranks the following countries as the top destinations for exports from Hungary:

- European Union: 78.3 percent
- Russian Federation: 3.6 percent
- United States: 2.3 percent
- Ukraine: 2.0 percent
- Croatia: 1.6 percent

What Does Your Economy Import?

Hungary imports machinery, equipment, fuels, electricity, food products, and raw materials.

According to the WTO, the country imports $78.2 million in goods and merchandise compared to only $15.9 million in commercial services. The WTO breaks down those imports as follows:

- Goods and Merchandise
  - Agricultural products: 6.6 percent
  - Fuels and mining products: 13.1 percent
  - Manufactures: 78.9 percent
- Commercial Services
  - Transportation: 18.0 percent
  - Travel: 22.8 percent
  - Other commercial services: 59.2 percent

From Whom Does Your Economy Import?

The WTO ranks the following countries as the top sources of imports to Hungary:

- European Union: 68.3 percent
- Russian Federation: 9.3 percent
- China: 5.6 percent
- Japan: 2.6 percent
- United States: 1.8 percent

Do You Have an Attractive Government Debt Market?

Hungary currently has a Moody's rating of A1. It received this latest rating on December 6, 2010. Unfortunately for Hungary, this most recent rating was a downgrade from the Aa2 rating that the country had held previously. This is not a positive sign for the country's government debt market.[25]

Do You Have an Attractive Equities Market?

Hungary has a small equities market. In fact, it is the sixty-third largest equities market in the world, with a total market value of $28.29 billion.[26]

Tell Me About Your Central Bank. What Are Its Mandates? How Much Gold and Foreign Currency Reserves Does It Hold?

The most important objective of economic policy as a whole is to ensure stable economic growth that is sustainable over the long term. To this end, the central bank keeps inflation at a low level through pursuing a predictable and credible monetary policy. This is what also underlies the Central Bank Act, which stipulates that

---

[25] http://www.moodys.com/credit-ratings/Hungary-credit-rating-600013466.
[26] https://www.cia.gov/library/publications/the-world-factbook/geos/hu.html.

"the primary objective of the MNB [Magyar Nemzeti Bank] shall be to achieve and maintain price stability," in line with EU regulations and international practice, and the bank is gaining ground to a growing extent.[27]

The Magyar Nemzeti Bank has foreign currency reserves of $43,154 million and gold deposits of $139 million.[28]

Do You Have an Overinvolved Government That Likes to Intervene in the Forex Market?

The Hungarian government is not known as an aggressive currency manipulator.

What Economic Announcements Are Important to You?

When you are watching the economic announcements coming out of Hungary, make sure that you keep your eye on the following:

- Interest rates
- Employment
- Inflation
- Gross domestic product (GDP)
- Trade balance

Are You a Safe-Haven Currency?

No, the Hungarian forint is not considered to be a safe-haven currency.

How Can I Trade You?

You can trade the Hungarian forint using either of the following:

- Spot Forex
- Forex futures

---

[27] http://english.mnb.hu/Monetaris_politika.
[28] http://www.imf.org/external/np/sta/ir/IRProcessWeb/data/hun/eng/curhun.htm.

CZECH KORUNA

The Czech koruna (CZK) is considered to be an exotic currency in the Forex market.

The Czech Republic is the world's forty-fourth largest economy.[29]

Does Your Economy Run a Trade Surplus or a Trade Deficit?

The Czech Republic runs a trade deficit of $5.956 billion, giving the country a ranking of 171 out of the 190 countries tracked by the CIA in *The World Factbook*.[30]

What Does Your Economy Export?

The Czech Republic exports machinery and transportation equipment, raw materials, fuel, and chemicals.

According to the World Trade Organization (WTO),[31] the Czech Republic exports $113.4 billion in goods and merchandise compared to only $20.3 billion in commercial services. The WTO breaks down those exports as follows:

- Goods and Merchandise
  - Agricultural products: 6.1 percent
  - Fuels and mining products: 5.3 percent
  - Manufactures: 88.3 percent
- Commercial Services
  - Transportation: 26.9 percent
  - Travel: 31.9 percent
  - Other commercial services: 41.1 percent

---

[29] https://www.cia.gov/library/publications/the-world-factbook/rankorder/2001rank.html.

[30] https://www.cia.gov/library/publications/the-world-factbook/geos/ez.html.

[31] http://stat.wto.org/CountryProfile/WSDBCountryPFView.aspx?Language=E&Country=CZ.

To Whom Does Your Economy Export?

The WTO ranks the following countries as the top destinations for exports from the Czech Republic:

- European Union: 84.7 percent
- Russian Federation: 2.3 percent
- Switzerland: 1.6 percent
- United States: 1.6 percent
- China: 0.7 percent

What Does Your Economy Import?

The Czech Republic imports machinery and transportation equipment, raw materials, fuel, and chemicals.

According to the WTO, the country imports $105.2 billion in goods and merchandise compared to only $18.9 billion in commercial services. The WTO breaks down those imports as follows:

- Goods and Merchandise
  - Agricultural products: 7.7 percent
  - Fuels and mining products: 12.3 percent
  - Manufactures: 79.8 percent
- Commercial Services
  - Transportation: 21.2 percent
  - Travel: 21.6 percent
  - Other commercial services: 57.2 percent

From Whom Does Your Economy Import?

The WTO ranks the following countries as the top sources of imports to the Czech Republic:

- European Union: 66.9 percent
- China: 10.1 percent
- Russian Federation: 5.1 percent
- Japan: 3.1 percent
- United States: 2.1 percent

Do You Have an Attractive Government Debt Market?

The Czech Republic currently has a Moody's rating of Aa1. It received this latest rating on May 24, 2006. This most recent rating was an upgrade from the A1 rating that the country had held previously. This is a positive sign for the country's government debt market.[32]

Do You Have an Attractive Equities Market?

The Czech Republic has an attractive equities market, but it is not very large. It is the fifty-third largest equities market in the world, with a total market value of $52.69 billion.[33]

Tell Me About Your Central Bank. What Are Its Mandates? How Much Gold and Foreign Currency Reserves Does It Hold?

According to the Czech Constitution and the Act on the Czech National Bank (CNB), the CNB's primary objective is to maintain price stability. Without prejudice to its primary objective, the CNB also supports the general economic policies of the government. The CNB achieves its primary objective, price stability, by making changes in key interest rates. The interest-rate decisions of the CNB Bank Board are based on the current macroeconomic forecast and an assessment of the risks to its fulfillment. Upon the Czech Republic's entry into the euro area, the CNB will cede its independent monetary policy to the European Central Bank.[34]

The Czech National Bank has foreign currency reserves of $39,284 million and gold deposits of $584 million.[35]

---

[32] http://www.moodys.com/credit-ratings/Czech-Republic-credit-rating-600013456.

[33] https://www.cia.gov/library/publications/the-world-factbook/geos/ez.html.

[34] http://www.cnb.cz/en/monetary_policy/.

[35] http://www.imf.org/external/np/sta/ir/IRProcessWeb/data/cze/eng/curcze.htm.

Do You Have an Overinvolved Government That Likes to Intervene in the Forex Market?

The Czech Republic is not known for being an aggressive currency manipulator.

What Economic Announcements Are Important to You?

When you are watching the economic announcements coming out of the Czech Republic, make sure that you keep your eye on the following:

- Interest rates
- Employment
- Inflation
- Gross domestic product (GDP)
- Trade balance

Are You a Safe-Haven Currency?

No, the Czech koruna is not considered to be a safe-haven currency.

How Can I Trade You?

You can trade the Czech koruna using either of the following:

- Spot Forex
- Forex futures

Navigating the Economic Calendar

ECONOMIC ANNOUNCEMENTS DRIVE FUNDAMENTAL OUTLOOKS

Forex traders keep a close watch on the economic calendar because they know that economic announcements provide the data that analysts and traders use to develop their outlooks on where they believe currency values are going to move in the future.

The nice part about the economic calendar is that the announcements are scheduled months in advance, so that everybody knows precisely which announcements are going to be released and when each announcement is going to be made. For instance, the U.S. government doesn't just decide one morning that it needs to announce the unemployment rate for the previous month. Instead, it develops a schedule and makes sure that everyone is aware of that schedule. After all, there are enough surprises that come out of these economic announcements. We don't need to be surprised by the timing as well.

If you take a look at any economic calendar, you will see announcements ranging from central bank interest rates to natural gas storage levels. Naturally, some economic announcements are more important than others. So to help you identify what you should be paying the most attention to, we will be covering the following announcements:

- Interest rates
- Employment
- Inflation
- Economic growth (GDP)
- Trade balance
- Foreign investment
- Consumer confidence
- Retail sales
- Business confidence
- Manufacturing
- Housing

Knowing which announcements to pay attention to is only half of the equation. You also need to know what you are looking for when you analyze an announcement. When you evaluate any economic announcement, you should be asking yourself how the announcement will affect expectations for the following five drivers of currency prices:

- Trade flows
- Investment flows
- Money supply
- Investor fear
- Government interventions

Unfortunately, there is no cut-and-dried method for calculating the impact that an economic announcement will have on any one of these five price drivers. When evaluating economic announcements, there is always room for interpretation. With that in mind, we are going to outline a few scenarios for each announcement to help you better understand the linear thought process that you need to go through when you analyze an announcement. The scenarios will walk through a series of cause-and-effect relationships that will look like this:

Rising Interest Rates → Increased Investment Flows → Increased Demand for the Currency → Increase in Value of the Currency → Less Competitive Exports → Decrease in Trade Flows

The "→" in these cause-and-effect relationships is shorthand for the phrase "lead(s) to" or "which leads to." So you would read the previous relationship as follows: rising interest rates lead to increased investment flows, which leads to increased demand for the currency, which leads to an increase in the value of the currency, which leads to less competitive exports, which ultimately leads to a decrease in trade flows.

Now that we know what we're looking for, let's get familiar with the major economic announcements that are going to be part of your Forex investing life from here on out. One thing you will notice as we go through this section is that it is fairly U.S.-centric. However, most of the concepts apply universally across various countries. And one more thing: if you have an economic calendar that you already use and are happy with, that's great. However, if you are interested in checking out some different calendars, here are a few that we think are worthy of your time:

- Forex Factory: www.Forexfactory.com/calendar.php (our personal favorite)
- FX Street: www.fxstreet.com/nou/continguts/economicalcal. asp
- Forex Economic Calendar: www.Forexeconomiccalendar.com

INTEREST RATES

The interest-rate announcement specifies the short-term target rate that the central bank will try to maintain in the future. Interest rates are one of the most important economic announcements on the calendar because the interest rate that a central bank sets for its economy has ripple effects that spread far and wide. You will also notice that many of the other economic announcements that we discuss gain some of their importance from the impact they have on a central bank's decision-making process when it sets interest rates.

Interest-rate data are released in one key announcement that you need to watch:

Central bank interest-rate announcements: Official announcements from a central bank stating what the

target short-term interest rate for the economy is going to
be

Impact on Trade Flows

Rising Interest Rates → Increased Investment Flows → Increased
Demand for Currency → Increase in Value of Currency → Less
Competitive Exports → Decrease in Trade Flows

Falling Interest Rates → Decreased Investment Flows →
Decreased Demand for Currency → Decrease in Value of
Currency → More Competitive Exports → Increase in Trade
Flows

Impact on Investment Flows

Rising Interest Rates → More Attractive Investment Returns →
Increased Investment Flows

Falling Interest Rates → Less Attractive Investment Returns →
Decreased Investment Flows

Impact on Money Supply

Rising Interest Rates → Decrease in the Money Supply
(see discussion of repos in Chapter 2)

Falling Interest Rates → Increase in the Money Supply
(see discussion of reverse repos in Chapter 2)

Impact on Investor Fear

Raising Interest Rates (When Inflation Is Rising) → Confident
Investors

Not Raising Interest Rates (When Inflation Is Rising) → Nervous Investors

Lowering Interest Rates (When the Economy Is Slowing) → Confident Investors

Not Lowering Interest Rates (When the Economy Is Slowing) → Nervous Investors

Typical Impact on the Currency

Rising Interest Rates → Stronger Currency

Falling Interest Rates → Weaker Currency

EMPLOYMENT

Employment announcements report on the number of new jobs that have been created in an economy and the percentage of workers who are unemployed. The employment announcements rank right up there with interest-rate announcements in terms of importance.

Employment data are released in multiple announcements every month. Here are the ones you are going to want to pay attention to (in order of importance):

1. **Nonfarm payrolls:** The number of new jobs not related to farming that were created during the previous month.
2. **Unemployment rate:** The percentage of the population that is actively looking for work but has been unable to find it.
3. **Weekly initial unemployment claims:** The number of people who applied for unemployment benefits for the first time during the previous week.
4. **ADP National Employment Report:** The number of new jobs that are not related to farming that were created during the previous month, according to payment-processing company ADP. This number is released two

days before the official nonfarm payrolls number from the Bureau of Labor Statistics (BLS).

Impact on Trade Flows

Rising Unemployment → Less Money in Consumers' Pockets → Decreased Demand for Imports

Falling Unemployment → More Money in Consumers' Pockets → Increased Demand for Imports

Impact on Investment Flows

Rising Unemployment → Central Bank Lowering Interest Rates to Stimulate the Economy → Lower-Yielding Government Debt Market → Decreased Investment Flows

Declining Unemployment → Central Bank Raising Interest Rates to Prevent the Economy From Overheating → Higher-Yielding Government Debt Market → Increased Investment Flows

Impact on Money Supply

Rising Unemployment → Central Bank Lowering Interest Rates to Stimulate the Economy → Increase in the Money Supply

Declining Unemployment → Central Bank Raising Interest Rates to Prevent the Economy From Overheating → Decrease in the Money Supply

Impact on Investor Fear

Rising Unemployment → Nervous Investors

Declining Unemployment → Confident Investors

Typical Impact on the Currency

Rising Unemployment → Weaker Currency

Falling Unemployment → Stronger Currency

INFLATION

Inflation announcements report on how quickly or slowly the general price level in the economy is rising. Monitoring inflation is important because inflation erodes buying power. Rising inflation is a sign that an economy may be expanding too rapidly. Falling inflation is a sign that an economy may be contracting too sharply.

Inflation data are released in a few different announcements, and it is important that you pay attention to each of them. Here are the three most important inflation announcements that you need to watch:

1. **Consumer price index (CPI):** Measurement of the price changes in a basket of goods and services that retail consumers purchase
2. **Personal consumption expenditures (PCE):** Another measurement of the price changes in goods and services that retail consumers purchase
3. **Producer price index (PPI):** Measurement of the price changes in goods and services that businesses purchase

Impact on Trade Flows

Rising Inflation → Less Money in Consumers' Pockets → Decreased Demand for Imports

Falling Inflation → More Money in Consumers' Pockets → Increased Demand for Imports

Impact on Investment Flows

Rising Inflation → Weakening Currency → Loss of Value of Domestic Assets for Foreign Investors → Decreased Investment Flows

Declining Inflation → Stabilizing Currency → No Loss of Value of Domestic Assets for Foreign Investors → Stable Investment Flows

Impact on Money Supply

Rising Inflation → Central Bank Raising Interest Rates to Prevent the Economy From Overheating → Decrease in the Money Supply

Declining Inflation → Central Bank Lowering Interest Rates to Stimulate the Economy → Increase in the Money Supply

Impact on Investor Fear

Rising Inflation → Nervous Investors

Declining Inflation → Confident Investors

Typical Impact on the Currency

Rising Inflation → Weaker Currency

Falling Inflation → Stronger Currency

ECONOMIC GROWTH: GROSS DOMESTIC PRODUCT (GDP)

Economic growth announcements report on how well a country's economy is doing. Economies can move in one of three directions: they can be growing, they can be stagnating, or they can be contracting. When an economy is growing, everything within the economy is able to function normally and profitably. When an economy is stagnating or contracting, however, all sorts of problems start to emerge, and the country's currency typically suffers.

Economic growth data are released in one key announcement that you need to watch:

- **Gross domestic product (GDP):** Measurement of the total economic output of a country

Impact on Trade Flows

Expanding Economy → More Money in Consumers' Pockets → Increased Demand for Imports

Contracting Economy → Less Money in Consumers' Pockets → Decreased Demand for Imports

Impact on Investment Flows

Expanding Economy → Profitable Companies → Bullish Stock Market → Increased Investment Flows

Expanding Economy → Rising Inflation → Higher Interest Rates → Attractive Government Debt Market → Increased Investment Flows

Contracting Economy → Struggling Companies → Bearish Stock Market → Decreased Investment Flows

Contracting Economy → Falling Inflation → Lower Interest Rates → Less Attractive Government Debt Market → Decreased Investment Flows

Impact on Money Supply

Expanding Economy → Central Bank Raising Interest Rates to Prevent the Economy From Overheating → Decrease in the Money Supply

Contracting Economy → Central Bank Lowering Interest Rates to Stimulate the Economy → Increase in the Money Supply

Impact on Investor Fear

Expanding Economy → Confident Investors

Contracting Economy → Nervous Investors

Typical Impact on the Currency

Expanding Economy → Stronger Currency

Contracting Economy → Weaker Currency

TRADE BALANCE

Trade balance announcements report on how much a country is exporting compared to how much it is importing. Countries that export more than they import have trade surpluses, while countries that import more than they export have trade deficits.

If you were to ask the leaders of any government whether they would rather have a trade surplus or a trade deficit, they would all choose a trade surplus. Unfortunately, not every country can export more than it imports. Some countries are net exporters, and other countries are net importers. Watching changes in the level of exports and imports, however, can give you a good idea as to how strong or weak the currency is going to be in the future.

Trade balance data are released in one key announcement that you need to watch:

Trade balance: Measurement of a country's exports compared to its imports

Impact on Trade Flows

Widening Trade Surplus (Due to Increased Exports) = Increase in Trade Flows

Widening Trade Surplus (Due to Decreased Imports) = Decrease in Trade Flows

Shrinking Trade Surplus (Due to Decreased Exports) = Decrease in Trade Flows

Shrinking Trade Surplus (Due to Increased Imports) = Increase in Trade Flows

Widening Trade Deficit (Due to Increased Imports) = Increase in Trade Flows

Widening Trade Deficit (Due to Decreased Exports) = Decrease in Trade Flows

Shrinking Trade Deficit (Due to Increased Exports) = Increase in Trade Flows

Shrinking Trade Deficit (Due to Decreased Imports) = Decrease in Trade Flows

Impact on Investment Flows

Widening Trade Surplus → Widening Imbalance in the Balance of Payments → Decrease in Investment Flows

Shrinking Trade Surplus → Widening Imbalance in the Balance of Payments → Increase in Investment Flows (Sometimes Driven by a Hike in Interest Rates)

Widening Trade Deficit → Widening Imbalance in the Balance of Payments → Increase in Investment Flows (Sometimes Driven by a Hike in Interest Rates)

Shrinking Trade Deficit → Widening Imbalance in the Balance of Payments → Decrease in Investment Flows

Impact on Money Supply

Widening Trade Surplus → Increase in the Money Supply

Shrinking Trade Surplus → Decrease in the Money Supply

Widening Trade Deficit → Decrease in the Money Supply

Shrinking Trade Deficit → Increase in the Money Supply

Impact on Investor Fear

Widening Trade Surplus → Confident Investors

Shrinking Trade Surplus → Cautious Investors

Widening Trade Deficit → Nervous Investors

Shrinking Trade Deficit → Cautiously Optimistic Investors

Typical Impact on the Currency

Widening Trade Surplus → Stronger Currency

Shrinking Trade Surplus → Weaker Currency

Widening Trade Deficit → Weaker Currency

Shrinking Trade Deficit → Stronger Currency

FOREIGN INVESTMENT

Foreign investment announcements report on how much foreign money is coming into an economy. Naturally, economies that are performing well and that have thriving financial markets tend to draw more foreign investment, and economies that are struggling and have lackluster financial markets tend to lose foreign investment to other economies.

In that regard, foreign investment can get caught in either a virtuous circle or a negative feedback loop. In the virtuous circle, economies that are doing well draw more foreign investment, which helps the economy grow even more, which draws more foreign capital. In the negative feedback loop, economies that are struggling lose foreign investment, which hurts the economy even more, which leads to further losses of foreign investment.

Foreign investment data are released in multiple announcements that you need to be aware of:

1. **Treasury International Capital (TIC) data:** Comparison between the total foreign assets purchased by U.S. citizens and the total domestic assets purchased by foreigners
2. **Foreign securities purchases:** Measurement of the total value of domestic stocks, bonds, and other financial assets purchased by foreigners
3. **Foreign direct investment:** Measurement of the total value of foreign investments in nonfinancial domestic assets, such as companies, real estate, and so on

Impact on Trade Flows

Increase in Foreign Investment → Widening Imbalance in the Balance of Payments → Decrease in Trade Flows

Decrease in Foreign Investment → Widening Imbalance in the Balance of Payments → Increase in Trade Flows

Impact on Investment Flows

Increase in Foreign Investment = Increase in Investment Flows

Decrease in Foreign Investment = Decrease in Investment Flows

Impact on Money Supply

Increase in Foreign Investment → Increase in the Money Supply

Decrease in Foreign Investment → Decrease in the Money Supply

Impact on Investor Fear

Increase in Foreign Investment → Confident Investors

Decrease in Foreign Investment → Nervous Investors

Typical Impact on the Currency

Increase in Foreign Investment → Stronger Currency

Decrease in Foreign Investment → Weaker Currency

CONSUMER CONFIDENCE

Consumer confidence announcements report on how confident the consumers within an economy are. Confident consumers tend to spend more because they believe that the economy is going to continue to grow, and that therefore they will have more money in the future. Insecure consumers tend to spend less because they are uncertain about their future income and the future of the economy.

Consumer confidence data are released in multiple announcements that you need to be aware of:

1. **Consumer Confidence Index (Conference Board):** Survey of 5,000 households that measures consumer confidence not only in current economic conditions but also in future economic conditions.

2. **Consumer Sentiment Index (University of Michigan):** Survey of 500 consumers that measures consumer confidence not only in current economic conditions but also in future economic conditions. The University of Michigan releases this data in a "preliminary" report and in a "revised" report.

3. **Foreign Direct Investment:** Measurement of the total value of foreign investments in nonfinancial domestic assets, such as companies, real estate, and so on.

Impact on Trade Flows

Rising Consumer Confidence → Increase in Consumer Spending → Increased Demand for Imports → Increase in Trade Flows

Falling Consumer Confidence → Decrease in Consumer Spending → Decreased Demand for Imports → Decrease in Trade Flows

Impact on Investment Flows

Rising Consumer Confidence → Increase in Consumer Spending → Increase in Corporate Profits → Rising, More Attractive Stock Market → Increase in Investment Flows

Rising Consumer Confidence → Increase in Consumer Spending → Rising Inflation → Central Bank Raising Interest Rates → More Attractive Government Debt Market → Increase in Investment Flows

Falling Consumer Confidence → Decrease in Consumer Spending → Decline in Corporate Profits → Falling, Less Attractive Stock Market → Decrease in Investment Flows

Falling Consumer Confidence → Decrease in Consumer Spending → Falling Inflation → Central Bank Lowering Interest Rates → Less Attractive Government Debt Market → Decrease in Investment Flows

Impact on Money Supply

Rising Consumer Confidence → Increase in Consumer Spending → Rising Inflation → Central Bank Raising Interest Rates → Decrease in the Money Supply

Falling Consumer Confidence → Decrease in Consumer Spending → Falling Inflation → Central Bank Lowering Interest Rates → Increase in the Money Supply

Impact on Investor Fear

Rising Consumer Confidence → Confident Investors

Falling Consumer Confidence → Nervous Investors

Typical Impact on the Currency

Rising Consumer Confidence → Stronger Currency

Falling Consumer Confidence → Weaker Currency

RETAIL SALES

Retail sales announcements report on how much money individual consumers are spending on retail goods. This is where the rubber meets the road in terms of translating consumer confidence into consumer action. Consumers can say that they are confident about the economy, but unless they follow it up with actual purchases, their confidence doesn't do much to grow the economy.

Retail sales data are released in multiple announcements that you need to be aware of:

1. **Retail sales:** Measurement of goods purchased by individual consumers
2. **Personal spending or personal consumption expenditures (PCE):** Another measurement of goods purchased by individual consumers
3. **Weekly chain-store sales snapshot:** Weekly measurement of sales at major department stores
4. **Johnson Redbook Index:** Another weekly measurement of sales at major department stores

Impact on Trade Flows

Rising Retail Sales → Increased Demand for Imports → Increase in Trade Flows

Falling Retail Sales → Decreased Demand for Imports → Decrease in Trade Flows

Impact on Investment Flows

Rising Retail Sales → Increase in Corporate Profits → Rising, More Attractive Stock Market → Increase in Investment Flows

Rising Retail Sales → Rising Inflation → Central Bank Raising Interest Rates → More Attractive Government Debt Market → Increase in Investment Flows

Falling Retail Sales → Decline in Corporate Profits → Falling, Less Attractive Stock Market → Decrease in Investment Flows

Falling Retail Sales → Falling Inflation → Central Bank Lowering Interest Rates → Less Attractive Government Debt Market → Decrease in Investment Flows

Impact on Money Supply

Rising Retail Sales → Rising Inflation → Central Bank Raising Interest Rates → Decrease in the Money Supply

Falling Retail Sales → Falling Inflation → Central Bank Lowering Interest Rates → Increase in the Money Supply

Impact on Investor Fear

Rising Retail Sales → Confident Investors

Falling Retail Sales → Nervous Investors

Typical Impact on the Currency

Rising Retail Sales → Stronger Currency

Falling Retail Sales → Weaker Currency

BUSINESS CONFIDENCE

Business confidence announcements report on how confident the business managers within an economy are. Confident business managers tend to hire more people and invest in business expansion, new products, and more inventory. Insecure business managers tend to hire fewer people (or even lay off employees) and invest less in business expansion, new products, and more inventory.

Business confidence data are released in multiple announcements that you need to be aware of:

1. **Institute for Supply Management (ISM) Manufacturing Business Survey:** Survey of purchasing managers' confidence in the economy based on new orders, production, employment, deliveries, inventories, and so on

2. **Chicago Purchasing Managers' Index (PMI):** Survey of the confidence of purchasing managers in the Chicago area
3. **German ZEW (Zentrum für Europäische Wirtschaftsforschung) Indicator of Economic Sentiment:** Survey of institutional investors' and analysts' confidence
4. **German IFO (Institut für Wirtschaftsforschung) Business Climate Index:** Survey of manufacturers', builders', wholesalers', and retailers' confidence
5. **Tankan Manufacturing Index (Japan):** Survey of manufacturers' confidence

Impact on Trade Flows

Rising Business Confidence → Increase in Corporate Spending → Increased Demand for Imports → Increase in Trade Flows

Falling Business Confidence → Decrease in Corporate Spending → Decreased Demand for Imports → Decrease in Trade Flows

Impact on Investment Flows

Rising Business Confidence → Increase in Corporate Spending → Increase in Corporate Profits → Rising, More Attractive Stock Market → Increase in Investment Flows

Rising Business Confidence → Increase in Corporate Spending → Rising Inflation → Central Bank Raising Interest Rates → More Attractive Government Debt Market → Increase in Investment Flows

Falling Business Confidence → Decrease in Corporate Spending → Decline in Corporate Profits → Falling, Less Attractive Stock Market → Decrease in Investment Flows

Falling Business Confidence → Decrease in Corporate
Spending → Falling Inflation → Central Bank
Lowering Interest Rates → Less Attractive Government Debt
Market → Decrease in Investment Flows

Impact on Money Supply

Rising Business Confidence → Increase in Corporate
Spending → Rising Inflation → Central Bank Raising Interest
Rates → Decrease in the Money Supply

Falling Business Confidence → Decrease in Corporate
Spending → Falling Inflation → Central Bank Lowering Interest
Rates → Increase in the Money Supply

Impact on Investor Fear

Rising Business Confidence → Confident Investors

Falling Business Confidence → Nervous Investors

Typical Impact on the Currency

Rising Business Confidence → Stronger Currency

Falling Business Confidence → Weaker Currency

MANUFACTURING

Manufacturing announcements report on how much manufacturing
activity is taking place within an economy. Manufacturing is one of
the most significant drivers of economic growth and job creation in
most economies, so seeing increasing levels of manufacturing activity is always a good sign. Conversely, seeing decreasing levels of
manufacturing activity is typically a negative sign for an economy.

Manufacturing data are released in multiple announcements that you need to be aware of:

1. **Factory orders:** Measurement of factory demand and activity
2. **Industrial production and capacity utilization:** Measurement of the goods produced in an economy and the spare production capacity of its manufacturers

Impact on Trade Flows

Increasing Manufacturing → More Jobs → Increased Consumer Spending → Increased Demand for Imports → Increase in Trade Flows

Increasing Manufacturing → Increased Demand for Raw Goods and Materials → Increased Demand for Imports → Increase in Trade Flows

Decreasing Manufacturing → Fewer Jobs → Decreased Consumer Spending → Decreased Demand for Imports → Decrease in Trade Flows

Decreasing Manufacturing → Decreased Demand for Raw Goods and Materials → Decreased Demand for Imports → Decrease in Trade Flows

Impact on Investment Flows

Increasing Manufacturing → More Jobs → Increased Consumer Spending → Increase in Corporate Profits → Rising, More Attractive Stock Market → Increase in Investment Flows

Increasing Manufacturing → More Jobs → Increased Consumer Spending → Rising Inflation → Central Bank Raising Interest Rates → More Attractive Government Debt Market → Increase in Investment Flows

Decreasing Manufacturing → Fewer Jobs → Decreased Consumer Spending → Decline in Corporate Profits → Falling, Less Attractive Stock Market → Decrease in Investment Flows

Decreasing Manufacturing → Fewer Jobs → Decreased Consumer Spending → Falling Inflation → Central Bank Lowering Interest Rates → Less Attractive Government Debt Market → Decrease in Investment Flows

Impact on Money Supply

Increasing Manufacturing → More Jobs → Increased Consumer Spending → Rising Inflation → Central Bank Raising Interest Rates → Decrease in the Money Supply

Decreasing Manufacturing → Fewer Jobs → Decreased Consumer Spending → Falling Inflation → Central Bank Lowering Interest Rates → Increase in the Money Supply

Impact on Investor Fear

Increasing Manufacturing → Confident Investors

Decreasing Manufacturing → Nervous Investors

Typical Impact on the Currency

Increasing Manufacturing → Stronger Currency

Decreasing Manufacturing → Weaker Currency

HOUSING

Housing announcements report on how healthy the housing sector of the economy is. Because such a large amount of the average person's net worth is tied up in the value of her home, the health of the housing market tends to have a dramatic effect on consumer confidence and the strength of the economy. A strong housing market typically leads to a strong economy.

Housing data are released in multiple announcements that you need to be aware of:

1. **Housing starts and building permits:** Measurement of the number of building permits that have been issued and the number of planned homes that have actually been started
2. **Existing home sales:** Measurement of the number of homes that have been lived in before that have been sold
3. **New home sales:** Measurement of the number of homes that have never been lived in before that have been sold
4. **Standard & Poor's/Case-Shiller Home Price Indices:** Measurement of home values

Impact on Trade Flows

Increasing Housing Prices/Activity → Increasing Consumer Confidence → Increasing Refinancing → Increasing Consumer Spending → Increased Demand for Imports → Increase in Trade Flows

Decreasing Housing Prices/Activity → Decreasing Consumer Confidence → Decreasing Refinancing → Decreasing Consumer Spending → Decreased Demand for Imports → Decrease in Trade Flows

Impact on Investment Flows

Increasing Housing Prices/Activity → Increasing Consumer Confidence → Increasing Refinancing → Increasing Consumer Spending → Increase in Corporate Profits → Rising, More Attractive Stock Market → Increase in Investment Flows

Increasing Housing Prices/Activity → Increasing Consumer Confidence → Increasing Refinancing → Increasing Consumer Spending → Rising Inflation → Central Bank Raising Interest Rates → More Attractive Government Debt Market → Increase in Investment Flows

Decreasing Housing Prices/Activity → Decreasing Consumer Confidence → Decreasing Refinancing → Decreasing Consumer Spending → Decline in Corporate Profits → Falling, Less Attractive Stock Market → Decrease in Investment Flows

Decreasing Housing Prices/Activity → Decreasing Consumer Confidence → Decreasing Refinancing → Decreasing Consumer Spending → Falling Inflation → Central Bank Lowering Interest Rates → Less Attractive Government Debt Market → Decrease in Investment Flows

Impact on Money Supply

Increasing Housing Prices/Activity → Increasing Consumer Confidence → Increasing Refinancing → Increasing Consumer Spending → Rising Inflation → Central Bank Raising Interest Rates → Decrease in the Money Supply

Decreasing Housing Prices/Activity → Decreasing Consumer Confidence → Decreasing Refinancing → Decreasing Consumer Spending → Falling Inflation → Central Bank Lowering Interest Rates → Increase in the Money Supply

Impact on Investor Fear

Increasing Housing Prices/Activity → Confident Investors

Decreasing Housing Prices/Activity → Nervous Investors

Typical Impact on the Currency

Increasing Housing Prices/Activity → Stronger Currency

Decreasing Housing Prices/Activity → Weaker Currency

CHAPTER 11

Indicators That Forex Traders Watch

THE VIX: CBOE VOLATILITY INDEX

The CBOE Volatility Index (VIX) is arguably the best gauge of risk and sentiment available to the investing public; it can be used effectively by any trader in the Forex market. The VIX is often nicknamed the "fear index," which is actually somewhat misleading, since it doesn't directly measure fear of any kind. The VIX is actually a measure of traders' expectations about volatility in the S&P 500. It is charted like an index, and the higher it goes, the higher traders' expectations for short-term market volatility are.

The VIX rises with higher market volatility because it measures the prices of the out-of-the-money S&P 500 index options. If option sellers think that volatility is going to increase in the near term, they will require larger premiums from option buyers. This increase in option prices is used in the calculation of the VIX index. Conversely, if they think that volatility is going to drop, option sellers will reduce their premiums to attract buyers. Falling option prices will be reflected in a falling VIX index.

The VIX tracks these changes in investor sentiment and option premiums in real time on each trading day. The VIX reading is an annualized number of how much traders think the S&P 500 will move during the next 30 days. If the VIX has a reading of 30, or 30 percent, it means that traders think the S&P 500 is likely to move about 2.5 percent (30 percent/12 months = 2.5 percent) during the next month.

Traders' expectations as shown on the VIX are directionless. In the previous example, we can recognize that traders are expecting a 2.5 percent move in one direction or the other, but not specifically whether it will be up or down. However, because unexpected market volatility is biased to the downside, a rising VIX is usually associated with bearish expectations. Remember that the market doesn't crash up, it only crashes down.

This means that if traders are expecting a lot of volatility, this is generally a bearish sign. That is one of the reasons that the VIX is often called a measure of fear. If investors are concerned that volatility is increasing, the VIX will rise. Conversely, if investors are expecting low volatility, the VIX will drop, which is considered to be a bullish sign. This rule is generally true, but you will see exceptions to it on a day-to-day basis.

The implications here are obvious. If the VIX is falling, investors are trading bullish strategies and taking on more risk. If the VIX is rising, traders may be shorting the market and trying to limit risk within their portfolio. Because the VIX is typically range bound, traders are particularly interested in periods when the index is hitting support or resistance levels.

How bearish or bullish traders feel based on the VIX is important because it indicates what is going on with their attitudes toward risk. Recently, increases in investor fear have been associated with falling stocks, rising bonds, and a stronger dollar. The opposite is also true.

The VIX can be used as an analytical tool to identify entry and exit opportunities or periods when market risk is likely to be higher or lower. This information is especially useful because it is not just another iteration of a price-and-time study but is derived from investor expectations for near-term volatility.

So what should you be watching for when you analyze the VIX? You should be looking for the following:

- When the VIX starts to rise, look for safe-haven currencies to appreciate in value.
- When the VIX starts to fall, look for riskier, higher-yielding currencies to appreciate in value.

10-YEAR BOND YIELD SPREADS

Monitoring 10-year bond spreads can give you a good idea of where investment flows may be headed in the future. Here's the thing, though: you can't just look for the country that has the highest yield and anticipate that the currency from that country is going to continue to move higher and higher. What you want to be looking for is a country whose bond yields are increasing. It is this change in bond yields that can lead to a change in investment flows, which can lead to an increase in the value of the currency.

For instance, if you are watching bond yields in Switzerland, and you notice that they are starting to move steadily higher, this is a great clue that the value of the Swiss franc may be appreciating. Now, if, at the same time, you notice that the bond yields in the United States are starting to decline, you should seriously consider looking at placing a trade that takes advantage of both a strengthening Swiss franc and a weakening U.S. dollar.

The *Financial Times* is an excellent resource for tracking these bond rates.[1]

STOCK MARKET PERFORMANCE

Monitoring stock market performance can also give you a good idea of where investment flows may be headed in the future. Here's the thing, though: just as with bond yield spreads, you can't just look for the country that has the strongest stock market and anticipate that the currency from that country is going to continue to move higher and higher. What you want to be looking for is a country whose stock market is getting stronger and stronger. It is this change in the strength of the stock market that can lead to a change in investment flows, which can lead to an increase in the value of the currency.

For instance, if you are watching the stock market performance in Japan, and you notice that the market is starting to move steadily higher, this is a great clue that the value of the Japanese yen may be appreciating. Now, if, at the same time, you notice

---

[1] http://markets.ft.com/markets/bonds.asp.

that the stock market in the United Kingdom is starting to decline, you should seriously consider looking at placing a trade that takes advantage of both a strengthening Japanese yen and a weakening British pound.

The *Financial Times* is an excellent resource for tracking the performance of various stock markets.[2]

FED FUNDS FUTURES

Traders can buy and sell futures based on the fed funds rate and their expectations for changes in that rate. When traders think that the Fed will raise rates in the future, they sell these futures contracts, and when traders think that the Fed will lower rates in the future, they buy these futures contracts. These contracts are a great way for institutional traders to hedge interest-rate risk and speculate on changes in the future.

The fed funds futures rate can be useful for Forex traders who are looking to understand what market expectations for the long-term trend are. If the fed funds futures rate were to show a rate that is lower than the current rate, it would indicate that traders are expecting a rate cut, which would typically be bad for the U.S. dollar. Conversely, if the fed funds futures rate were to show a rate that is higher than the current rate, it would indicate that traders are expecting a rate hike, which would typically be good for the U.S. dollar.

If you are used to trading other futures contracts, the way these fed funds futures are priced can be a little confusing at first. The calculation for the price is 100 minus the expected fed funds rate. For instance, if the current price is 96, then you know that traders expect the fed funds rate to be 4 percent (100 − 4 = 96).

Similarly, if the fed funds futures rate rises from 96 to 98, then it shows that traders believe that the rate will change from 4 percent (100 − 4 = 96) to 2 percent (100 − 2 = 98). These kinds of moves happen over the long term, of course, and the fed funds futures rate can channel in a very tight range for a long time.

---

[2] http://markets.ft.com/ft/markets/worldEquities.asp.

It is important to remember that the fed funds futures chart is showing what traders think will happen to the rate in the near future, not what it is right now. The fed funds futures chart is something that analysts and traders will refer to frequently, and it can be a great resource when you are trying to understand where interest rates are likely to go. You can find the fed funds futures chart at the Web site for the CME. There is also a great discussion of the predictive power of options on the fed funds futures at the Web site of the Cleveland Federal Reserve.

So what should you be watching for when you analyze the fed funds futures rate? You should be looking for the following:

- When the rate starts to rise, look for the U.S. dollar to lose value.

- When the rate starts to fall, look for the U.S. dollar to gain value.

COMMITMENT OF TRADERS (COT)

Traders have access to a special market report each week that provides a snapshot of the positions of large institutional traders and small speculators in each commodity futures category, including Forex. This information is called the Commitment of Traders, or COT, report, and it is provided by the Commodity Futures Trading Commission (CFTC).

The COT report is a great analytical tool for traders in any market because it provides up-to-date information about the trend and the strength of the commitment that traders have toward that trend in each of the commodities markets.

The COT report essentially shows the net long or short positions for each available futures contract for three different types of traders: commercial traders, noncommercial traders, and nonreporting traders. If traders are overwhelmingly long or are increasing their long positions, then they have a bullish bias on the market. Similarly, if traders are short or are increasing their short positions, then they have a bearish bias.

Not all traders in the report are of equal importance. In fact, of the three types of traders, investors usually pay attention to the one type with requirements most like those of other individual traders: noncommercial traders.

Commercial Traders: These traders represent companies and institutions that use the futures market to offset risk in the cash or spot market. For example, a Japanese auto manufacturer that has accounts receivable from a firm in the United States may short U.S. dollar futures contracts to protect its profits in the event that the value of the U.S. dollar falls in the near term. This class of trader is not going to be very helpful for retail investors, and we don't pay much attention to them.

Noncommercial Traders: This category includes large institutional investors, hedge funds, and other entities that are trading in the futures market for investment and growth. They are typically not involved directly in the production, distribution, or management of the underlying commodities or assets. We pay the most attention to this category.

Nonreporting Traders: This is the catchall category for traders who are too small to be required to report their positions to the CFTC. We don't know how many individual traders there are in this category or what kind of investors they represent because they are nonreporting. Most market professionals assume that a major percentage of the traders in this category are individual speculators. They are notoriously bad traders, and you will more often see this category betting against the trend than with it. We don't pay any attention to this category.

So what should you be watching for when you analyze the COT report? You should be looking for the following:

- When the net long position is expanding or the net short position is contracting, look for the currency represented in the report to appreciate in value.
- When the net short position is expanding or the net long position is contracting, look for the currency represented in the report to depreciate in value.

Investment Vehicles for Trading Forex

THE $4 TRILLION FOREX INSTRUMENTS

Yes, as we discussed in the introduction, nearly $4 trillion changes hands in the Forex market every day. The question is, how is that money changing hands? What investment vehicles are traders using to participate in the Forex market? According to the "2010 Triennial Central Bank Survey," conducted by the Bank for International Settlements (BIS), traders used the following five groups of instruments to trade currencies:[1]

- Spot transactions, accounting for $1,490 billion
- Outright forwards, accounting for $475 billion
- Foreign exchange swaps, accounting for $1,765 billion
- Currency swaps, accounting for $43 billion
- Currency options, currency swaptions, and currency warrants, accounting for $207 billion

As a retail Forex trader, the only two instruments from this list that you are likely to actually be involved with are spot transactions and currency options, but we think it is a good idea for you to at least be aware of how the other contracts work as well because they drive a lot of the trading and price activity in the Forex market.

---

[1] http://www.bis.org/press/p100901.htm.

Spot Transactions

Spot transactions are the immediate purchase or sale of one currency for another. The price of the transaction, or the *spot rate*, is the current market price of the currency pair, which is determined when the purchase or sale takes place, but delivery of the currency usually takes about two days. We'll cover spot transactions in much greater detail in just a moment.

Outright Forwards

Outright forwards are similar to spot transactions, except that the exchange rate is not based on the current market price of the currency pair. The two parties involved in the contract agree upon an exchange rate for some time in the future (more than two business days later).

For example, suppose you want to buy a EUR/USD contract 10 days from now. Right now, this contract is trading at a rate of 1.3500, but you believe that it will be trading at 1.3300 10 days from now.

Foreign Exchange Swaps

Foreign exchange swaps are transactions involving the actual exchange of two currencies in which the parties involved agree not only to the immediate purchase or sale of one currency for another for an agreed-upon amount, as they do in a spot transaction, but also to the future resale or repurchase of the same currency for an agreed-upon amount (which is usually different from the first amount).

Currency Swaps

Currency swaps are contracts that commit two counterparties to exchange streams of interest payments in different currencies for an agreed-upon period of time and to exchange principal amounts in different currencies at an agreed-upon exchange rate at maturity.

Currency Options, Currency Swaptions, and Currency Warrants

Currency options are contracts that give the buyer the right to buy or sell a currency with another currency at a specified exchange rate during a specified period. This category also includes exotic foreign exchange options such as average-rate options and barrier options.

Currency swaptions are option contracts that give the buyer the right to enter into a currency swap contract.

Currency warrants are option contracts with maturities longer than one year.

Now that we've at least scratched the surface on the types of transactions that the Bank for International Settlements (BIS) uses in its calculations—and digging any deeper into many of them is beyond the scope of this book—let's spend some time getting to know and understand the investment vehicles that you might actually use to invest in the Forex market. In doing so, we will be covering the following:

- Spot Forex
- Forex futures
- Exchange-traded funds (ETFs)
- Exchange-traded notes (ETNs)
- Spot Forex options
- Exchange-traded Forex options

SPOT FOREX

Spot transactions are the immediate purchase or sale of one currency for another. As stated earlier, the price, or spot rate, of the transaction is the current market price of the currency pair and is determined when the purchase or sale takes place. Whenever you hear people quoting the current exchange rate, they are talking about the spot rate.

Although the purchase or sale transaction takes place immediately, delivery of the currency usually takes about two days. So when you talk about spot Forex contracts, there are two dates that you need to be aware of: the trade date and the settlement date. The *trade date* is the day you enter a trade—the day you place your order for a trade and the order is accepted by your broker. The *settlement date* is the day on which the transaction is settled. You will also hear this date referred to as the "value date" or the "delivery date."

The settlement date is typically two good business days (which is often depicted as T + 2) after the trade date because it takes time to settle these international transactions. The exceptions to this rule are trades based on the U.S. dollar vs. either the Canadian dollar (USD/CAD) or the Mexican peso (USD/MXN). Because these pairs deal with two currencies that are both in North America, settlement usually takes only one good business day (T + 1).

A good business day is a day that is not a holiday or a weekend in either country represented by the currency pair. Because different countries have different holidays, this can sometimes lead to a value date that is six or seven days from the trade date, particularly at the beginning and end of the year.

Because the Forex market is a 24-hour market that never sleeps, you may be wondering when the official "end" of the trading day is. By convention, the "end" of the trading day is 5 p.m. Eastern time. This means that if you place a trade on the EUR/USD at 2 p.m. Eastern time on a Monday, it will settle the following Wednesday at 5 p.m. Eastern. However, if you placed a similar trade at 6 p.m. Eastern on a Monday, it would not settle until the following Thursday at 5 p.m. Eastern because you technically placed the trade on a Tuesday, as far as the days on a Forex market calendar are concerned.

Rollover

As a spot Forex trader, you most likely are never going to take delivery of the currencies you are trading. Let's face it, that's not what we're interested in doing when we dive into the Forex market. We want to be able to trade into and out of currencies and reap the rewards that come as prices change. So what should you do if you don't want to end up with 100,000 euros at your house?

Luckily, you don't have to do anything. Forex dealers know that you don't want to take delivery of the currency, so they take care of it for you by rolling over the contracts you are trading each and every day. Here's how it works.

At the end of each trading day, which we've already established is at 5 p.m. Eastern time, your dealer will automatically close the trades you are in and will roll over the proceeds into new, identical trades for the following day. This all happens instantaneously, so you don't lose any money in the process. For example, if you buy five full-size EUR/USD lots on Tuesday at 2 p.m. Eastern, the trade date for your transaction is Tuesday. Well, at 5 p.m. Eastern on Tuesday, your dealer will instantaneously sell your five full-size EUR/USD lots and buy five new full-size EUR/USD lots. This effectively changes the trade date for your position from Tuesday to Wednesday. Because you no longer own five lots with a trade date of Tuesday, you don't have to worry about a settlement date on Thursday. As you continue to hold the trade, your dealer will continue to roll the position over from one day to the next to keep you one step ahead of having to take delivery.

Interest Payments (Rollover Rate)

Rollover also affects the interest payments that you receive from your Forex investments. When you trade currency pairs, you earn interest on the currency that you buy, and you must pay interest on the currency that you sell. The interest rate that you either earn or pay is typically the short-term interest rate set by the country's central bank. When the interest rate offered by both currencies is the same, they net each other out in the transaction. However, when one interest rate is higher than the other, you will end up either paying more interest on one side of the trade than you bring in on the other side or bringing in more interest on one side of the trade than you pay on the other side.

This difference in interest rates is called the *rollover rate*. When the interest rate on the currency that you buy is higher than the interest rate on the currency that you sell, you will end up with positive net interest, or a *positive roll*. This is the underlying premise for a trading strategy called the *carry trade*. When the interest rate on the currency that you buy is lower than the interest rate on the currency that you sell, you will end up with negative net interest, or a *negative roll*.

If you are in a trade that has a positive roll, a payment equal to the interest-rate differential will be credited to your account when the trade rolls over at 5 p.m. Eastern. If you are in a trade that has a negative roll, a charge equal to the interest-rate differential will be debited from your account when the trade rolls over at 5 p.m. Eastern. For instance, if you are long the Australian dollar vs. the U.S. dollar (AUD/USD) and the Reserve Bank of Australia (RBA) has an interest rate of 5.5 percent while the Federal Reserve has an interest rate of 1.5 percent, you will receive a credit in your account based on an interest-rate differential of 4.0 percent (5.5% – 1.5% = 4.0%). On the flip side, if you are short the AUD/USD and the Reserve Bank of Australia (RBA) has an interest rate of 5.5 percent while the Federal Reserve has an interest rate of 1.5 percent, you will pay a debit from your account based on an interest-rate differential of 4.0 percent (1.5% – 5.5% = –4.0%).

The credit you receive or the debit you pay will be calculated on an annualized basis. To determine how large your credit or debit will be, simply use the following equations:

$$\text{Credit on Long Currency} = \text{Contract Size} \times \text{Exchange Rate} \times \text{Interest Rate} \times (1/360)$$

$$\text{Debit on Short Currency} = \text{Contract Size} \times \text{Exchange Rate} \times \text{Interest Rate} \times (1/360)$$

$$\text{Rollover Rate} = \text{Credit} - \text{Debit}$$

Here's how it would play out using the numbers from the AUD/USD scenario just given if you were *long* one full-size contract (we'll discuss these shortly) and the current exchange rate was 1.0135:

$$\text{Credit on Long Currency (AUD)} = 100{,}000 \times 1.0135 \times 0.055 \times (1/360) = \$15.48$$

$$\text{Debit on Short Currency (USD)} = 100{,}000 \times 1.0135 \times 0.015 \times (1/360) = \$4.22$$

$$\text{Rollover Rate} = \$15.48 - \$4.22 = \$11.26$$

Here's how it would play out using the numbers from the AUD/USD scenario just given if you were *short* one full-size contract and the current exchange rate was 1.0135.

$$\text{Credit on Long Currency (USD)} = 100{,}000 \times 1.0135 \times 0.015 \times (1/360) = \$4.22$$

$$\text{Debit on Short Currency (AUD)} = 100{,}000 \times 1.0135 \times 0.055 \times (1/360) = \$15.48$$

$$\text{Rollover Rate} = \$4.22 - \$15.48 = -\$11.26$$

Of course, there are a few caveats regarding the daily rollover that you will see in your account. First, your dealer does not do all this for free. Your dealer will charge you a small interest payment on both the currency that you buy and the currency that you sell. These interest charges will eat into the interest-rate differential that you earn with a positive roll and will add to the interest-rate differential that you must pay with a negative roll. Make sure to check with your broker to determine what rates you will be charged.

Second, since trades don't get rolled over on the weekends, those rollover credits and debits need to be assessed somewhere. To that end, there is one rollover that is three times the size of all the other rollovers—one regular rollover plus two weekend rollovers, one for each day of the weekend.

Trading Spot Forex

Now that you understand the characteristics of spot Forex contracts, let's talk about how you can actually trade these contracts. As we do so, we will cover the following topics:

- Available currency pairs
- Lot (contract) sizes
- Buying and selling spot Forex
- Trading hours
- Margin and leverage
- Liquidity

Available Currency Pairs

To get an idea of just how many different currency pairs you have access to as a spot Forex retail trader, take a look at Table 12-1, where you will see more than 120 available pairs.

TABLE 12-1

127 Available Currency Pairs (Based on Offerings at GFT*)

USD/AED	EUR/AUD	GBP/AUD	CHF/CZK	AUD/CAD	CAD/CHF	NZD/CAD	DKK/CZK	CZK/HUF
USD/CAD	EUR/CAD	GBP/CAD	CHF/DKK	AUD/CHF	CAD/DKK	NZD/CHF	DKK/HUF	CZK/JPY
USD/CHF	EUR/CHF	GBP/CHF	CHF/HKD	AUD/CZK	CAD/HKD	NZD/CZK	DKK/JPY	
USD/CZK	EUR/CZK	GBP/CZK	CHF/HUF	AUD/DKK	CAD/JPY	NZD/DKK	DKK/PLN	HKD/JPY
USD/DKK	EUR/DKK	GBP/DKK	CHF/JPY	AUD/HKD	CAD/NOK	NZD/HKD	DKK/SEK	MXN/JPY
USD/HKD	EUR/GBP	GBP/HKD	CHF/NOK	AUD/JPY	CAD/PLN	NZD/HUF	DKK/SGD	NOK/DKK
USD/HUF	EUR/HKD	GBP/HUF	CHF/PLN	AUD/NOK	CAD/SEK	NZD/JPY	DKK/THB	NOK/JPY
USD/ILS	EUR/HUF	GBP/JPY	CHF/SEK	AUD/NZD	CAD/SGD	NZD/PLN	DKK/ZAR	NOK/SEK
USD/JPY	EUR/JPY	GBP/NOK	CHF/SGD	AUD/PLN		NZD/SEK		
USD/MXN	EUR/MXN	GBP/NZD	CHF/TRY	AUD/SEK		NZD/SGD		PLN/JPY
USD/NOK	EUR/NOK	GBP/PLN	CHF/ZAR	AUD/SGD		NZD/THB		
USD/PLN	EUR/NZD	GBP/SEK		AUD/THB		NZD/USD		SEK/JPY
USD/RON	EUR/PLN	GBP/SGD		AUD/USD		NZD/ZAR		SEK/PLN
USD/SAR	EUR/RON	GBP/THB		AUD/ZAR				
USD/SEK	EUR/SEK	GBP/TRY						SGD/HKD
USD/SGD	EUR/SGD	GBP/USD						SGD/JPY
USD/THB	EUR/THB	GBP/ZAR						THB/JPY
USD/TRY	EUR/TRY							TRY/JPY
USD/ZAR	EUR/USD							ZAR/JPY
	EUR/ZAR							

*http://www.gftForex.com/Markets-And-Pricing/Forex-Spreads/Default.aspx.

Lot (Contract) Sizes
Spot Forex lots, or contracts, come in three standard sizes: full-size lots, mini lots, and micro lots.

- Full-size lots control 100,000 units of the base currency.
- Mini lots control 10,000 units of the base currency.
- Micro lots control 1,000 units of the base currency.

Some dealers allow you to customize the size of your lots (so that you could control 18,234 units of the base currency if you wanted to), but most trading is conducted using fixed lot sizes.

Buying and Selling Spot Forex
You can either buy or sell lots in the spot Forex market. If you believe that a currency pair is going to be increasing in value, you should buy the pair to take advantage of the price appreciation. If you believe that a currency pair is going to be losing value, you should sell the pair to take advantage of the price drop.

Trading Hours
The spot Forex market is open from 5 p.m. Eastern time on Sunday through 5 p.m. Eastern time on Friday. It does not close at any time during that period.

Margin and Leverage
When you trade spot Forex, you are required to post margin with your dealer. Margin is a good-faith deposit that shows your broker that you have the wherewithal to make good on your obligations if you should ever need to.

When investors talk about margin, you will often hear the term *post* your margin. All posting your margin means is showing your dealer that the money you are providing is unencumbered. In other words, it shows that you have not committed the money that you are going to use as margin to any other trades.

The amount of margin you are required to post as a spot Forex trader will depend on the level of leverage that you choose to use in your trading. When you use leverage in your spot Forex trading, it means that you are borrowing money in order to place a trade. Why would you borrow money in order to place a trade, you ask? The answer is simple: you can dramatically increase your profits.

Here's how it works. Suppose you have $10,000 and you want to buy the EUR/USD contract, but you are not going to use any leverage (that is, borrow any money). Well, you can't buy a full-sized lot because $10,000 definitely isn't enough to pay for 100,000 euros. You can't even buy a mini lot because 10,000 euros cost more than $10,000. You will only be able to deal in micro lots and earn micro profits.

Now suppose you have $10,000, you want to buy the EUR/USD contract, and you are going to use leverage. This opens up all sorts of opportunities for you because you can now buy full-sized and mini lots, which are going to put a lot more money in your pocket if you guess right on your trades.

Leverage and margin go hand in hand. A leverage of 50:1 corresponds to a margin requirement of 2 percent (1 divided by 50 is 0.02, or 2 percent). A 2 percent margin requirement means that if you wish to open a new position, you must have 2 percent of the size of that position available as margin. In other words, you can place a $50 trade with every $1 you have in margin.

Before October 18, 2010,[2] Forex dealers offered leverage levels ranging from 100:1 to 400:1. In case you are having a difficult time picturing what that means, with 400:1 leverage, you could control four full-size contracts (the equivalent of 400,000 units of currency) with just $1,000. That's like saying that you could buy a share of Apple (AAPL) stock, which is currently trading at approximately $345, for just over $0.85 per share. That is incredible.

The sky was the limit when you were determining how much leverage you wanted to use. Of course, these levels of leverage were extremely dangerous, and many traders blew up their accounts because they didn't understand how to handle that much leverage. You have to remember that leverage is a double-edged sword. It can boost your profits when you are right, but it can also accelerate your losses when you are wrong. That's why the Commodity Futures Trading Commission (CFTC) changed the rules.

Based on the new CFTC rules that went into effect on October 18, 2010, your dealer will now require a minimum margin of 2 percent (which gives you a maximum leverage of 50:1) when both currencies in a currency pair are in the following list:

---

[2] http://www.cftc.gov/PressRoom/PressReleases/pr5883-10.html.

- U.S. dollar (USD)
- Euro (EUR)
- Japanese yen (JPY)
- British pound (GBP)
- Swiss franc (CHF)
- Australian dollar (AUD)
- Canadian dollar (CAD)
- New Zealand dollar (NZD)
- Norwegian krone (NOK)
- Swedish krona (SEK)
- Danish krone (DKK)

If one or both of the currencies in a currency pair is not in this list, your dealer will require a minimum margin of 5 percent, which gives you a maximum leverage of 20:1.

Liquidity

When you are trading spot Forex through a dealer, liquidity is generally not an issue. If you want to buy or sell a currency pair, all you have to do is click on the "buy" or "sell" button and your trade will be executed for you because your dealer is acting as the counterparty to your trade. The place where you will see some liquidity-based differences is in the spread between the "sell" and "buy" (or "bid" and "ask") prices.

The less liquid a currency pair is in the interbank market, the wider the spread on the currency pair is going to be. For instance, looking at OANDA,[3] one of the largest retail foreign exchange dealers (RFEDs), the spread on the EUR/USD is 1.5 pips and the spread on the EUR/NZD is 7.0 pips. This makes sense because the trading volume on the EUR/USD is so much higher than that on the EUR/NZD, which means that it is easier for your dealer to offset the EUR/USD trade.

FOREX FUTURES

Forex (FX) futures are contracts that allow a trader to buy or sell a set amount of foreign currency at a specific price on a specific date in

---

[3] http://fxtrade.oanda.com/why/spreads/live.

the future (expiration date). For example, if you buy the December 2011 EUR/USD futures contract for 1.3645, you have the right to buy 125,000[4] euros at a rate of 1.3645 (regardless of what the exchange rate is at the time) when the contract expires in December 2011.

Looking at this definition, you may be thinking that Forex futures look a lot like Forex forwards. That's very astute of you. Forex futures operate exactly the way Forex forwards do. The main difference between the two is that futures are standardized contracts while forwards are not, and this standardization offers a lot of flexibility for futures traders.

A futures contract is more flexible because you can easily close out of any trade you are in simply by entering an offsetting trade. For instance, if you buy one EUR/USD futures contract, then all you have to do to close out of the trade is sell one EUR/USD futures contract. These two transactions cancel each other out and discharge all obligations that you may have had based on the contract.

This flexibility is made possible because all futures contracts are settled through a centralized clearinghouse. Through a process known as *novation*, the clearinghouse intermediates itself as the seller to every buyer of a futures contract and as the buyer to every seller. This means that the clearinghouse acts as the counterparty to every trade, which reduces your settlement risk.

Characteristics of Forex Futures

Now that you've got a basic understanding of what a Forex futures contract is, let's dive in a little deeper and take a look at the following characteristics of these contracts:

- Expiration
- Settlement
- Pricing

Expiration
Forex futures contracts operate on a set expiration schedule, with one contract expiring in each of the following four months:

---

[4]http://www.cmegroup.com/trading/fx/g10/euro-fx_contract_specifications. html.

- March (H)
- June (M)
- September (U)
- December (Z)[5]

You can tell in which month and which year a contract is going to expire by looking at its ticker symbol. For instance, the ticker symbol for the EUR/USD contract is EC. So if you were looking at a Forex futures contract with the symbol ECZ11, you would know that it was the following contract:

- EC = EUR/USD currency pair
- Z = December
- 11 = 2011

The day of the month on which the contract expires depends on the currency pair that the contract is based on. For most contracts, trading ceases at 9:16 a.m. Central time on the second business day immediately preceding the third Wednesday of the contract month, which is usually a Monday. This may seem like a weird way to describe the day, but it is accurate.

There are a few exceptions to this time frame.

- Trading ceases at 9:16 a.m. Central time on the business day immediately preceding the third Wednesday of the contract month, which is usually a Tuesday, for the CAD/USD, E-micro USD/CAD, and E-micro CAD/USD contracts.
- Trading ceases at 2:00 p.m. Central time on the last business day of the month for the Central Bank of Brazil immediately preceding the contract month for the BRL/USD contract.
- Trading ceases at 3:30 p.m. Seoul time on the second business day immediately preceding the third Wednesday of the contract (usually Monday), which would be either 12:30 a.m. Central time (standard time) or 1:30 a.m. Central time (daylight saving time) on the second business day

---

[5]http://www.cmegroup.com/trading/fx/g10/euro-fx_product_calendar_futures.html.

preceding the third Wednesday of the contract month (usually early Monday morning Central time) for the KRW/USD contract.

- Trading ceases at 11:00 a.m. Moscow time on the fifteenth day of the month, or, if this is not a business day, on the next business day for the Moscow interbank foreign exchange market for the RUB/USD contract.
- Trading ceases at 9:00 a.m. Beijing time on the first Beijing business day immediately preceding the third Wednesday of the contract month (usually Tuesday in Beijing), which is 7:00 p.m. Central time (standard time) or 8:00 p.m. Central time (daylight saving time) on the second Chicago business day preceding the third Wednesday of the contract month (usually Monday evening Central time) for the RMB/USD, RMB/EUR, and RMB/JPY contracts.
- Trading ceases at 12:30 a.m. Central time on the business day immediately preceding the third Wednesday of the contract month (usually early on Tuesday morning Central time, which is 8:30 a.m. Istanbul/Ankara time on Tuesday) for the USD/TRY and EUR/TRY contracts.

Settlement

Forex futures contracts are settled either by the buyer's taking physical delivery of the currency or by the buyer's receiving a cash settlement. Most contracts are settled via physical delivery. The exceptions are the BRL/USD, KRW/USD, RMB/USD, RMB/EUR, RMB/JPY, and RUB/USD contracts, which are cash settled.

Pricing

Forex futures are priced based on the current spot value of the currency pair and the interest-rate differential between the two currencies in the pair, also referred to as the "cost of carry." For example, if the European Central Bank (ECB) had set its minimum bid rate at 4.50 percent and the Fed's Federal Open Market Committee (FOMC) had set the federal funds rate at 2.50 percent, the currency pair would have an interest-rate differential of 2 percent (4.50 − 2.50 = 2.00).

If the interest rate for the country that is listed first in the currency pair is higher, the futures contracts will get cheaper and cheaper the farther out in the expiration cycle you go. Conversely, if the interest rate for the country that is listed first in the currency pair is lower, the futures contracts will get more and more expensive the farther out in the expiration cycle you go.

Looking at the EUR/USD contract example just given, where the interest rate in Europe is higher than it is in the United States, the futures prices would look something like this:

- Spot price: 1.3617
- March 2011 contract: 1.3611
- June 2011 contract: 1.3597
- September 2011 contract: 1.3573
- December 2011 contract: 1.3559

In this scenario, the buyer of the contract is willing to accept a lower value for a longer-term contract because he knows that he will be receiving a cash deposit in his account each day based on the interest-rate differential between the two currencies. The seller of the contract, on the other hand, demands a lower value for a longer-term contract because she knows that she will be enduring a cash withdrawal from her account each day based on the interest-rate differential between the two currencies.

If this interest-rate scenario were reversed and the ECB had set its minimum bid rate at 2.50 percent while the FOMC had set the federal funds rate at 4.50 percent, the futures prices would look something like this:

- Spot price: 1.3617
- March 2011 contract: 1.3629
- June 2011 contract: 1.3642
- September 2011 contract: 1.3668
- December 2011 contract: 1.3691

In this scenario, the buyer of the contract demands a higher value for a longer-term contract because she knows that she will be enduring a cash withdrawal from her account each day based on the interest-rate differential between the two currencies. The seller of the contract, on the other hand, is willing to accept a higher value for a longer-term contract because he knows that he will be receiving a cash deposit in his account each day based on the interest-rate differential between the two currencies.

When you talk about futures pricing, you also have to address contango and backwardation.

Contango in the futures market refers to the situation in which the contracts are more expensive than they should be if they were based solely on the interest-rate differential between the two currencies. Some other force is at work. The market typically goes into contango when there is a general underlying belief that the spot price is going to be rising in the future. Based on that belief, sellers of the futures contracts demand a higher premium for the higher risk they believe they are taking, and buyers of the futures contracts are willing to pay a higher premium for the higher return they believe they are going to make.

To explain contango, let's look at the scenario in which the ECB had set its minimum bid rate at 4.50 percent and the FOMC had set the federal funds rate at 2.50 percent. If the market was in contango, instead of the futures prices looking like this:

- Spot price: 1.3617
- March 2011 contract: 1.3611
- June 2011 contract: 1.3597
- September 2011 contract: 1.3573
- December 2011 contract: 1.3559

They would look something like this:

- Spot price: 1.3617
- March 2011 contract: 1.3616
- June 2011 contract: 1.3608
- September 2011 contract: 1.3595
- December 2011 contract: 1.3587

As you can see, the prices are still affected by the interest-rate differential (the longer-term contracts have a lower price than the shorter-term contracts), but the entire price curve has been shifted higher.

Contango can also happen when the interest rate offered by the first currency in the pair is lower than the interest rate offered by the second currency in the pair. Let's look at the scenario in which the ECB had set its minimum bid rate at 2.50 percent and the FOMC had set the federal funds rate at 4.50 percent. If the market was in contango, instead of the futures prices looking like this:

- Spot price: 1.3617
- March 2011 contract: 1.3629
- June 2011 contract: 1.3642
- September 2011 contract: 1.3668
- December 2011 contract: 1.3691

They would look something like this:

- Spot price: 1.3617
- March 2011 contract: 1.3639
- June 2011 contract: 1.3652
- September 2011 contract: 1.3678
- December 2011 contract: 1.3701

As you can see, the prices are still affected by the interest-rate differential (the longer-term contracts have a higher price than the shorter-term contracts), but the entire price curve has been shifted higher once again.

Backwardation in the futures market refers to the situation in which the contracts are less expensive than they should be if they were based solely on the interest-rate differential between the two currencies. The market typically goes into backwardation when there is a general underlying belief that the spot price is going to be falling in the future. Based on that belief, sellers of the futures contracts are willing to take a lower premium for the lower return they believe they are going to make, and buyers of the futures contracts demand a higher premium for the higher risk they believe they are taking.

To explain backwardation, let's look once again at the scenario in which the ECB had set its minimum bid rate at 4.50 percent and the FOMC had set the federal funds rate at 2.50 percent. If the market was in backwardation, instead of the futures prices looking like this:

- Spot price: 1.3617
- March 2011 contract: 1.3611
- June 2011 contract: 1.3597

- September 2011 contract: 1.3573
- December 2011 contract: 1.3559

They would look something like this:

- Spot price: 1.3617
- March 2011 contract: 1.3601
- June 2011 contract: 1.3587
- September 2011 contract: 1.3563
- December 2011 contract: 1.3549

As you can see, the prices are still affected by the interest-rate differential, (the longer-term contracts have a lower price than the shorter-term contracts), but the entire price curve has been shifted down.

Backwardation can also happen when the interest rate offered by the first currency in the pair is lower than the interest rate offered by the second currency in the pair. Let's look one last time at the scenario in which the ECB had set its minimum bid rate at 2.50 percent and the FOMC had set the federal funds rate at 4.50 percent. If the market was in backwardation, instead of the futures prices looking like this:

- Spot price: 1.3617
- March 2011 contract: 1.3629
- June 2011 contract: 1.3642
- September 2011 contract: 1.3668
- December 2011 contract: 1.3691

They would look something like this:

- Spot price: 1.3617
- March 2011 contract: 1.3623
- June 2011 contract: 1.3632
- September 2011 contract: 1.3658
- December 2011 contract: 1.3681

As you can see, the prices are still affected by the interest-rate differential (the longer-term contracts have a higher price than the shorter-term contracts), but the entire price curve has been shifted down.

Trading Forex Futures

Now that you understand the characteristics of Forex futures contracts, let's talk about how you can actually trade these contracts. As we do so, we will cover the following topics:

- Available currency pairs
- Buying and selling futures contracts
- Trading hours
- Margin
- Liquidity

Available Currency Pairs

When it comes to Forex futures, there is no shortage of contracts you have available to you as a trader. Here's a sampling of the various currency pairs you can trade in the Forex futures market (see Table 12-2).

Buying and Selling Futures Contracts

You can either buy or sell contracts in the futures market. If you believe that a currency pair is going to be increasing in value, you should buy the futures contract in order to take advantage of the price appreciation. If you believe that a currency pair is going to be losing value, you should sell the futures contract in order to take advantage of the price drop.

Trading Hours

Forex futures trade around the world on the Chicago Mercantile Exchange (CME), the Singapore Exchange (SGX), and the London International Financial Futures Exchange (LIFFE). This means that you can trade Forex futures virtually around the clock. Here are the hours of operation for the CME Globex electronic exchange (all times are Central time):

- Opens for the week on Sunday at 5 p.m.
- Closes each trading day from 4 p.m. to 5 p.m.
- Closes for the week on Friday at 4 p.m.[6]

---

[6]http://www.cmegroup.com/trading/fx/files/FX-Product-Guide-and-Calendar.pdf.

TABLE 12-2

127 Available Currency Pairs (Based on Offerings at CME Globex*)

G-10 Currencies		Emerging Currencies		E-Minis and E-Micros	
Symbol	Contract	Symbol	Contract	Symbol	Contract
EC	EUR/USD	TRY	USD/TRY	E7	EUR/USD
RF	EUR/CHF	RA	ZAR/USD	J7	JPY/USD
KE	EUR/SEK	RU	RUB/USD	M6S	USD/CHF
CN	EUR/NOK	PZ	PLN/USD	MSF	CHF/USD
RY	EUR/JPY	MP	MXN/USD	M6J	USD/JPY
CC	EUR/CAD	KRW	KRW/USD	MJY	JPY/USD
RP	EUR/GBP	FR	HUF/USD	M6E	EUR/USD
CA	EUR/AUD	Z	PLN/EUR	M6C	USD/CAD
JY	JPY/USD	R	HUF/EUR	MCD	CAD/USD
BP	GBP/USD	K	CZK/EUR	M6B	GBP/USD
BF	GBP/CHF	TRE	EUR/TRY	M6A	AUD/USD
BY	GBP/JPY	RMY	RMB/JPY		
AD	AUD/USD	RME	RMB/EUR		
AN	AUD/NZD	BR	BRL/USD		
AJ	AUD/JPY				
AC	AUD/CAD				
SJ	CHF/JPY				
SE	SEK/USD				
UN	NOK/USD				
NE	NZD/USD				
CD	CAD/USD				
CY	CAD/JPY				
FXD	$ INDEX				

*http://www.cmegroup.com/trading/fx/.

Margin

When you trade Forex futures, you are required to post margin with your broker. Margin is a good-faith deposit that shows your broker that you have the wherewithal to make good on your obligations if you should ever need to.

When investors talk about margin, you will often hear the term *post* your margin. All posting your margin means is showing your broker that the money is unencumbered. In other words, it shows that you have not committed the money that you are going to use as margin to any other trades. Some brokers will allow you to post assets as margin, which means that if you have bonds worth $10,000, you could use those as collateral against your Forex futures trade.

Futures contracts have two different margin requirements that you should be aware of: initial margin and maintenance margin. *Initial margin* is the amount of money you have to post when you first enter a trade. *Maintenance margin* is the amount of money you must keep unencumbered with your broker after you have entered the trade. For example, at the time of this writing, the initial margin that you have to post when you buy the EUR/USD contract as a speculator is $4,320, and the maintenance margin that you have to hold once you are in the trade is $3,200.[7]

Interestingly enough, if you are using Forex futures as a hedging instrument and not as a speculative instrument, you don't have to post quite as much margin. Hedgers who buy the EUR/USD contract have to post initial margin of only $3,200. However, the maintenance margin level does not drop for hedgers. It remains at $3,200.

Because futures contracts are marked to market on a daily basis, the amount of money you are required to post as margin may fluctuate. You will need to check with your broker to find out what the exact amount you need to post is.

Liquidity

Forex futures provide the most liquidity for the contracts with the shortest maturity—the "front month" contract. The farther out you go in the expiration cycle, the less liquidity and the wider spreads you will see.

EXCHANGE-TRADED FUNDS

Many retail investors are interested in adding Forex to diversify their portfolio, but they're not interested in setting up a separate trading account to trade spot Forex contracts or Forex futures

---

[7] http://www.cmegroup.com/wrappedpages/clearing/pbrates/performancebond. html?group=FX&type=OutrightRates&h=2&reporttype=marginrate.

contracts. Instead, they would rather be able to trade currencies in the same accounts that they use to trade stocks, mutual funds, and bonds. In most cases, if you have a 401(k) or an individual retirement account (IRA), you will be unable to trade spots or futures contracts. However, thanks to a burgeoning supply of various currency-related exchange-traded funds (ETFs), you can trade currencies right within your IRA or 401(k) accounts.

ETFs burst onto the scene a few years ago and have become increasingly popular with investors. ETFs are investment funds that are traded on stock markets. They are not mutual funds, yet they offer all the benefits of diversification that you would expect from a mutual fund. ETFs also enjoy all the benefits of liquidity that you have from trading individual shares.

As you get ready to start investing in currency-based ETFs, you need to answer the following five questions:

1. Do you want to invest in one currency at a time or in multiple currencies?
2. What assets does the ETF hold to gain exposure to the currency market?
3. Does the ETF use leverage?
4. What are the fees associated with the ETF?
5. How are the profits you earn on your ETFs going to be taxed?

Once you know the answers to these questions, you will know whether the ETF you are looking at is suitable for you or not.

This may seem obvious, but the easiest way to look at the differences among ETFs is to look at a bunch of different ETFs. To that end, we're going to be looking at currency ETFs from three different fund families: CurrencyShares, PowerShares, and WisdomTree. These are three of the dominant fund families in the currency ETF space at the time of this writing. Naturally, if the number of ETFs continues to grow as rapidly in the future as it has in the past, investors will be able to choose from many more ETFs in the coming years. But gaining an understanding of the differences in the ETFs in these fund families should give you the foundation you need to make intelligent investment decisions.

One Currency or Multiple Currencies?

The first decision you have to make as a currency ETF investor is whether you want to invest in a single currency at a time or in multiple currencies at the same time. When you invest in a single currency, you are investing in the value of that currency compared to the U.S. dollar. When you invest in multiple currencies, you are investing in the value of the U.S. dollar compared to that basket of currencies.

If you want to invest in individual currencies, you will most likely be focusing on the CurrencyShares and WisdomTree fund families. For example, here is a current list of the single-currency ETFs (and their ticker symbols) offered by CurrencyShares:

- CurrencyShares Euro Trust (FXE)
- CurrencyShares British Pound Sterling Trust (FXB)
- CurrencyShares Japanese Yen Trust (FXY)
- CurrencyShares Swiss Franc Trust (FXF)
- CurrencyShares Canadian Dollar Trust (FXC)
- CurrencyShares Australian Dollar Trust (FXA)
- CurrencyShares Mexican Peso Trust (FXM)
- CurrencyShares Swedish Krona Trust (FXS)
- CurrencyShares Russian Ruble Trust (XRU)

Using CurrencyShares ETFs, you can invest in anything from the euro to the British pound or from the Australian dollar to the Japanese yen.

Of course, if you want to focus more on the currencies from emerging economies, like China, India, and Brazil, you may want to look at the WisdomTree family of funds. Here is a current list of the single-currency ETFs offered by WisdomTree:

- WisdomTree Dreyfus Euro Fund (EU)
- WisdomTree Dreyfus Japanese Yen Fund (JYF)
- WisdomTree Dreyfus Chinese Yuan Fund (CYB)
- WisdomTree Dreyfus Brazilian Real Fund (BZF)
- WisdomTree Dreyfus Indian Rupee Fund (ICN)
- WisdomTree Dreyfus New Zealand Dollar Fund (BNZ)
- WisdomTree Dreyfus South African Rand Fund (SZR)

If you want to invest in multiple currencies at the same time, you will most likely be focusing on the WisdomTree and PowerShares fund families. Here is a current list of the multiple-currency ETFs offered by WisdomTree:

- WisdomTree Dreyfus Emerging Currency Fund (CEW)
- WisdomTree Dreyfus Commodity Currency Fund (CCX)

The WisdomTree Dreyfus Emerging Currency Fund currently invests in the Mexican peso, Brazilian real, Chilean peso, South African rand, Polish zloty, Israeli shekel, Turkish new lira, Chinese yuan, South Korean won, New Taiwan dollar, Indian rupee, and Malaysian ringgit.

The WisdomTree Dreyfus Commodity Currency Fund currently invests in the Australian dollar, Brazilian real, Canadian dollar, Chilean peso, Norwegian krone, New Zealand dollar, Russian ruble, and South African rand.

Here is a current list of the multiple-currency ETFs offered by PowerShares:

- PowerShares DB G10 Currency Harvest Fund (DBV)
- PowerShares DB USD Bull Fund (UUP)
- PowerShares DB USD Bear Fund (UDN)

The PowerShares DB G10 Currency Harvest Fund invests in the currencies that are tracked in the Deutsche Bank G10 Currency Future Harvest Index, which include the U.S. dollar, euro, Japanese yen, Canadian dollar, Swiss franc, British pound, Australian dollar, New Zealand dollar, Norwegian krone, and Swedish krona.

The PowerShares DB USD Bull Fund invests in the currencies that are tracked by the Deutsche Bank Long US Dollar Index (USDX®), which include the euro (57.6%), Japanese yen (13.6%), British pound (11.9%), Canadian dollar (9.1%), Swedish krona (4.2%), and Swiss franc (3.6%).

The PowerShares DB USD Bear Fund invests in the currencies that are tracked by the Deutsche Bank Short US Dollar Index (USDX®), which includes the euro (57.6%), Japanese yen (13.6%), British pound (11.9%), Canadian dollar (9.1%), Swedish krona (4.2%), and Swiss franc (3.6%).

Now that you've had a chance to look at some of the available currency ETFs, you have probably noticed that some currencies, like the euro, have multiple ETFs that track their performance. At first blush, this may seem redundant, but actually it's not. Here's the key: while there are multiple ETFs that track the euro, they don't all invest in the same assets.

Assets Held by the ETF

The next decision you have to make is what type of assets you want the fund to hold. Do you want the fund to hold cash in a bank account in London, or do you want the fund to invest in futures contracts? Do you want the fund to invest in currency forwards or swaps, or do you want the fund to invest in investment-grade assets (such as bonds and certificates of deposit) that are denominated in the currency of your choice?

The answers to these questions will have an important impact on the fees charged by the fund and the taxes you will be required to pay on profits generated by the fund.

As you evaluate currency ETFs, you will be able to choose among funds that invest in one of the following three asset groups:

1. Cash
2. Futures, forwards, and swaps
3. Money market instruments

Cash

When an ETF invests in cash, the fund literally holds cash deposits in a bank account somewhere. For example, the CurrencyShares Euro Trust (FXE) holds 100 euro in the London branch of JPMorgan Chase for every outstanding share of FXE.

Futures, Forwards, and Swaps

When an ETF invests in futures contracts, forwards, and swaps, the fund deposits money into a trading account and then uses that money to purchase the appropriate contracts. For example, the PowerShares DB USD Bull Fund (UUP) puts money into a trading account and then buys futures contracts.

In most cases, the fund manager will not be able to deploy all of the money that is in the account. Chances are good that based on the price of the contracts that the manager is willing to buy and the total amount of money that is available, some is going to be left over. When that happens, the excess cash is usually invested in high-quality bonds, like U.S. Treasuries.

Money Market Instruments

When an ETF invests in money market instruments, the fund also deposits money into a trading account and then uses that money to purchase the appropriate assets.

Leverage

Leverage can be appealing, but it can also be dangerous. Leveraged ETFs seek to deliver multiples of the performance of the index or benchmark that they track. To accomplish their objectives, leveraged ETFs pursue a range of investment strategies through the use of swaps, futures contracts, and other derivative instruments.

Most leveraged ETFs "reset" daily, meaning that they are designed to achieve their stated objectives on a daily basis. Their performance over longer periods of time (weeks, months, or years) can differ significantly from the performance of their underlying benchmark during the same period of time. This effect can be magnified in volatile markets. As the following examples demonstrate, an ETF that is set up to deliver twice the performance of a benchmark from the close of trading on Day 1 to the close of trading on Day 2 will not necessarily achieve that goal over weeks, months, or years.

How can this apparent breakdown between longer-term returns and ETF returns happen? Here's a hypothetical example. Let's say that on Day 1, an index starts with a value of 100 and a leveraged ETF that seeks to double the return of the index starts at $100. If the index drops by 10 points on Day 1, it has a 10 percent loss and a resulting value of 90. Assuming that it achieved its stated objective, the leveraged ETF would therefore drop 20 percent on that day and have an ending value of $80. On Day 2, if the index rises 10 percent, the index value would increase to 99. For the ETF, its value for Day 2 would rise by 20 percent, which means that the

ETF would have a value of $96. On both days, the leveraged ETF did exactly what it was supposed to do: it produced daily returns that were two times the daily index returns. But let's look at the results over the two-day period: the index lost 1 percent (it fell from 100 to 99), while the two times leveraged ETF lost 4 percent (it fell from $100 to $96). That means that over the two-day period, the ETF's negative returns were 4 times as much as the two-day return of the index instead of 2 times the return.

As you can see, the tracking errors that can arise by investing in leveraged ETFs can be significant, so make sure that you use caution when investigating these investments.

Fees, Fees, Fees

Anytime you invest in a managed fund—whether it's an actively managed fund or a passively managed fund—you know that you are going to be paying fees. Typically, passively managed funds have lower fees than actively managed funds. And the assets that the fund holds play a significant role in how actively the fund needs to be managed. For instance, if an ETF simply holds onto cold, hard cash denominated in a single currency, there isn't a lot of active management that has to be done. On the other hand, if an ETF holds futures contracts on 10 different currencies at the same time, the fund managers will have to be much more active to maintain an appropriate balance of contracts in the fund and to roll over contracts that are expiring and move those funds into new futures contracts.

Adding leverage to a fund also tends to increase the fees associated with that fund because leverage isn't free. When a fund manager borrows money to invest in an asset like a forward contract or a futures contract, the fund often has to pay fees and other costs associated with the borrowing and will always have to make interest payments on the money that it borrowed. These expenses are then passed along to the fund's investors in the form of higher fees.

Of the four fund families that we are evaluating here, CurrencyShares has the lowest average fees and ProShares has the highest average fees. At the time of this writing, CurrencyShares charges a fee of 0.40 percent for its individual-currency ETFs,

WisdomTree charges fees ranging from 0.35 percent to 0.55 percent, PowerShares charges a fee of 0.75 percent for its multiple-currency ETFs (it also passes along brokerage fees that average 0.05 percent), and ProShares charges a fee of 0.95 percent for its leveraged funds.

Typically, fees are quoted on an annualized basis, such as 0.40 percent per year, but they accrue on a daily basis and are paid on a monthly basis.

Some funds will try to downplay the fees that they are charging by telling you that the fees will be paid out of the interest earned on the fund's investments or on any excess cash within the fund, but that is a nonsensical argument. You have to remember that if the fees weren't being taken out of the earned interest of the fund, that money would be coming to you in the form of additional profits. When it comes to paying fees, it doesn't matter whether the money is coming out of your left pocket or out of your right pocket. It is still coming out of your pocket.

Tax Implications

Any time you receive a *distribution*, typically a payout based on the interest that the assets have earned, from a non-futures-based currency ETF, you will need to pay taxes on that distribution (unless your investment is held in a tax-exempt account). Those distributions will be taxed as *ordinary income*.

Whenever you *sell* a non-futures-based currency ETF, you will have to pay *capital gains tax*. The amount you pay will be determined by how long you held the ETF. In most cases, if you held the ETF for less than one year, you will have to pay taxes based on the current short-term capital gains rate, which is the same as your ordinary-income tax rate. If you held the ETF for more than one year, you will have to pay taxes based on the current long-term capital gains rate, which is currently 15 percent.

Futures-based ETFs are taxed as *1256 investments*, which means that all capital gains are marked to market at the end of each calendar year. When an asset is marked to market, the IRS treats the investment as if you had sold the fund on December 31 and realized the gains. Luckily, with 1256 investments, 60 percent of the gains are taxed as *long-term capital gains* (which typically have a lower tax rate) and only 40 percent are taxed as *short-term capital gains*.

EXCHANGE-TRADED NOTES

Exchange-traded funds are not the only way to diversify your portfolio into the Forex market without leaving the comfortable confines of your IRA or 401(k). You can get many of the same benefits you would enjoy with ETFs by investing in exchange-traded notes (ETNs). Now, you may be thinking that ETFs and ETNs sound pretty similar, but they are actually quite different.

ETNs are actually senior, unsubordinated debt instruments issued by asset managers. When you buy an ETN, you are not buying a share of assets, you are buying debt—similar to a bond, except that a currency ETN doesn't have a set face value. Instead, the value of an ETN is based on the performance of a currency pair. However, the issuer of the ETN does not have to own any of the currency pairs on which the ETN is based. It just has to make good on its obligations.

This issuer obligation adds a wrinkle to your investing. Although it is a remote possibility, there is a chance that the issuer of the ETN may default on its debt. Again, it's a remote possibility, but you should at least keep it in the back of your mind.

As you get ready to start investing in currency-based ETNs, you need to answer the following three questions:

1. Do you want to invest in one currency at a time or in multiple currencies?
2. What are the fees associated with the ETN?
3. How are the profits you earn on your ETNs going to be taxed?

Once you know the answers to these questions, you will know whether the ETN you are looking at is suitable for you or not.

We're going to analyze ETNs the same way we looked at ETFs; we're going to be looking at currency ETNs from three different asset managers: iPath, Market Vectors, and Barclays GEMS. These are the three dominant asset managers in the currency ETN space at the time of this writing. Gaining an understanding of the differences in the ETNs from these three asset managers should give you the foundation you need to make intelligent investment decisions.

One Currency or Multiple Currencies?

Just as with ETFs, the first decision you have to make as a currency ETN investor is whether you want to invest in a single currency at a time or in multiple currencies at the same time. When you invest in a single currency, you are investing in the value of that currency compared to the U.S. dollar. When you invest in multiple currencies, you are investing in the value of the U.S. dollar compared to that basket of currencies.

Here is a current list of the single-currency ETNs (and their ticker symbols) offered by iPath:

- iPath EUR/USD Exchange Rate ETN (ERO)
- iPath GBP/USD Exchange Rate ETN (GBB)
- iPath JPY/USD Exchange Rate ETN (JYN)

Here is a current list of the single-currency ETNs (and their ticker symbols) offered by Market Vectors:

- Market Vectors Chinese Renminbi/USD ETN (CNY)
- Market Vectors Indian Rupee/USD ETN (INR)

Of course, if you are interested in a leveraged or an inverse ETN, you can also get one from Market Vectors:

- Market Vectors Double Long Euro ETN (URR)
- Market Vectors Double Short Euro ETN (DRR)

Keep in mind that ETN issuers don't have to invest in the underlying assets on which the prices of their ETNs are based, so ETNs don't tend to suffer from the same tracking errors as leveraged ETFs do.

If you want to invest in multiple currencies at the same time, you will most likely be focusing on Barclays GEMS and iPath. Here is a current list of the multiple-currency ETFs offered by these two managers:

- Barclays GEMS Index ETN (JEM)
- Barclays GEMS Asia-8 ETN (AYT)

- Barclays Asian and Gulf Currency Revaluation ETN (PGD)
- iPath Optimized Currency Carry ETN (ICI)

The Barclays GEMS Index ETN invests in the Hungarian forint, Polish zloty, Russian ruble, Turkish lira, South African rand, Argentine peso, Brazilian real, Chilean peso, Colombian peso, Mexican peso, Indian rupee, Indonesian rupiah, South Korean won, Philippine peso, and Thai baht.

The Barclays GEMS Asia-8 ETN invests in the Indonesian rupiah, Indian rupee, Philippine peso, South Korean won, Thai baht, Malaysian ringgit, New Taiwan dollar, and Chinese yuan.

The Barclays Asian and Gulf Currency Revaluation ETN invests in the Chinese yuan, Hong Kong dollar, Saudi Arabian riyal, Singapore dollar, and United Arab Emirates dirham.

The iPath Optimized Currency Carry ETN invests in the U.S. dollar, euro, Japanese yen, Canadian dollar, Swiss franc, British pound, Australian dollar, New Zealand dollar, Norwegian krone, and Swedish krona.

Fees, Fees, Fees

ETNs, just like ETFs, charge fees. Of the three asset managers we are evaluating here, iPath has the lowest average fees and Barclays GEMS has the highest average fees. This isn't too surprising, as the Barclays GEMS ETNs all track multiple currencies, which is more expensive for the issuer to hedge against. At the time of this writing, iPath charges a fee of 0.40 percent for its individual-currency ETNs and a fee of 0.65 percent for its multiple-currency ETN. Market Vectors charges a fee of 0.55 percent. Barclays GEMS charges a fee of 0.89 percent for its multiple-currency ETNs.

Typically, fees are quoted on an annualized basis, such as 0.40 percent per year, but they accrue on a daily basis and are paid on a monthly basis.

Tax Implications

Paying taxes on currency ETNs is fairly straightforward. Whether the ETN pays a monthly interest payment or the manager rolls any proceeds into the value of the ETN instead of distributing them (as the iPath ETNs do), the money you make on your ETN investment is treated as ordinary income.

Here's the one twist. Just as ETFs that invest in futures contracts are marked to market at the end of each year and you are required to pay taxes on any gains, realized or unrealized, ETNs that roll their proceeds into the value of the ETN are treated as if they were marked to market, and you are responsible for paying taxes on any gains.

FOREX OPTIONS

Forex options are unique, multidimensional trading tools and are available in two varieties: spot Forex options and exchange-traded options. Spot Forex options are offered by your dealer, and your dealer serves as counterparty to the trade, just as it does with spot Forex contracts. Exchange-traded options are similar to Forex futures because they trade on an exchange and are cleared by a central clearing agent. Both types of options give you tremendous flexibility in your investing. If you want to use them successfully in your own portfolio, however, you need to become familiar with their distinctive traits.

Forex options consist of two types of contracts: calls and puts.

Call options give the buyer of the option the right, but not the obligation, to buy a currency pair at a certain price on or before a certain date. Conversely, call options obligate the seller of the option to sell a currency pair at a certain price on or before a certain date, if the buyer of the call option chooses to exercise the call.

Put options give the buyer of the option the right, but not the obligation, to sell a currency pair at a certain price on or before a certain date. Conversely, put options obligate the seller of the option to buy a currency pair at a certain price on or before a certain date, if the buyer of the put option chooses to exercise the put.

Every Forex option contract has the following three characteristics:

1. **Strike price:** The price at which you can buy a currency pair (if you have bought a call option or sold a put option) or the price at which you can sell a currency pair (if you have bought a put option or sold a call option).

2. **Expiry date:** The date on which the option expires, or becomes worthless, if the option buyer fails to exercise it. This is typically the Saturday following the third Friday of the expiration month.

3. **Premium:** The price you pay when you buy an option and the price you receive when you sell an option.

For example, you can buy a call option on the EUR/USD with a *strike price* of 1.3300 and an *expiry date* of August 21 by paying a *premium* of $1,800. By doing so, you have paid $1,800 for the right to buy the EUR/USD currency pair at 1.3300 at any time before August 21.

Option Values

As you look at the price of an option contract, you need to be aware that the price is made up of two components: intrinsic value and time value.

Intrinsic value is the value of the option if you were to exercise it right now. It is the price of the underlying asset minus the strike price of the option (for a call option; for a put, it is just the opposite). Theoretically, one could argue that the forward rate of the underlying asset should be used instead of its spot rate, but market convention is to use the spot rate.

Time value is the amount by which the value of the option exceeds the intrinsic value. The volatility of the underlying asset has a significant bearing on the time value. Time value increases as volatility increases because of the profit/loss scenario for an option. The potential upside for an option holder is unlimited, while the downside is limited to the premium paid. Hence, an option on an asset that is more likely to take on extreme values is much more valuable than an option on a less volatile asset.

Let's say that you hold a EUR/USD call option with a 1.2000 strike price, and that the market price of EUR/USD has risen to 1.2155. Your option is worth 225 pips 30 days before the option's expiration date. The intrinsic value is the difference between the strike price for the underlying asset in the option contract (1.2000) and the market price (1.2155). If you hold a call option, which gives you the right to buy EUR/USD at 1.2000, and the market price is

1.2155, the intrinsic value of the option is 155 pips. So the price of the option is the intrinsic value plus the time value (in this case, 70 pips).

Option Styles

Options come in two styles: American and European. *American-style options* can be exercised at any time before their expiration date. This gives option buyers much more flexibility because they get to choose when they exercise their options, but it subjects option sellers to much more risk because they have no idea when an option is going to be exercised or even if it is going to be exercised.

European-style options can be exercised only at expiration. This gives option buyers much less flexibility because they have no say in when they exercise their options, but it also subjects option sellers to much less risk because they know exactly when an option is going to be exercised if it is going to be exercised.

Some Forex options are American-style options, while others are European-style options.

Making Money with Options

Forex option traders can be either option buyers or option sellers. *Option buyers* are those traders who enter a trade by buying either a call or a put option. *Option sellers* are those traders who enter a trade by selling either a call or a put option. Your decision to buy or to sell an option contract will be based on whether you are bullish or bearish on a currency pair.

You can make money with Forex options whether currency pairs are going up, down, or sideways.

- **Up:** If your fundamental and technical analysis tells you that the currency pair is going to be moving up, you can either buy a call option or sell a put option.
- **Down:** If your fundamental and technical analysis tells you that the currency pair is going to be moving down, you can either buy a put option or sell a call option.
- **Sideways:** If your fundamental and technical analysis tells you that the currency pair is going to be moving sideways, you can either sell a call option or sell a put option.

Buying a call option or a put option allows you to achieve virtually unlimited profits so long as the currency pair continues moving higher if you bought a call option or moving lower if you bought a put option. However, the currency pair does have to move far enough to overcome the initial premium that you paid for the option.

Selling a call or a put option allows you to collect your profits up front and keep the full profit so long as the currency pair remains below the strike price of the call that you have sold or above the strike price of the put that you have sold. However, if the currency pair does move past your strike price, you can lose more money than you collected by selling the option.

Option Greeks

The value of an option is affected by five factors, each of which has a Greek name to represent it. Let's take a moment and get acquainted with the following five Greeks:

1. Delta
2. Gamma
3. Theta
4. Vega
5. Rho

Delta describes how the value of an option changes as a result of small changes in the price of the underlying currency pair. When you buy a call or sell a put, your position will have a positive delta. When you sell a call or buy a put, your position will have a negative delta.

Gamma describes how the delta of the option changes with the price of the underlying currency pair. When you buy a call or a put, your position will have a positive gamma. When you sell a call or a put, your position will have a negative gamma.

Theta describes how the value of an option changes as a result of time passing. The theta (sensitivity) is often noted in pips lost per day that passes. When you buy a call or a put, your position will have a negative theta. When you sell a call or a put, your position will have a positive theta.

Vega describes how the value of an option changes as a result of changes in the volatility of the underlying currency pair. The wider the price swings of the underlying currency pair, the higher the volatility. When you buy a call or a put, your position will have a positive vega. When you sell a call or a put, your position will have a negative vega.

Rho describes how the value of an option changes as a result of changes in the interest rate of either currency in the pair. When you buy a call or sell a put, your position will have a positive rho. When you sell a call or buy a put, your position will have a negative rho.

Reading a Risk Graph

Risk graphs are a simple tool that you can use to visualize what the result of your option trade will be in various market situations. Risk graphs illustrate what the result of your option trade will be if the currency pair does any of the following:

- Goes up
- Remains flat
- Goes down

As you look at a risk graph (see Figure 12-1), you will see the following components (we will use a risk graph for a long call to illustrate):

- **Profit/loss axis:** The vertical axis on the left of the chart shows the profit or loss that you will receive. For example, Point C shows a profit along the profit/loss axis, while Point D shows a loss along the profit/loss axis.
- **Currency price axis:** The horizontal axis that runs through the middle of the chart represents the price of the currency pair. Prices run lower to higher from left to right. For example, the price at Point C is higher price than that at Point D.
- **Profit/loss line:** The line that runs through the chart shows the profit or loss that you will receive at any given price along the chart. For example, Point C shows that you will receive a profit when the currency pair is at a higher price,

FIGURE 12-1

Risk Graph

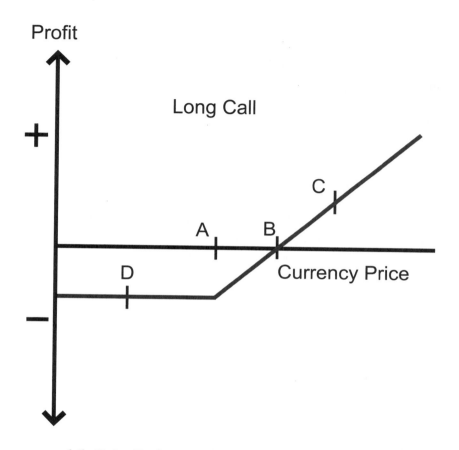

while Point D shows that you will receive a loss when the currency pair is at a lower price.

- **Strike price:** This is the price at which the option holder can exercise an option. The strike price is represented by Point A on the chart. Remember, calls become profitable above the strike price, while puts become profitable below the strike price.

- **Breakeven point:** This is the point at which you neither make money nor lose money on your option trade. The breakeven point is represented by Point B on the chart.

Remember, the breakeven point for calls is always above the strike price, while the breakeven point for puts is always below the strike price.

Exchange-Traded vs. Spot Forex Options

While exchange-traded options and spot options have a lot in common, they do have a few differences. We have already covered the differences in where transactions take place and who serves as counterparty to the trades, but there is still one other important difference to discuss.

The pairing convention of exchange-traded options varies from that used with spot options. With spot Forex options, the pairing convention is the same as the convention used for the spot currency contracts. Exchange-traded Forex options, on the other hand, switch the pairing convention depending on the option.

Let's take a look at Forex options listed on the following exchanges to better understand the differences:

- International Securities Exchange (ISE)
- Philadelphia Exchange (PHLX)
- Chicago Mercantile Exchange (CME)

International Securities Exchange Forex Options
The Forex options listed on the International Securities Exchange (see Table 12-3) are European-style options. All of the FX options list the U.S. dollar (USD) first in the currency pairing, while all of the spot options list the USD second in the currency pairing.

Philadelphia Exchange Forex Options
The Forex options listed on the Philadelphia Exchange (see Table 12-4) are European-style options. All of the Forex options list the U.S. dollar (USD) second in the currency pairing.

Chicago Mercantile Exchange (CME) Forex Options
The Forex options listed on the Chicago Mercantile Exchange (see Table 12-5) are American-style options. All of the Forex options list the U.S. dollar (USD) second in the currency pairing.

TABLE 12-3

Forex Options Listed on the International Securities
Exchange (ISE)

Symbol	Name	Convention
AUX	ISE FX Australian dollar	USD/AUD
BRB	ISE FX Brazilian real	USD/BRL
BPX	ISE FX British pound	USD/GBP
CDD	ISE FX Canadian dollar	USD/CAD
EUI	ISE FX euro	USD/EUR
YUK	ISE FX Japanese yen	USD/JPY
PZO	ISE FX Mexican peso	USD/MXN
NZD	ISE FX New Zealand dollar	USD/NZD
SKA	ISE FX Swedish krona	USD/SEK
SFC	ISE FX Swiss franc	USD/CHF
AUM	ISE Spot AUD/USD	AUD/USD
EUU	ISE Spot EUR/USD	EUR/USD
GBP	ISE Spot GBP/USD	GBP/USD
NDO	ISE Spot NZD/USD	NZD/USD

FINDING THE RIGHT PRODUCT FOR YOUR INVESTING GOALS

With all of these different investment vehicles for accessing the Forex market, you may be wondering which one is right for you. We're so glad you asked.

When it comes to trading currencies, you have to ask yourself the following four questions:

1. What are your currency-trading objectives?
2. How aggressive do you want to be?
3. What investment accounts do you have?
4. Do you want to open additional accounts?

What Are Your Currency-Trading Objectives?

The first question you have to answer for yourself is exactly what you are hoping to get out of your currency trading. Do you want to trade currencies as a speculator who is seeking big profits? Do you

TABLE 12-4

Forex Options Listed on the Philadelphia Exchange

Symbol	Name	Convention
XDA	PHLX U.S. dollar–settled Australian dollar currency options	AUD/USD
XDB	PHLX U.S. dollar–settled British pound currency options	GBP/USD
XDC	PHLX U.S. dollar–settled Canadian dollar currency options	CAD/USD
XDE	PHLX U.S. dollar–settled euro currency options	EUR/USD
XDN	PHLX U.S. dollar–settled Japanese yen currency options	JPY/USD
XDM	PHLX U.S. dollar–settled Mexican peso currency options	MXN/USD
XDZ	PHLX U.S. dollar–settled New Zealand dollar currency options	NZD/USD
XDV	PHLX U.S. dollar–settled Norwegian krone currency options	NKK/USD
XEV	PHLX U.S. dollar–settled South African rand currency options	SAR/USD
XEH	PHLX U.S. dollar–settled Swedish krona currency options	SEK/USD
XDS	PHLX U.S. dollar–settled Swiss franc currency options	CHF/USD

want to trade currencies as a way to add some passive diversification to your portfolio? Do you want to trade currencies to hedge other trades that you are making?

Once you can answer this question, you will be much better prepared to move on to the following questions.

How Aggressive Do You Want to Be?

Your aggressiveness is going to be driven largely by your trading objectives. If you are looking to make a lot of money as a currency speculator, you are probably going to be much more aggressive than if you are looking to add a layer of diversification to a passive portfolio of investments.

TABLE 12-5

Forex Options Listed on the Chicago Mercantile Exchange (CME)

Symbol/Convention	Name
AUD/USD	Australian dollar
BRL/USD	Brazilian real
CAD/USD	Canadian dollar
CHF/USD	Swiss franc
CZK/EUR	Czech koruna/euro
CZK/USD	Czech koruna
EUR/CHF	Euro/Swiss franc
EUR/GBP	Euro/British pound
EUR/JPY	Euro/Japanese yen
EUR/USD	Euro
GBP/USD	British pound
HUF/EUR	Hungarian forint/euro
HUF/USD	Hungarian forint
ILS/USD	Israeli shekel
JPY/USD	Japanese yen
KRW/USD	South Korean won
MXN/USD	Mexican peso
NZD/USD	New Zealand dollar
PLN/EUR	Polish zloty/euro
PLN/USD	Polish zloty
RMB/EUR	Renminbi/euro
RMB/JPY	Renminbi/Japanese yen
RMB/USD	Renminbi
RUB/USD	Russian ruble

If you want to be more aggressive in your currency trading, you should consider focusing on spot Forex, Forex futures, and Forex options. Each of these investment vehicles allows you to take advantage of some degree of leverage, which naturally makes these investments more aggressive.

If you want to be more conservative in your currency trading, you should consider focusing on exchange-traded funds (ETFs) and exchange-traded notes (ETNs). Of course, you will need to identify funds and notes that don't employ any leverage when making their investments if you want your trades to remain conservative.

What Investment Accounts Do You Have?

The investment accounts you already have may be a factor as you decide which Forex products to invest in, because different products are compatible with different account types. For instance, if you have a company 401(k) plan in which you want to do your Forex investing, you may be out of luck. Most 401(k) plans only offer a limited number of mutual funds to account holders, and there usually isn't a Forex-related fund.

On the other hand, if you have a more liberal 401(k) plan or an individual retirement account (IRA) with a stock brokerage like Scottrade, Vanguard, or Fidelity, you will have more choices available to you, but you will probably have to stick with currency exchange-traded funds (ETFs) and exchange-traded notes (ETNs).

Some brokers—like OptionsHouse, tradeMONSTER, and thinkorswim—will allow you to trade exchange-traded Forex options or Forex futures, but you will have to apply for these privileges.

Only if you have an account with a retail foreign exchange dealer (RFED), or with a broker that has an integrated spot-currency platform, will you be able to trade spot Forex products.

Do You Want to Open Additional Accounts?

If you want to trade a currency product that you are currently unable to trade in one of your accounts, you may have to open another trading account. This isn't a difficult process, but it is one you should weigh carefully. Managing multiple accounts adds a layer of complexity to your overall financial planning. It's one more set of login credentials to remember, and one more set of paperwork to account for at tax time.

Now, don't take this the wrong way. We're not trying to discourage you from opening additional accounts. We have additional trading accounts ourselves. We just want to make sure you jump into Forex trading with your eyes wide open.

CHAPTER 13

Effective Technical
Analysis Techniques

We have covered various aspects of fundamental analysis at great length in this book, and that is how it should be. Being aware of the fundamental forces (such as fear and changes in supply and demand) and other fundamental factors (such as central banks, hedge funds, economic announcements, and intermarket influences) that drive currency prices higher and lower is crucial to your long-term success in the Forex market. However, we would be doing you an incredible disservice if we talked only about fundamental analysis and completely ignored technical analysis.

Technical analysis is the process of looking at the price chart of a currency pair and trying to determine where the price of that currency pair might be going in the future and where it probably won't be going in the future.

Some investors try to disparage technical analysis by calling it voodoo or other derogatory terms, but these investors need to catch up with the times. Technical analysis may not have been as widely accepted a few decades ago because it was so difficult to do without computers. But now that any retail Forex investor with a paper-trading account has access to incredibly flexible price charts, technical analysis has been widely adopted across the industry.

Technical analysis has become something of a self-fulfilling prophecy. You see, the big players in the Forex market, like hedge funds, are all using technical analysis when they make their trading decisions. And since these traders have the ability to push market prices, especially if they are all looking at similar price points on their charts, currency prices will change as these traders place their orders at these price points, thus fulfilling what the technical analysts thought was going to happen at those prices points.

So why should you learn about technical analysis? You should learn about it because the major players who move the Forex market utilize it in their trading, which means that you need to be aware of what they are watching so that you don't get caught off guard.

With that in mind, we will be covering the following technical analysis concepts in this chapter:

- Following the trends
- Recognizing support and resistance levels
- Identifying price patterns
- Utilizing technical indicators

FOLLOWING THE TRENDS

The key to making money in the Forex market is to identify a trend and trade with it. Trends tell you where prices are most likely to be going in the future. If the trend of a currency pair is pointing up, you need to buy the currency pair if you are to make money. If the trend of a currency pair is pointing down, you need to sell the currency pair if you are to make money. If the trend of a currency pair is pointing sideways, you need to either alternate between buying and selling or wait until the trend points up or down if you are to make money. Whatever you do, never fight the trend. It will be an expensive battle if you do.

Trends do not move straight up or straight down. They usually move in one direction for a while, then retrace part of their previous movement before turning back around and continuing in the previous direction. Every time a currency pair turns around and begins moving in the opposite direction, it forms a new high or a new low. New highs form when a currency pair moves higher and then turns around and moves lower. New lows form when a currency pair moves lower and then turns around and moves higher.

Identifying these highs and lows allows you to identify whether a currency pair is in an uptrend, a downtrend, or a sideways trend.

Uptrends: Currency pairs that are trending upward form a series of higher highs and higher lows (see Figure 13-1).

Downtrends: Currency pairs that are trending downward form a series of lower highs and lower lows (see Figure 13-2).

Sideways Trends: Currency pairs that are trending sideways form a series of highs that are at approximately the same price level and a series of lows that are at approximately the same price level (see Figure 13-3).

RECOGNIZING SUPPORT AND RESISTANCE LEVELS

You will increase your trading profitability if you can accurately identify levels of support and resistance—areas where prices may stop and turn around in the future. Knowing where a currency pair may stop and turn around helps you enter and exit your trades at the most profitable times.

Support is a price level at which a currency pair tends to stop moving down, then turns around and starts moving back up.

So what causes a support level to form? Sometimes support levels form when traders who missed an earlier buying opportunity

FIGURE 13-1

Uptrend

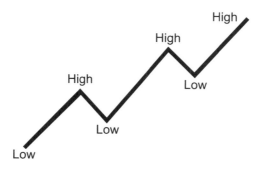

FIGURE 13-2

Downtrend

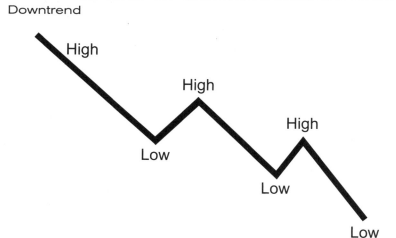

when the currency pair was at the same price level decide that this gives them a great second chance to get into the trade. Support levels also form when traders who are already in a trade decide to add to, or double up on, their trade. Finally, support levels can form when traders who are short a currency pair decide that this is a good time to take profits and buy back the currency pair to close out of the trade.

Resistance is a price level at which a currency pair tends to stop moving up, then turns around and starts moving back down.

FIGURE 13-3

Sideways Trend

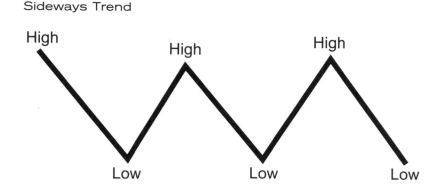

So what causes a resistance level to form? Sometimes resistance levels form when traders who missed an earlier selling opportunity when the currency pair was at the same price level decide that this gives them a great second chance to get into the trade. Resistance levels also form when traders who are already in a trade decide to add to, or double up on, their trade. Finally, resistance levels can form when traders who are long a currency pair decide that this is a good time to take profits and sell the currency pair to close out of the trade.

Support and resistance levels are not precise price points. Rather, they are general price ranges. For example, you are only going to frustrate yourself if you try to pinpoint a price level of 1.3617 on the EUR/USD as support. You will be much better off if you identify a price range of 1.3600 to 1.3630 or 1.3605 to 1.3625 as support. Think of drawing your support and resistance levels with a big, fat crayon instead of a fine-point pen. This will help you remember to give these levels the flexibility they demand.

You will find that support and resistance levels come in varying forms. To become a successful Forex investor, you will need to learn to recognize the following:

- Horizontal support and resistance
- Diagonal support and resistance

Horizontal Support and Resistance

Horizontal support and resistance levels are perhaps the easiest levels to identify. As you look at the charts of the currency pairs that you are interested in trading, you will begin to notice that the currency pairs will often rise and fall to the same price levels before turning around and moving back in the opposite direction. These price levels are horizontal support and resistance levels.

Looking at the GBP/USD chart, for instance, you can see that certain price levels (indicated by bold lines) acted as strong levels of support and resistance. During 2010, the GBP/USD bounced back and forth between a support level at about 1.5350 and a resistance level at about 1.6000 (see Figure 13-4).

Suppose you had bought the GBP/USD at 1.5350 as it was bouncing off of support, and it was now approaching 1.6000.

FIGURE 13-4

Horizontal Support and Resistance

Knowing that this level has been a significant resistance level, you might consider exiting your GBP/USD trade so that you can realize your profits before the currency pair turns around and begins moving lower.

Once you feel comfortable identifying horizontal support and resistance levels, you can move on to diagonal support and resistance levels.

Diagonal Support and Resistance

Diagonal support and resistance levels can be more difficult to identify when you are just getting started. However, diagonal support and resistance levels are usually the most important levels when you are analyzing a currency pair that is trending. Remember, you want to find trending currency pairs because it is much easier to make profitable trades when a currency pair is trending.

As you look at the charts of the currency pairs you are interested in trading, you will begin to notice that the currency pairs will often rise and fall in a stair-step pattern. These patterns form higher highs and higher lows or lower highs and lower lows. The lines that connect these highs and lows are your diagonal support and resistance levels.

Looking at the same GBP/USD chart, for instance, you can see that the currency pair was creating a series of lower highs and lower lows in November and December of 2010. If you connect all the highs with a diagonal line and all the lows with another diagonal line (indicated by bold lines), you will be able to see the diagonal levels of support and resistance that were affecting the GBP/USD (see Figure 13-5).

If you were watching the GBP/USD, you would wait until you saw the currency pair rise to the downtrending resistance level before you sold it. Once you were in your trade, you could then watch for the GBP/USD to drop down to the downtrending support level before you exited the trade and took your profits.

The real trick to using support and resistance levels to invest effectively is to combine both horizontal and diagonal levels in

FIGURE 13-5

Diagonal Support and Resistance

your analysis. Your currency charts have a wealth of information locked within them, and they are waiting for you to unlock that information with simple, but effective, technical analysis techniques.

IDENTIFYING PRICE PATTERNS

Price patterns are a lot like the brake lights on the cars around you when you are driving in traffic. When you see the brake lights on the car in front of you come on, you know that the car is slowing down and that you need to slow down too unless you want to crash into it. What you don't know is whether the car is going to accelerate and continue moving in the same direction after it slows down, or whether it is going to come to a complete stop and change direction.

When you see a price pattern starting to form on a Forex chart, you know that the pair is starting to slow down, or consolidate, and that you need to slow down, take a step back, and evaluate what may happen to it. What you don't know is whether the currency pair is going to break out and continue moving in the same direction after it slows down, or whether it is going to turn around and change direction.

Price patterns are an underutilized and extremely valuable tool in your Forex-trading arsenal. It may take you a little while to get comfortable with dealing with the subtle nuances and occasional ambiguity that are a part of price patterns, but once you do, you will feel like you are able to see into the future.

Price patterns are visual representations of market psychology. They tell you when traders in the market are excited and moving, when they need to take a moment and catch their breath and regroup, and when they are ready to get moving again.

Attributes of Price Patterns

All price patterns are made up of the following four pieces (see Figure 13-6):

1. **Old trend:** The trend that the currency pair is in as it starts to form the price pattern

FIGURE 13-6

Price Pattern Attributes

2. **Consolidation zone:** A constrained area defined by set support and resistance levels in which the trend is undefined or channeling
3. **Breakout point:** The point at which the currency pair breaks from the consolidation zone
4. **New trend:** The trend that the currency pair enters coming out of the consolidation zone

Types of Price Patterns

Price patterns are divided into two major categories: continuation patterns and reversal patterns.

1. *Continuation patterns* tell you that the new trend is going to continue in the same direction as the old trend was moving.

2. *Reversal patterns* tell you that the new trend is going to reverse directions and move in the opposite direction from that in which the old trend was moving.

The only real difference between continuation patterns and reversal patterns is the direction in which the new trend is moving. Both types of patterns have an old trend, a consolidation zone, a breakout point, and a new trend.

Continuation Patterns

Road trips are some of our favorite vacations. You jump in the car, head out on the open highway, and soak in all the scenery that you miss when you fly somewhere. Of course, every once in a while you have to interrupt your cruising to take a pit stop—to put some gas in your car and buy some snacks.

Pit stops are part of the adventure. And let's face it, driving would get pretty old after a while if you didn't stop and take a break every now and then. At the same time, nobody wants to spend his entire vacation at the rest stop. So once you've had a chance to stretch your legs and fill up the gas tank, you jump back into the car and head back out on the open road.

Currency pairs take exciting road trips all the time. They cruise along for a while, passing support and resistance levels and other significant price points along the way, but every once in a while, they need to take a pit stop. After big price moves, the traders who are pushing these currency pairs higher and lower have to stop to catch their breath. Don't get too comfortable, though. The pit stop isn't going to last forever.

If the currency pair is really in the middle of a road trip, a continuation pattern will form while the currency pair consolidates in its pit stop. Continuation patterns tell you that the currency pair is going to resume its previous trend after it breaks out of the continuation pattern.

Identifying Continuation Patterns

Continuation patterns, like all price patterns, are made up of the following four pieces (see again Figure 13-6):

1. **Old trend:** The trend that the currency pair is in as it starts to form the price pattern
2. **Consolidation zone:** A constrained area defined by set support and resistance levels
3. **Breakout point:** The point at which the currency pair breaks out of the consolidation zone
4. **New trend:** A resumption of the old trend that the currency pair enters as it comes out of the consolidation zone

Continuation patterns form in a few different shapes, but for the most part, they look quite similar. The only real difference you will see is in the shape of the consolidation zone. The consolidation zones of some continuation patterns have support and resistance levels that converge as the pattern forms, while others have support and resistance levels that remain parallel. Every other aspect of the price pattern is identical.

Continuation Patterns During an Uptrend
The following are the most common continuation patterns you will see during an uptrend.

Pennants: These form during an uptrend when the uptrending support level and the downtrending resistance level that encompass the consolidation zone converge.

Flags: Flags form during an uptrend when the horizontal or downtrending support level and the horizontal or downtrending resistance level that encompass the consolidation zone remain parallel.

Wedges: When the downtrending support level and the downtrending resistance level that encompass the consolidation zone converge during an uptrend, you see a wedge.

Ascending triangles: Ascending triangles form during an uptrend when the uptrending support level and the horizontal resistance level that encompass the consolidation zone converge.

Continuation Patterns During a Downtrend

The following are the most common continuation patterns you will see during a downtrend.

> **Pennant:** Pennants form during a downtrend when the uptrending support level and the downtrending resistance level that encompass the consolidation zone converge.
>
> **Flags:** Flags form during a downtrend when the horizontal or uptrending support level and the horizontal or uptrending resistance level that encompass the consolidation zone remain parallel.
>
> **Wedges:** Watch for wedges during a downtrend when the uptrending support level and the uptrending resistance level that encompass the consolidation zone converge.
>
> **Descending Triangles:** Descending triangles form during a downtrend when the horizontal support level and the downtrending resistance level that encompass the consolidation zone converge.

Learning to identify price patterns enables you to get a glimpse into the future price movement of the currency pair. Once you have identified a breakout point, you can get a pretty good idea of where the price is going to go in the near future, and you can take advantage of that potential movement.

Reversal Patterns

As you learned in the continuation patterns lesson, road trips are some of our favorite vacations. You jump in the car, head out on the open highway, and soak in all the scenery that you miss when you fly somewhere.

Unfortunately, every road trip has to come to an end at some point, and you have to turn around and drive back home. Sometimes you just turn around and head back immediately, but sometimes you delay heading home for a little bit and cruise around a little longer. But either way, you end up turning around.

Currency pairs turn around and end their road trips, too. They run into support or resistance levels, and eventually they turn around and start moving back in the opposite direction. Sometimes they turn around immediately, and sometimes they test the support or resistance level in front of them a few times before finally giving up and turning around. Either way, they eventually end up turning around.

If the currency pair really is at the end of its road trip and is ready to turn around and head home, a reversal pattern will form while the currency pair consolidates. Reversal patterns tell you that the currency pair is going to turn around and reverse its previous trend after it breaks out of the continuation pattern.

Identifying Reversal Patterns

Reversal patterns, like all price patterns, are made of the following four pieces (see Figure 13-7):

1. **Old trend:** The trend that the currency pair is in as it starts to form the price pattern
2. **Consolidation zone:** A constrained area defined by set support and resistance levels
3. **Breakout point:** The point at which the currency pair breaks out of the consolidation zone
4. **New trend:** A reversal of the old trend that the currency pair enters as it comes out of the consolidation zone

Reversal patterns come in a few different shapes, but for the most part, they look quite similar. The only real difference you will see is in the shape of the consolidation zone. The consolidation zones of some reversal patterns have a single level of support and a single level of resistance, while others have multiple levels of support and multiple levels of resistance. Every other aspect of the price pattern is identical.

Reversal Patterns During an Uptrend

The following are the most common reversal patterns that you will see during an uptrend.

>   **Double tops:** Double tops form during an uptrend when the uptrending currency pair hits the same resistance level twice in the consolidation zone.

FIGURE 13-7

Reversal Pattern Attributes

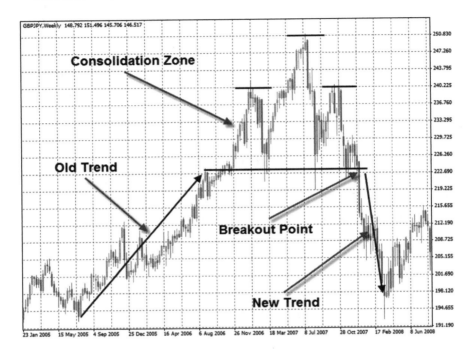

Triple tops: Triple tops form during an uptrend when the uptrending currency pair hits the same resistance level three times in the consolidation zone.

Head-and-shoulders tops: Head-and-shoulders tops form during an uptrend when the uptrending currency pair hits a lower resistance level, then hits a higher resistance level, and then hits the lower resistance level a second time in the consolidation zone.

Reversal Patterns During a Downtrend

The following are the most common reversal patterns you will see during a downtrend.

Double bottoms: Double bottoms form during a downtrend when the downtrending currency pair hits the same support level twice in the consolidation zone.

Triple bottoms: Triple bottoms form during a downtrend when the downtrending currency pair hits the same support level three times in the consolidation zone.

Head-and-shoulders bottoms: Head-and-shoulders bottoms form during a downtrend when the downtrending currency pair hits a higher support level, then hits a lower support level, and then hits the higher support level a second time in the consolidation zone.

UTILIZING TECHNICAL INDICATORS

Once you have a good grip on the concepts of trends and support and resistance, and only then, can you move on and start looking at the potential for using technical indicators in your analysis. You may be wondering why we are starting with such a strong word of caution regarding technical indicators. After all, you have probably heard that technical indicators are simple and easy to use. You have probably even heard that technical indicators are the magic bullet that can unlock the secret to fabulous riches in the Forex market. Well, that is exactly why we are being so forceful here.

Technical indicators are not the be-all and end-all of technical analysis. They certainly provide clues to where the market may be going in the future, but they are by no means infallible. As we discuss these indicators, it is important to remember that they are based on past data, so they inherently lag what is currently happening in the market. In other words, they are not a crystal ball.

So with that out of the way, let's take a look at the following four technical indicators, which should give you a basic overview of the various types of indicators:

- Simple moving average
- Moving-average convergence/divergence (MACD)
- Stochastic oscillator
- Bollinger bands

Simple Moving Average

The simple moving average is the most basic of technical indicators. It is also one of the most popular indicators because it is so easy to use.

To help you better understand what the simple moving average is and how you can use it in your investing, we will discuss the following:

- Interpreting the simple moving average
- Evaluating support and resistance levels with the simple moving average
- Identifying trading signals generated by the simple moving average

Interpreting the Simple Moving Average

A simple moving average is a fully customizable trending indicator that consists of a single line that plots the mean stock price over a specified period of time. For example, a 30-day simple moving average will plot the average price of the currency pair during the last 30 trading periods, including the current period on the price chart.

You can see in Figure 13-8 that the simple moving average is illustrated with a line that moves up and down as it follows the stock price.

The simple moving average shows the relationship of the currency pair's current price to the average price of the pair in the past. If the current price is above the moving average, you know that the price of the currency pair is moving higher than it was in the past. If the current price is below the moving average, you know that the price of the currency pair is moving lower than it was in the past. You can see an example of both scenarios in Figure 13-9.

Traders use the simple moving average to determine whether the currency pair is in an uptrend or a downtrend. If the simple moving average is trending higher and the price of the currency pair is above it, the currency pair is considered to be in an uptrend. If the simple moving average is trending lower and the price of the currency pair is below it, the currency pair is considered to be in a downtrend.

FIGURE 13-8

Simple Moving Average

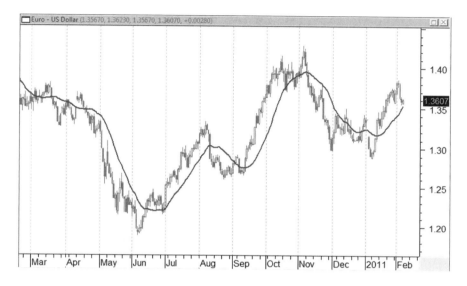

FIGURE 13-9

Relationship of Price to Simple Moving Average

Of course, many traders are looking for much more specific information from a technical indicator than whether the currency pair appears to be in an uptrend or in a downtrend. The simple moving average provides this. Let's take a look.

Evaluating Support and Resistance Levels with the Simple Moving Average

Traders also use the simple moving average to identify potential levels of support and resistance. If the price of the currency pair is above an uptrending simple moving average, as you can see in Figure 13-10, the simple moving average can act as a potential support level.

Similarly, if the price of the currency pair is below a downtrending simple moving average, as you can see in Figure 13-11, the simple moving average can act as a potential resistance level.

However, when the simple moving average is trending sideways, it typically will not provide any reliable information on where the support and resistance levels are. As you can see in Figure 13-12, when the simple moving average is moving

FIGURE 13-10

Simple Moving Average Acting as Support

FIGURE 13-11

Simple Moving Average Serving as Resistance

sideways, it tends to cut through the middle of the price action, not be above or below it.

Knowing where potential levels of support or resistance are forming can inform your trading decisions and help you determine potential entry and exit signals.

Now that you've seen how the simple moving average can help you identify potential levels of support and resistance, let's take a look at how you can use the simple moving average to identify specific trading signals.

Identifying Trading Signals Generated by the Simple Moving Average

The simple moving average produces trading signals when you see support and resistance bounces off the moving average.

Buy Signals

The simple moving average generates buy signals when you see the price of the currency pair bounce up off an *uptrending* moving average; see Figure 13-13.

FIGURE 13-12

Moving Average During Sideways Trend

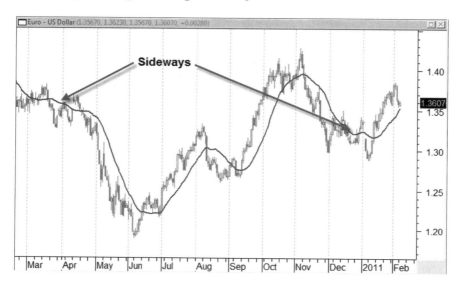

FIGURE 13-13

Simple Moving Average Buy Signals

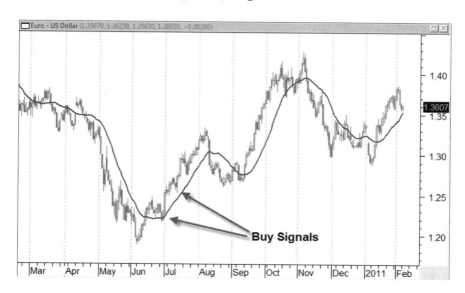

While this may seem like a small detail, it is important that the moving average be in an uptrend when you are looking for buy signals. If the moving average is trending sideways or downward, it will not provide reliable buy signals.

Sell Signals

The simple moving average generates sell signals when you see the stock price bounce down off a *downtrending* moving average; see Figure 13-14.

While this may seem like a small detail, it is important that the moving average be in a downtrend when you are looking for sell signals. If the moving average is trending sideways or upward, it will not provide reliable sell signals.

Conclusion

The simple moving average is an efficient technical indicator that is relatively simple to understand and extremely easy to use. You

FIGURE 13-14

Simple Moving Average Sell Signals

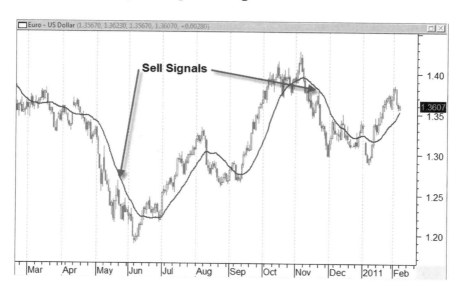

can use it to identify not only bullish and bearish trends, but also specific levels of support and resistance.

Of course, like any other technical indicator, the simple moving average is a lagging indicator because it is based on price data from the past. Use caution when interpreting any lagging indicator, because what happened in the past is not a guarantee of what will happen in the future.

Moving-Average Convergence/Divergence (MACD)

Gerald Appel is generally credited with creating and popularizing the moving-average convergence/divergence (MACD) indicator in the 1960s. This indicator is one of the most popular oscillating indicators used by traders and is often displayed as two intersecting lines below the price chart. The MACD is primarily a trend-following indicator and can also be used to generate buy or sell signals.

To help you better understand what the MACD is and how you can use it in your investing, we will discuss the following:

- Interpreting the MACD
- Using the MACD as a trend-following indicator
- Using MACD divergences to identify potential trend changes

Interpreting the MACD

The MACD indicator consists of two lines. The first one is called the *MACD line* and represents the difference between two exponential moving averages. If the market is moving very fast, the difference between these two exponential moving averages will be very large, and the MACD line will be moving up or down very quickly.

The second line on the MACD indicator is an exponential moving average of the MACD line. This line is called the *signal line*. Because the signal line is an exponential moving average of the MACD line, it will always lag the MACD line.

When the MACD line crosses above the signal line, it is a bullish signal. When the MACD line crosses below the signal line, it is a bearish signal. You can see in Figure 13-15 what the MACD looks like when the market is in a downtrend versus an uptrend.

FIGURE 13-15

Moving-Average Convergence/Divergence

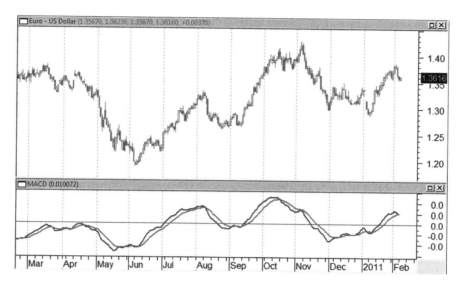

The general rule of thumb is that traders are buying when the MACD line is above the signal line and shorting the market, or selling, when the MACD is below the signal line. Let's start learning how to use the MACD to identify potential trend-following opportunities.

Using the MACD as a Trend-Following Indicator

The MACD is an oscillator, which means that it (like all oscillators) can be very volatile in a channeling or flat market and less so in a trending market. Therefore, it is not wise to arbitrarily take all signals that the MACD generates. Rather, you should use the MACD to filter opportunities and to help you understand the underlying momentum within the current trend.

As mentioned previously, if the MACD is above the signal line, traders will most likely be buying into the currency pair that they are analyzing. For example, in Figure 13-16, you can see that the MACD was above the signal line in September, indicating a

FIGURE 13-16

Narrowing MACD

bullish market, but that the distance between the lines began to narrow in October. This indicates a weakening trend and would be a good time to pay more attention to risk control.

Once the MACD line actually crosses the signal line, as happened in late October, technical traders may consider exiting the trade. The same analysis can be done in reverse to find shorting opportunities in the market.

As you can see in the figures in the next section, the MACD can move above and below its signal line frequently when the market is more flat. Using each of these crosses as a buy or sell signal could lead to overtrading and excessive losses. This is why it is wise to use the MACD in combination with other analytical methods.

Using MACD Divergences to Identify Potential Trend Changes

The MACD can identify potential trend changes when the sequential highs or lows of the oscillator do not match the corresponding highs and lows of the price chart. Bullish divergences indicate a potential change from a downtrend to an uptrend, and bearish divergences indicate a potential change from an uptrend to a downtrend.

A bearish divergence consists of a series of at least two higher highs on the price chart that coincide with a series of lower highs on the MACD oscillator. Bearish divergences indicate that the trend is weakening and may change in the near term. You can see an example of what this looked like during the months of September through November in Figure 13-17.

A bullish divergence consists of at least two sequentially lower lows on the price chart that coincide with sequentially higher lows on the MACD oscillator. Bullish divergences indicate that the downtrend is weakening and may change in the near term. You can see an example of what this looked like during the months of May and June in Figure 13-18.

FIGURE 13-17

MACD Bearish Divergence

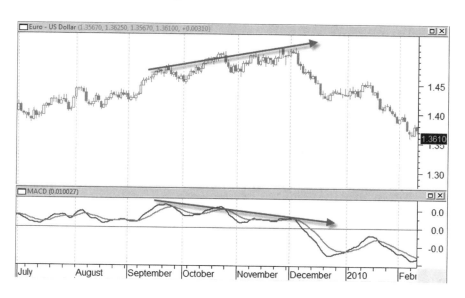

FIGURE 13-18

MACD Bullish Divergence

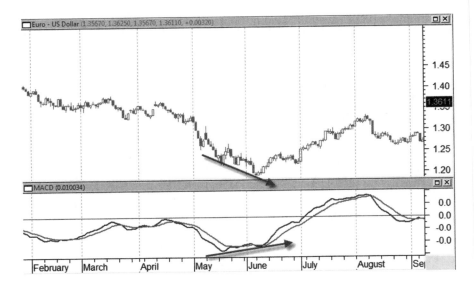

The MACD produces divergence signals for bearish or bullish trades in the following two scenarios:

1. A bullish divergence is indicated by sequentially lower lows on the price chart with coinciding higher lows on the MACD indicator. Bullish divergences signal the potential for a new uptrend.

2. A bearish divergence is indicated by sequentially higher highs on the price chart with coinciding lower highs on the MACD indicator. Bearish divergences signal the potential for a new downtrend.

Divergences indicate that prices are overextended to the upside or the downside. This overextension makes a correction or change in price direction more likely. Traders use divergences both to signal trade entries and exits and to identify periods of time when risk control is more important.

Conclusion

The MACD is one of the most common technical indicators and has been used by traders for more than 40 years. Although the MACD is an oscillator, it can be used both to find changes in trend (through divergences) and as a trend-following indicator. The MACD is easy to customize and can be used the same way each and every time, regardless of whether you are analyzing currencies, individual stocks, or stock indexes.

Stochastic Oscillator

The stochastic oscillator, which comes in three variations (fast, slow, and full), was originally developed by George C. Lane in the late 1950s, but it is still a favorite of many traders and technical analysts nearly 50 years later. Two of the reasons that the full stochastic oscillator has gained in popularity are that it is easy to read and that it provides clear buy and sell signals.

To help you better understand what the full stochastic oscillator is and how you can use it in your investing, we will discuss the following:

- Interpreting the full stochastic oscillator
- Evaluating momentum with the full stochastic oscillator
- Identifying trading signals generated by the full stochastic oscillator

Interpreting the Full Stochastic Oscillator

The full stochastic oscillator is a fully customizable momentum indicator that consists of two lines, %K and %D, that move back and forth and crisscross over each other in a range between 0 and 100.

You can see in Figure 13-19 that %K always turns and changes direction first and %D always follows and turns after %K has made its turn. You can also see that %K is the leader and %D is the follower, so when you are evaluating the full stochastic indicator, most of your attention should be focused on %K.

The full stochastic oscillator shows the relationship of the currency pair's current closing price to the currency pair's trading

FIGURE 13-19

Stochastic Oscillator

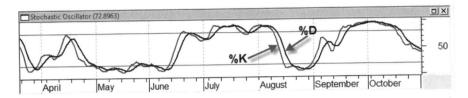

range in the past. If the current closing price is toward the top of the past trading range, %K will move higher. If the current closing price is toward the bottom of the past trading range, %K will move lower. You can see an example of both scenarios in Figure 13-20.

Traders use the full stochastic oscillator to determine whether there is bullish or bearish momentum behind a currency pair and to determine specific entry and exit points for their trades. Let's start by taking a look at how you can use the full stochastic oscillator to determine momentum, and then we will look at how you can use it to identify trading signals.

Evaluating Momentum with the Full Stochastic Oscillator

Not all traders use technical indicators to identify specific buy and sell signals. Many traders use technical indicators to give them an indication of whether a currency pair has bullish or bearish momentum behind it. The full stochastic indicator does a marvelous job of providing this information. When %K is above %D, as you can see in Figure 13-21, the full stochastic oscillator is showing bullish momentum.

FIGURE 13-20

%K Movement

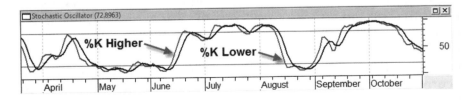

FIGURE 13-21

Bullish Momentum on the Stochastic Oscillator

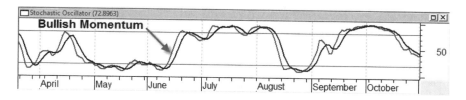

When %K is below %D, as you can see in Figure 13-22, the full stochastic oscillator is showing bearish momentum.

Also, when %K is above 80, it is showing that the market may be overbought, and when %K is below 20, it is showing that the market may be oversold. (See Figure 13-23.)

Knowing when a currency pair has bullish or bearish momentum behind it or when it may be overbought or oversold can inform your trading decisions. Of course, many traders are looking for much more specific information from a technical indicator than whether or not the stock appears to have bullish or bearish momentum. These traders are looking for trading signals, and the full stochastic oscillator is more than happy to oblige. Let's take a look.

Identifying Trading Signals Generated by the Full Stochastic Oscillator

The full stochastic oscillator produces trading signals in the following two scenarios:

FIGURE 13-22

Bearish Momentum on the Stochastic Oscillator

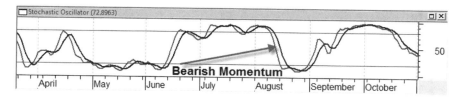

FIGURE 13-23

Overbought and Oversold Readings on the Stochastic Oscillator

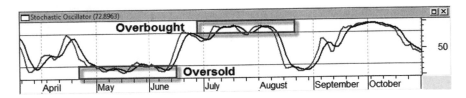

1. **Reversals:** When %K enters and exits its upper and lower reversal zones
2. **Divergences:** When %K diverges from the price action of the stock

Let's start by looking at what happens when %K enters and exits its upper and lower reversal zones.

Reversals

The upper reversal zone is the area of the indicator that lies between 80 and 100. The lower reversal zone is the area of the indicator that lies between 0 and 20. Entry trading signals come either when %K rises up above 80 and then crosses back down below 80 or when %K drops down below 20 and then crosses back up above 20, as you can see in Figure 13-24.

Exit trading signals come when, after having moved out of the upper or lower reversal zone, %K crosses back over %D, as you can see in Figure 13-25.

Now let's take a look at the trading signals that are generated by divergences between %K and the price of the stock.

FIGURE 13-24

Entry Signals

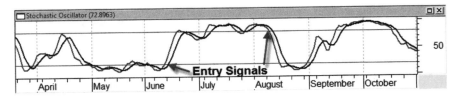

FIGURE 13-25

Exit Signals

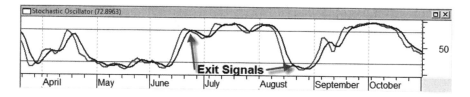

Divergences

In fact, %K does not always follow the price movement of the currency pair. At times, the currency pair price will be creating higher highs or lower lows while %K is creating lower highs or higher lows. When this happens, %K is diverging from the price of the currency pair, and you have a trading signal.

Divergences come in two forms: bullish divergences and bearish divergences. Bullish divergences occur when the price of the currency pair is creating lower lows, but %K is creating higher lows, as seen in Figure 13-26.

FIGURE 13-26

Bullish Divergence on the Stochastic Oscillator

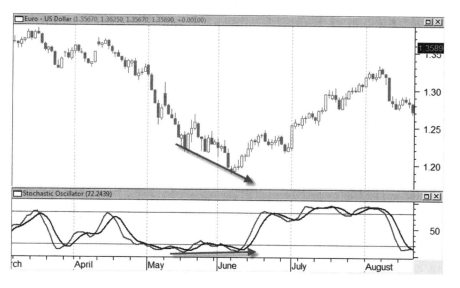

Bearish divergences occur when the price of the currency pair is creating higher highs, but %K is creating lower highs. A bullish or bearish divergence is completed—and you receive your trading signal—when %K crosses over %D after having formed the higher low or the lower high, as you can see in Figure 13-27.

Exit trading signals come the same way that they come in reversal trades—when %K crosses back over %D, as you can see in Figure 13-28.

Conclusion

The full stochastic oscillator is an efficient technical indicator that is relatively simple to understand and extremely easy to use. You can use it to identify not only bullish and bearish momentum, but also specific entry and exit trading signals.

Of course, like any other technical indicator, the full stochastic oscillator is a lagging indicator because it is based on price data from the past. Use caution when interpreting any lagging indicator, because what happened in the past is not a guarantee of what will happen in the future.

FIGURE 13-27

Bearish Divergence on the Stochastic Oscillator

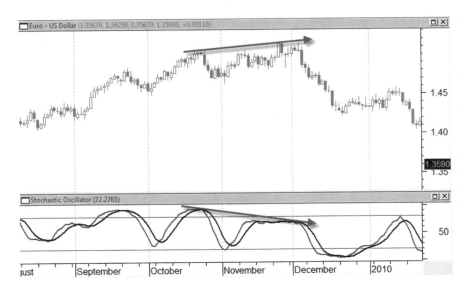

FIGURE 13-28

Exit Signal on the Stochastic Oscillator

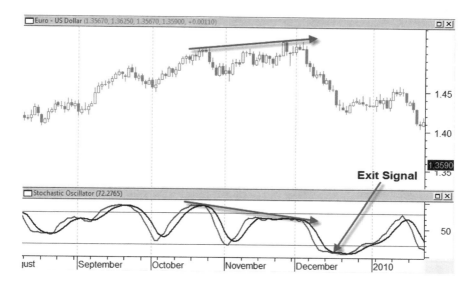

Bollinger Bands

Bollinger bands have been a popular indicator since their development by John Bollinger in the early 1980s. The bands are customizable and are used to identify both periods of relatively high price volatility and periods of relatively low price volatility compared to the recent past.

To help you better understand what Bollinger bands are and how you can use them in your investing, we will discuss the following:

- Interpreting Bollinger bands
- Identifying potential volatility breakouts with Bollinger bands
- Using Bollinger bands as a trend-following tool

Interpreting Bollinger Bands

Bollinger bands consist of a moving average and two volatility bands that are displayed equidistant above and below the moving average. The bands are typically placed two standard deviations away from the moving average, but they can be customized to be farther away from the moving average by increasing the number of standard deviations or closer to the moving average by decreasing the number of standard deviations. The moving average is typically a 20-period moving average, but it can also be customized to be more sensitive to price movements by decreasing the number of periods or less sensitive to price movements by increasing the number of periods.

You can see in Figure 13-29 that the moving average is illustrated with a line that bisects two other lines on the price chart. The upper and lower lines that surround the moving average are the two Bollinger bands.

Bollinger bands show the relative price volatility over the moving-average period. When prices are near the upper band, it means that upward price volatility is greater than it has been over the last 20 periods. When prices are near or at the lower price band, it means that there has been more price volatility to the downside

FIGURE 13-29

Bollinger Bands

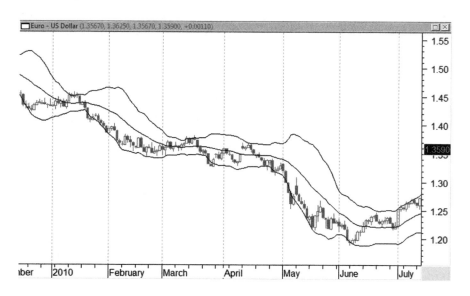

than at other times over the 20 periods. You can see an example of both scenarios in Figure 13-30.

Traders use Bollinger bands to identify both potential volatility breakouts and trend formations. Bollinger bands point to potential volatility breakouts when the bands narrow, and they point to potential trend formations when prices are following, or "walking" along, either the upper or the lower band.

Let's start by taking a look at how you can use the Bollinger bands to identify potential price breakouts, and then we will look at how you can use them to identify trend-following signals.

Identifying Potential Volatility Breakouts with Bollinger Bands
While Bollinger bands are not usually used to trigger a trade, they can be an excellent filter for identifying a potential opportunity. Filtering for potential volatility breakouts can help you identify periods in which there is a high likelihood that the market will make a large move up or down in the near term.

Volatility, or wide price swings, is a normal condition for the financial markets. When volatility slows or declines, it is usually

FIGURE 13-30

Price Volatility and Bollinger Bands

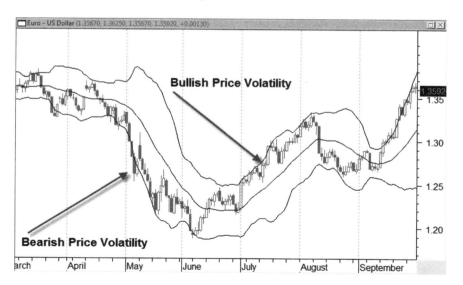

a temporary situation that will often end with a dramatic move in one direction or the other. During periods of low price volatility, the Bollinger bands will narrow and move closer to the moving average. Traders will often call an extreme narrowing of the Bollinger bands a "squeeze."

In Figure 13-31, you can see a squeeze appearing at the beginning of March on the currency pair featured in the chart. The width of the bands was narrower than it had been for several months. Toward the end of March, the bands started to widen again, but they quickly began to contract once more in early April. It is not uncommon to see fake outs like this followed by a new contraction.

Traders are interested in these periods of very low volatility as an indicator that large price movements are imminent. However, the Bollinger bands cannot tell us specifically when or in which direction the breakout will occur.

Traders are usually looking for the first few large trading periods following a squeeze to trigger a trade in the direction of the breakout. This is important. As you saw in the fake out in March in

FIGURE 13-31

Bollinger Band Squeeze

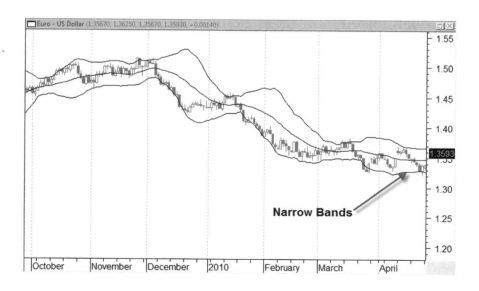

Figure 13-31, one-day moves can reverse themselves quite quickly. If you wait for a confirmation of the breakout, you can avoid many of the fake outs. You can see the squeeze in April featured in Figure 13-31 resolve into a short but fast move to the downside in Figure 13-32 after confirming the breakout by moving lower for consecutive days.

Traders will often use other technical indicators, like a stochastic oscillator or the MACD, to trigger the actual trade following the volatility breakout. One note of caution regarding volatility breakouts: watch out for "head fakes." Head fakes, or fake-outs, occur when the currency pair breaks out from a squeeze in one direction and then immediately reverses course. Using appropriate risk management and stop losses in your trading is critical if you want to avoid the large losses that can result from head fakes.

Using Bollinger Bands as a Trend-Following Tool

Bollinger bands can also help you identify strong momentum within a trend. For example, when prices are near the upper band, traders assume that there is strength behind an uptrend. Conversely, if

FIGURE 13-32

Volatility Breakout

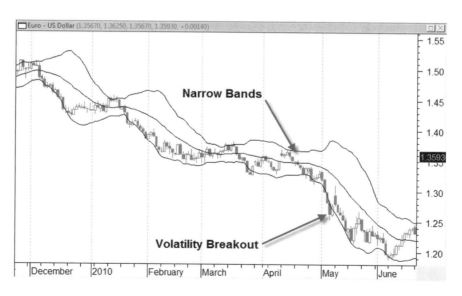

prices are near the lower band while the market in general is in an uptrend, traders assume that the trend is weak.

Bollinger bands produce trend signals for bullish trades in the following two scenarios:

1. A strong trend occurs when the overall market trend is up and prices are at or near the upper Bollinger band.
2. A weak trend occurs when the overall market trend is up and prices are at or near the lower Bollinger band.

In Figure 13-33, you can see how these two scenarios look in the live market. Traders will enter a long trade when the trend is strong, and they will cover their positions or reduce their risk exposure when the trend is weak.

Bollinger bands can also be useful in grading the strength of a downtrend. This is useful for traders who are selling currency pairs or for option traders who are buying puts. Traders will wait to enter new bearish trades until the trend is strong and will cover or exit a short position when the trend is weak.

FIGURE 13-33

Strong and Weak Uptrends

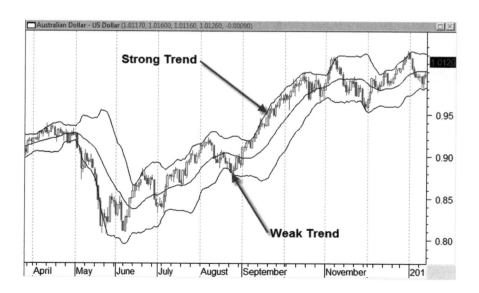

Bollinger bands produce trend signals for bearish trades in the following two scenarios:

1. A strong trend occurs when the overall market trend is down and prices are at or near the lower Bollinger band.
2. A weak trend occurs when the overall market trend is down and prices are at or near the upper Bollinger band.

You can see an example of these kinds of bearish trend signals in Figure 13-34.

Conclusion

Bollinger bands are ideally suited to be a filtering indicator. They can help traders understand current volatility within the context of the recent past. This is useful as a tool to identify buying opportunities in an uptrend or shorting opportunities in a downtrend. Bollinger bands are especially useful when they are combined with an indicator that is more suited for creating buy or sell signals.

FIGURE 13-34

Strong and Weak Downtrends

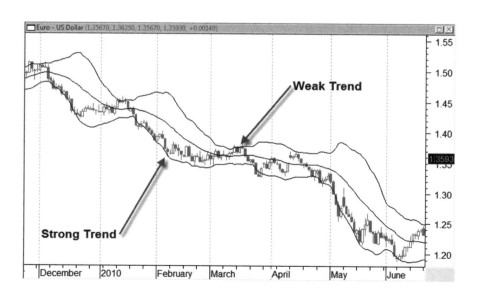

Like any other technical indicator, Bollinger bands are a lagging indicator, which means that they are based on price data from the past. Use caution when interpreting any lagging indicator because what happened in the past is not a guarantee of what will happen in the future.

CHAPTER 14

Getting Started as a Forex Trader

CHOOSING A FOREX DEALER

This is a topic that most traders are passionate about. There are significant differences among Forex dealers, and you need to understand these differences in order to pick a preferred dealer. In this section, we will discuss both the internal characteristics and the external benefits that you should look for in choosing a dealer.

Looking Under a Dealer's Hood — Internal Qualities

You would never buy a new car based on the paint job and the rims alone. You need to look under the hood and make sure you are not buying a lemon. The same principle applies when selecting a Forex dealer. You should never put your money with a dealer simply because it offers low spreads and a wide selection of tradable currency pairs. You need to make sure the dealer you are going to use is in good standing with its regulators and has a strong financial foundation.

Regulation

The Forex market is nearly unregulated, and this means that there are plenty of small "bucket shops" out there soliciting business. Recently, there have been some changes in regulations in the

United States and Australia that have cleaned up the dealer market somewhat. This is helping good dealers stand out from bad ones.

Dealers usually have to register with some regulatory agency or association. You can find out a lot of information about a dealer—including the principals' names, history, disciplinary problems, and complaints—by checking out the regulatory agency's Web site. The following list gives the best places to look for that information. If your dealer does not appear in any system, that is a big red flag. If you don't know where, or if, a dealer is registered, call him and find out.

- **United States:** The National Futures Association (NFA), http://www.nfa.futures.org/basicnet/
- **United Kingdom:** The Financial Services Authority (FSA), http://www.fsa.gov.uk/register/home.do
- **Australia:** The Australian Securities and Investments Commission (ASIC), http://www.search.asic.gov.au/fsr/flb.html

Capitalization

As a registered financial services provider, a dealer is required to maintain a minimum level of capitalization, or money in reserve. This has a direct impact on the dealer's ability to remain solvent and is a good indication of the size of the company and its ability to remain in business.

Net capitalization requirements for Forex dealers in the United States just went up to $5,000,000, which has been a good way to clean out some of the seedier operations. You can find out what your dealer's capitalization levels are on the Commodity Futures Trading Commission (CFTC) Web site (see Table 14-1).

If a dealer can't meet minimum capital requirements or keeps its capitalization private, you should worry about that dealer's ability to remain solvent in adverse market conditions.

Service

The most common complaint I get from traders about their dealer's service is that the dealer is abrupt and rude, or that she can't answer difficult questions. Investigate a dealer's service and its

TABLE 14-1

List of RFEDs by Adjusted Net Capital*

Retail Foreign Exchange Dealer (RFED)	Adjusted Net Capital
OANDA Corporation	$168,923,482
Global Futures & Forex Ltd. (GFT)	$77,435,995
GAIN Capital Group LLC	$65,206,853
Forex Capital Markets LLC	$43,161,405
FX Solutions LLC	$40,515,513
Interbank FX LLC	$26,846,244
FX Direct Dealer LLC	$26,237,585
MB Trading Futures, Inc.	$25,196,840
Alpari (US) LLC	$22,606,782
Forex Club Financial Company, Inc.	$20,419,739
Advanced Markets LLC	$20,401,823
Capital Market Services, LLC	$16,048,102

*http://www.cftc.gov/marketreports/financialdataforfcms/.

dealing or execution departments. You can do this by doing some research and calling the service department at different times of the day with difficult questions. Make sure that you opt for the dealing desk or execution department a few times to get a feel for how the people there treat you. You can learn a lot about a dealer by calling it a few times.

Judging a Book by Its Cover—External Qualities

Dealers are not all created equal. Dealers' product lines differ in two main areas:

1. **Pairs offered:** Some dealers offer close to 100 different crosses, which can be great for fundamental or strategy traders.

2. **Product offerings:** Some dealers offer futures, commodities, and options as well as spot Forex. We are big advocates of using options in your Forex activities, so this may be an important factor for you as well.

Spread and Rollover

The spread between bid and ask prices on the majors tends to be relatively uniform across most major dealers. The largest differences exist in the crosses. Be aware that most dealers offer one of the following two spread models:

1. **Fixed spread:** A fixed spread means that you always pay the same spread, regardless of market conditions.

2. **Variable spread:** A variable spread is narrower on average than a fixed spread, often one pip or less on the majors, but it can become very wide during periods of market volatility. Very short-term traders may lose a trade because the spread widened rather than because the market price actually reached their stop limit.

For more fundamental or longer-term traders, the spread is less of an issue, so competitive spreads are usually sufficient.

Rollover, interest payments, and the "tomorrow-next policy" are all terms for the interest charge/payment offered by dealers on individual pairs. This subject is covered extensively in Chapter 12 because it is so important. Call the dealer to determine its policy and whether higher payment rates and lower charges are available with lower margin levels, higher balances, or just upon request.

Charting and Execution Platform

Dealing platforms fall into two basic categories.

1. **Execution-based platforms:** These platforms are oriented toward speed of order entry and execution. You will often see them advertised as "one-click trading." This is great for scalpers and day traders. Dealers using platforms of this type make executing an order very fast and specialize in simple trading interfaces.

2. **Information-based platforms:** These platforms place a much heavier emphasis on charting and research technology. Some of the benefits of dealers using the second type of platform are as follows:

   - Customizable charting and system development
   - Display of positions, orders, and P/L on the charts

- Mechanical system execution
- Chart pattern search and identification
- Institutional-grade news feed and analysis

Making Your Pick: Tips for Choosing a Dealer

Now that you know more about Forex dealers than most traders out there, it is time to choose one. Here are a few suggestions to help get you started.

Don't Pick One Dealer, Pick a Few

We think you should avoid limiting yourself to one dealer. Picking a dealer isn't a marriage, so feel free to shop around and trade with dealers that suit each strategy you use in your portfolio. This is also a great way to add some diversification to your trading. While it is rare for a big broker or dealer to go out of business, it has happened. When it does, the results are catastrophic for traders who have all their "eggs" in one basket. Many Forex traders who are interested in options may have to split their account between an options broker and a Forex dealer anyway.

Prioritize Qualities Based on What Is Important to You

You cannot compromise on the internal qualities that we listed earlier, but the external qualities depend on what you want and need as a trader. Long-term traders may value a higher-quality news feed and charting research tool more than short-term traders or scalpers do. Many dealers will say that they are a one-size-fits-all solution, but we have not found this to be true.

Paper Trade

Paper trading is not just for new traders. Paper trading a dealer's application is a critical step before making a decision. Almost all dealers will allow you to set up a paper account to really test the technology and service levels. Spend the time to get to know an application before you make a decision. Too many traders are impressed with surface features in a day or two of paper trading and then make a bad decision.

IGNORE MONEY MANAGEMENT AT YOUR PERIL

Position sizing is the process of determining how much to invest, or risk, in any single trade. The benefit of position sizing is that it can help you predict and control the effect that your trades have on your portfolio's value. Too many traders invest inconsistent amounts in each trade.

Being inconsistent, or overinvesting in a single trade, will lead to drawdowns in your account that could wipe you out. Knowing how much you have at risk in a single trade compared to your total portfolio will help your investing become much more stable.

Good traders sometimes differ on how to calculate the risk, or maximum risk, of any particular position. We believe that using the distance between your entry point and your stop loss is the most effective way to determine the maximum risk amount.

To size your position, you need to know how much money you have in your account, what percentage of your account you are willing to risk, and what your stop loss is. Imagine that you have an account with $10,000 in it and you are willing to lose 2 percent in a bad trade. You are considering a long position on the EUR/USD at 1.5000, and you feel you need a 50-pip stop loss for that trade. You are now ready to calculate your position's size. The formula for calculating a position's size is

$$(\text{Account Value} \times \text{Portfolio Risk \%}) / \$ \text{ Value of Stop Loss} = \text{Position Size}$$

$$(\$10,000 \times 2\%) / \$50 = 4 \text{ mini lots}$$

We use the stop loss to calculate the maximum risk in the Forex market because a Forex position is a margin position. That means that there is an obligation on the trader's part to make good on losses, but there isn't a transfer of ownership in the currency. You are not actually taking possession of $10,000 worth of currency when you trade a mini lot. What you really own is your obligation, and therefore your position sizing should be based on this rather than on the entire notional value. This is unlike a stock trade, where you could ask for delivery of the stock certificate itself.

Position Sizing FAQ

Here are answers to some common questions that we get about position sizing.

What if I Have Only $1,000 in My Account?

We know that there are many traders who are in love with the Forex who have very small account balances. This is not uncommon. Many dealers report average account balances of less than $10,000. If you are in this situation and you want to keep your risk low while you keep depositing money in your account, work with a dealer that offers fractional lot sizes. Many dealers have lot sizes much smaller than 10,000 units.

Why Not Increase the Percentage at Risk When I Am Very Confident in My Trade?

The key to effective trading is consistency. If you have a particular setup or system that you are extra confident about, make sure you have the experience to back that up. If you have a high-probability trade, always trade the same fixed risk amount in that trade. Inconsistency will disrupt your equity growth and can hurt your trading mentality.

How Do I Account for Slipped Stops?

We have made a big assumption here by assuming that the amount between your entry price and your stop loss is the most you can lose. We realize that stops can be slipped. It's rare, but when the market gets really volatile, it can happen. You will find that this is much more common with very tight stops during periods of extreme market volatility. The wider your stop is, which usually accompanies a longer-term outlook, the less likely you are to experience slippage.

This is one argument for the use of options as a speculative alternative. The maximum loss on a long option position is capped at the amount you paid for the option. You cannot lose more than what you paid.

If you were trading a long position on the EUR/USD and you simultaneously bought a long put option to protect the position, you could calculate your maximum loss as the time value portion of what you paid for the put. If all the other variables were held constant and the premium for the put was $100 per mini lot, you would be able to buy 1 mini lot.

$$(\$10,000 \times 2\%)/\$100 = 2 \text{ minis}$$

You can use any method you choose to protect your trades and calculate your position sizing; just make sure you use some method.

BENEFITS OF LONGER-TERM FOREX INVESTING

In this section, we will show you how long-term trading has the potential to be more profitable and provide more risk control than short-term trading. In addition, it is typically easier for new traders to learn and get started with longer-term trading strategies.

Let's just make sure we're on the same page with regard to what we consider a short-term trade as opposed to a long-term trade. We classify a short-term trade as anything with a holding period of less than a week. Short-term trading includes day traders and scalpers, who may hold a position for a few seconds or minutes, as well as short-term swing traders, who may hold a position for a few days. A great way to tell the difference between short-term and long-term traders is the chart period they favor. Longer-term traders tend to use daily charts. Short-term traders may use anything from hourly charts to 1-minute charts to tick charts.

A long-term trader falls outside the short-term horizon and is identified not only by the period that the trade lasts, but also by how the position is managed throughout the holding period. Being a long-term trader does not mean that you are a static trader who does not actively manage a position. A long-term trader may actively manage a position for several weeks to several months. Just to be clear, long-term trading is not the same thing as "buy and hold."

Key Differences Between Long- and Short-Term Trading

Here are the differences that we see between the two types of trading and what you need to be aware of as you make your trading decisions.

Spread

Short-term Forex traders immediately face a disadvantage because they trade more and therefore have to overcome the spread more often. To make a 1,000-pip profit when trading the EUR/USD pair, a short-term Forex trader who makes 50 trades must make a total of 1,100 pips (assuming that the spread on the EUR/USD is 2 pips) because he has to overcome the spread 50 times (once for each trade) before he can make a profit.

On the other hand, to make a 1,000-pip profit when trading the EUR/USD, a long-term Forex trader who makes only one trade must make a total of 1,002 pips (again, assuming that the spread on the EUR/USD is 2 pips) because she has to overcome the spread only one time before she can make a profit.

Looking at this example, a short-term trader has to earn an additional 98 pips, or be approximately 10 percent more effective than a long-term trader has to be, to earn the same profit.

At this point, we hope you are asking yourself the question, "Why would I want to make my Forex investing experience 10 percent harder than it has to be?" The numbers in this example can be modified to fit any scenario, but the point is, more transactions equal more transaction costs. That is good for your dealer, but it is not so good for you.

Overfocus

We find that many traders suffer from market tunnel vision. They are watching one or two pairs in the short term and are unable to see what is happening in the rest of the market around them. The amount of attention it takes to manage one or two short-term trades with entries, exits, and stops can prevent the short-term trader from seeing the trading opportunities on other pairs. Short-term traders who miss these trading opportunities are unable to leverage the benefits of diversification and portfolio management to control risk, which longer-term traders routinely take advantage of.

Flexibility

Short-term traders will often deal with bracket orders out of necessity. A bracket order, or one-cancels-the-other (OCO) order, means that you have predetermined your exits and have entered those orders at the same time you entered the position.

Long-term traders have a greater ability to adjust their expectations, manage their trades, and employ risk control as new information, price patterns, and opportunities arise.

Most technical analysts agree that the validity of a trading signal is independent of its time frame. Therefore, if the quality of the trading signal is the same, regardless of its time frame, isn't it better to give yourself more time, rather than less time, to make decisions? We think so.

Miscellaneous
Short-term traders miss out on other benefits of operating in the Forex market as well. Short-term traders often miss out on rollover, or interest premiums, on a daily basis, depending on when they enter and exit their positions. Longer-term traders can create trades and groups of positions that benefit from interest payments in the long term.

Long-term trading is typically also less time-consuming, since you don't have to watch the live market all day every day. Many new traders are working a full-time job, raising a family, and having a life while they learn this market. Checking in on your trades and making adjustments every once in a while, rather than constantly watching the live market throughout the duration of the trade, requires a lot less time and can be easily scheduled around your daily routine.

Short-term trading requires a lot more attention to the market on a continuous basis. A much-talked-about aspect of trading is the toll that it can take on you emotionally. The longer you are in front of your trading screen watching the market zigzag back and forth between your limit and your stop, the more tempting it can be to interfere with your strategy. This emotional toll increases the stress of trading and can make the whole experience unpleasant.

Ultimately, the most important thing you can do is find a trading strategy that best fits your personality and meets your investing needs. But we hope you won't discount longer-term strategies simply because they aren't as sexy or exciting on the surface. You just may find that they are the best thing for you and your portfolio.

HARD-CURRENCY SCAMS: THE IRAQI DINAR

Like most financial markets, the Forex has no shortage of scams designed to take advantage of inexperienced traders. One of these strategies, known as a *hard-currency scam*, is particularly popular in the Forex market because it is extremely difficult to prosecute the scammers. A hard-currency scam involves the sale of physical currency that usually doesn't have an over-the-counter, or exchange-traded, market. The currency involved is typically low-valued, and the promise (or scam) is that this depreciated currency will rise dramatically as its economy improves.

The most popular hard-currency scam over the last few years involves "investments" in the Iraqi dinar (IQD). Investors are told that if they buy Iraqi dinars today, they will profit when the economy becomes stable again and the currency starts to appreciate. The victim usually buys dinars with U.S. dollars and then holds them—waiting for a potential revaluation, or appreciation, in his favor.

The scammers promise that millions of dollars in profits are virtually guaranteed if you buy the dinars at today's value (as of this writing, it was 1,200 dinar to 1 U.S. dollar) and then exchange the dinars back for dollars at a later date once the exchange rate has improved. Although it is theoretically possible for the dinar to improve in value against the dollar, there are some fundamental problems with the scam that potential buyers should be aware of before they begin investing in one of the most illiquid currency markets in the world.

Lack of Registration

In the United States and most other major economies, it is illegal to market an investment without appropriate securities registration and disclosure. The scammers get around this requirement in two ways. First, it is technically legal to sell hard currency for its numismatic value. In other words, it is possible to sell hard currency as a "collector's item." Second, some dealers will register with the U.S. Treasury as a money service business (MSB), which gives them the appearance of being sanctioned by the government. An MSB is a company that exchanges physical currency, which is technically what these outfits are doing when they take your dollars and give you virtually worthless dinars.

You have probably seen legitimate MSB companies at the airport, and you may have used one when you returned home from a vacation or business trip and traded in the euros, pesos, or Canadian dollars that were still in your pocket. However, the difference between a legitimate MSB and dinar dealers is that a real MSB is not marketing an investment, it is providing a service.

The fact that several large U.S. banks will exchange dinars for dollars also tends to cloud the issue and inadvertently adds credibility to the claims of the scammers. "After all," these dinar scammers will ask, "if it were really a scam, would Citigroup be participating?" We're going to let that question hang in the air for a bit while you reflect on the financial crisis of 2008. It's not that we don't appreciate many of the services that are offered by these large financial institutions, because we do. We just don't think they are the best barometer to use when trying to determine if something makes credible financial sense.

Dinars Are Sold Based on Misleading Hype

The potential value of an investment in dinars is often illustrated with references to what happened to the Kuwaiti dinar following the first Gulf War and the German deutsche mark following World War II. In both cases, the currency seemed to appreciate a few thousand percent against the U.S. dollar following the end of the war. These would be good examples, except that neither one was a free-floating currency at the time, so the value was a function of policy making and official currency management. You should also know that in both cases, the prewar currency was not the same thing as the postwar currency. They had the same name, but the old currency had been demonetized and replaced with new currency.

Even if those examples of currency appreciation were entirely legitimate, no rational investor would base an investment decision solely on two instances of past data, one of which occurred more than 60 years ago, without considering all the times that this investing strategy did not pay off. The vast majority of currencies with extremely low values compared to the U.S. dollar never recover. They either are demonetized or end up collapsing completely.

Much of the argument behind a potential rise in the value of the dinar rests on the fallacy that a growing economy will result in a stronger currency. As the U.S. economy has illustrated during the past several decades of continuous economic growth, a currency can decline even if its economy is prospering. Even economies with double-digit economic growth and expanding oil industries, such as Venezuela, Turkey, and Mexico, are much more likely to see their currencies grow weaker and weaker as a result of inflation than they are to see them get stronger and stronger.

But let's say for just a moment that the dinar does start to regain some of its lost value. A currency that starts to rise in value too quickly is a problem for the government. And as you know, one surefire method that a government has at its disposal to bring the value of a currency back down is to print more money.

So you have to ask yourself, will the Iraqi government pursue a policy of currency appreciation in the future, or will it try to keep the value of the dinar low? Since an appreciating currency makes funding your brand-new government and paying off past debts more expensive, it seems unlikely that the government will pursue this option. An economy in Iraq's situation is more likely to experience a currency crash or intentional devaluation than a sudden and dramatic appreciation.

What to Consider if You Decide to "Invest" in Hard Currencies Anyway

Assume that you are determined to "invest" in dinars despite the shadowy and misleading dealers that you will have to work with. You should be aware of the following risks that you are not likely to hear from a dealer.

Liquidity

There is currently no active market for dinars. You can buy them, but can you sell them? We surveyed several dealers and found that the difference between the price at which they will sell you Iraqi dinars and the price at which they will buy those same dinars back from you is approximately 20 percent. This means that the dinar will have to appreciate by at least 25 percent before you can sell it back and break even on the transaction. Here's how the math works on that one.

One dinar dealer is currently advertising that it will sell you 1,000,000 dinars for $1,180. On the other hand, that same dealer is currently advertising that it will buy 1,000,000 dinars from you for anywhere between $780 and $900. Now, for argument's sake, let's say you can get $900. That is a spread of $280 ($1,180 − $900 = $280), or 24 percent ($280/$1,180 = 0.24), based on the price that you will have to pay for your dinars. However, the currency will have to increase in value by at least 31 percent ($280/$900 = 0.31) for you to sell it back at a breakeven price of $1,180 if the dealer maintains the same spread of $280.

Currencies with Extremely Low Values Are Often Demonetized

It is quite common for countries with currencies that have very low exchange rates to demonetize their existing hard currency and issue new currency with new values. For example, Venezuela, another oil economy, demonetized the bolivar (which was trading at 2,150 bolivar per U.S. dollar) in 2008 and allowed currency owners to exchange 1,000 of the old bolivar for 1 new bolivar. The new bolivar began trading at 2.15 bolivar per U.S. dollar, but it has since depreciated—again—and is trading at 4.30 bolivar per U.S. dollar in 2011. This demonetization and revaluation process has been carried out over and over again in modern history. People who owned 1,000 bolivar before the revaluation received 1 bolivar after the revaluation, with no increase in total value. This is how a revaluation in the dinar would be conducted as well.

In addition to the inherent problems associated with revaluation, you will face some difficulty with the process of actually getting your hard-currency dinars exchanged for a second issue of new dinars at a new value. If there is an extremely illiquid market today, there is probably going to be one later as well. It may even be something that can only be completed in Iraq—which could make the process extremely expensive.

Inflation

Currently, the Iraqi Central Bank is reporting inflation rates that vary, depending on the month, anywhere from −4 percent to +8 percent. If the government and the economy become more unstable than they are at present, those inflation rates could skyrocket. Hyperinflation destroys the value of hard currency, and extreme volatility often precedes a complete currency collapse. For example, by the time the Turkish government revalued in 2008, the lira had inflated to 1.5 million lira to the U.S. dollar.

The bottom line is that buying hard currency is an investment opportunity that is marketed by unregistered advisors to mostly unsophisticated currency investors. No risks are disclosed, historical data are fabricated, and the cost of trading the currency is 25 percent or more. This investment is a gamble at best.

CONCLUSION

The Forex market is one of the most exciting and liquid markets in the world, and you can jump in right now and take advantage of it in many different ways. Whether you are looking to diversify your investment portfolio or to leverage up and swing for the fences, there is a Forex investment for you.

Just make sure that you understand what you are getting into before you dive in headfirst. We've seen friends and colleagues make great money by investing in the Forex market. Unfortunately, we have seen far too many people get chewed up and spit out by this thrilling, but unforgiving, market. So don't become another casualty of the Forex market. Take the time to really study, learn, and apply the concepts in this book. If you do, you will be much better off than many of the people who wander blindly into the market.

Good luck.

INDEX

ABOUT THE AUTHORS

John Jagerson has worked in the capital markets and private equity for most of his career—including investing, writing, education, and money management. He was a vice president for thinkorswim Group, Inc. (SWIM) and is currently a cofounder of LearningMarkets.com.

John has a bachelor of science degree in business administration from Utah Valley University and completed the Program for Leadership Development (PLD) at Harvard Business School in 2006. He is actively involved in managing his own stock, options, futures, and Forex portfolio.

John is also the coauthor of the book *Profiting with Forex*, published in 2006 by McGraw-Hill, and has written for numerous online and offline financial publications. John's commentary, videos, and educational articles are regularly featured across the Web and at LearningMarkets.com.

S. Wade Hansen is an internationally recognized investing-education expert. He has created online training programs for some of the world's largest stock, option, and Forex brokers and has written for Yahoo! Finance, Forbes.com, Nasdaq.com, BloggingStocks. com, and more.

Wade has a bachelor's degree from Brigham Young University and an MBA from the University of Utah. During his career, he has served as a principal for a commodity trading advisor (CTA) and as a registered representative for a large securities firm.

Wade is a cofounder of the investment Web site LearningMarkets.com. He is also the coauthor of *Profiting with Forex*.